LEARNING
Animal Behavior
and Human Cognition

McGraw-Hill Series in Psychology

Consulting Editors
Norman Garmezy
Lyle V. Jones

Guion   *Personnel Testing*
Haire   *Psychology in Management*
Hetherington and Park   *Child Psychology: A Contemporary Viewpoint*
Hirsch   *Behavior-Genetic Analysis*
Hirsh   *The Measurement of Hearing*
Horowitz   *Elements of Statistics for Psychology and Education*
Hulse, Deese, and Egeth   *The Psychology of Learning*
Hurlock   *Adolescent Development*
Hurlock   *Child Development*
Hurlock   *Developmental Psychology*
Jackson and Messick   *Problems in Human Assessment*
Krech, Crutchfield, and Ballachey   *Individual in Society*
Lakin   *Interpersonal Encounter: Theory and Practice in Sensitivity Training*
Lawler   *Pay and Organizational Effectiveness: A Psychological View*
Lazarus, A.   *Behavior Therapy and Beyond*
Lazarus, R.   *Adjustment and Personality*
Lewin   *A Dynamic Theory of Personality*
Lewin   *Principles of Topological Psychology*
Maher   *Principles of Psychopathology*
Marascuilo   *Statistical Methods for Behavioral Science Research*
Marx and Hillix   *Systems and Theories in Psychology*
Miller   *Language and Communication*
Morgan   *Physiological Psychology*
Mulaik   *The Foundations of Factor Analysis*
Novick and Jackson   *Statistical Methods for Educational and Psychological Research*
Nunnally   *Introduction to Statistics for Psychology and Education*
Nunnally   *Psychometric Theory*
Overall and Klett   *Applied Multivariate Analysis*
Porter, Lawler, and Hackman   *Behavior in Organizations*
Restle   *Learning: Animal Behavior and Human Cognition*
Robinson and Robinson   *The Mentally Retarded Child*
Rosenthal   *Genetic Theory and Abnormal Behavior*
Ross   *Psychological Disorders of Children: A Behavioral Approach to Theory, Research and Therapy*
Schwitzgebel and Kolb   *Changing Human Behavior: Principles of Planned Intervention*
Shaw   *Group Dynamics: The Psychology of Small Group Behavior*
Shaw and Costanzo   *Theories of Social Psychology*
Shaw and Wright   *Scales for the Measurement of Attitudes*
Sidowski   *Experimental Methods and Instrumentation in Psychology*
Siegel   *Nonparametric Statistics for the Behavioral Sciences*
Spencer and Kass   *Perspectives in Child Psychology*
Stagner   *Psychology of Personality*
Steers and Porter   *Motivation and Work Behavior*
Townsend   *Introduction to Experimental Methods for Psychology and the Social Sciences*
Vinacke   *The Psychology of Thinking*
Wallen   *Clinical Psychology: The Study of Persons*
Warren and Akert   *Frontal Granular Cortex and Behavior*
Winer   *Statistical Principles in Experimental Design*
Zubek and Solberg   *Human Development*

LEARNING
Animal Behavior
and Human Cognition

Frank Restle

Professor of Psychology
Indiana University

McGRAW-HILL BOOK COMPANY

New York   St. Louis   San Francisco   Auckland   Düsseldorf
Johannesburg   Kuala Lumpur   London   Mexico   Montreal   New Delhi
Panama   Paris   São Paulo   Singapore   Sydney   Tokyo   Toronto

Library of Congress Cataloging in Publication Data

Restle, Frank.
    Learning: animal behavior and human cognition.

    (McGraw-Hill series in psychology)
      1. Learning, Psychology of. 2. Animal
intelligence. I. Title. [DNLM: 1. Behavior,
Animal. 2. Cognition. 3. Learning. 4. Psychology,
Educational. LB1051 R436L]
LB1051.R478   153.1'5   74-16006
ISBN 0-07-051910-2

LEARNING
Animal Behavior and Human Cognition

1234567890DODO798765

This book was set in Times Roman by Black Dot, Inc.
The editors were Richard R. Wright and Susan Gamer;
the cover was designed by Nicholas Krenitsky;
the production supervisor was Dennis J. Conroy.
The drawings were done by Vantage Art, Inc.
R. R. Donnelley & Sons Company was printer and binder.

To Barbara and the Kids

Contents

Preface

The purpose of this book is to join three major streams of psychological thought: cognitive psychology, learning theory, and animal behavior. Each of these has its supporters and its critics; each has an essential contribution to make to our understanding; and each has been extended beyond its natural compass. My goal is not to compare but to integrate them.

The plan of the book is simple. Chapters 1 and 2 set up the theoretical framework. Chapters 3 to 8 deal with animal behavior, both in the wild and in the laboratory. These chapters cover most of the standard topics, such as classical and instrumental conditioning, discrimination learning, schedules of reinforcement, avoidance, and learning sets. Chapters 9 to 15 deal with human cognitive processes—pattern recognition, memory, concept formation, and language.

Each of these topics is interesting; indeed, one of the great mysteries of higher education is that the usual course in learning is taken like medicine, because it is good for you. The instructor in such a course is usually caught in a conflict, however. If he presents only the most interesting material, his course is often rather superficial and disorganized and fails to build the intellectual discipline that students need. If he teaches a systematic course, he finds himself enmeshed in old controversies and specialized experiments that turn away many of his students. In this book I have tried to give a disciplined, systematic, and self-consistent course based on recent work and on interesting and surprising experimental findings.

Psychologists in the study of human and animal behavior develop an approach that can make an important contribution to the world. They seek causes for human action not in such vague substances as "human nature" but in specific areas: stimulation, attention, expectancy, goals, and cognitive structures. Their concern is less with the nature of evil than with the redirection of energies, less with who is responsible than with how the situation can be improved. The strength of modern society lies in its ability to organize the efforts and thoughts of its members. The use of force, economic need, and social pressures is limited. Newer, more precise, more effective, and more humane methods are needed. I believe that just as lawyers dominate the building of large societal structures, psychologists will come to dominate the process of running them smoothly. To take this role in society, psychologists will need disciplined minds and a precise and coherent theory, powerful enough to handle practical problems. This book is intended as a step on the way, an elementary yet serious presentation of systematic psychology.

Recent research in human cognition leads us to the conclusion that comprehension is a process of picking out the organized meaning of a passage, and that the success of long-term memory depends mainly on how clearly the learner understands the material and how intimately he can relate it to his own body of knowledge. I have tried to apply this idea in writing this book. First, I have worked seriously on the theory so that the book would make sense and have a coherent, organized meaning. Then at various points I have suggested to the reader how he might relate this meaning to his own knowledge.

Acknowledgments

My thanks to many colleagues who patiently answered my endless questions, read, criticized, supplied references, loaned precious books, and always broadened and tempered my views. The entire psychology faculty at Indiana University has been helpful, especially Richard Shiffrin, Conrad Mueller, William Timberlake, Lloyd Peterson, Eliot Hearst, George Hiese, and David Pisoni. The editing, typing, organizing, and management were in the hands of Ramona Rhodes, who also took the roles of critic, protector, and cheerleader. Finally, and most, to my wife, who assumed a hundred extra burdens while I wrote this, and my children, whose steadiness and self-reliance I have needed, I express my love and appreciation.

Frank Restle

LEARNING
Animal Behavior
and Human Cognition

Introduction

This book is about learning and the cognitive processes. Aristotle, in founding our thinking about psychology, divided the functions of the mind into three broad categories: cognition, the process of knowing; conation, the process of willing; and emotion, the feelings. These three aspects join together in every significant act or experience of a human being or an animal; but in this book we shall concentrate on the cognitive processes.

What is a cognitive process? The cognitive processes include perception, the acquisition of knowledge through the senses; memory, the storage and retrieval of information from the past; problem solving, the generation and testing of hypotheses; and thinking, the rehearsal of past events and the imagining of future ones. These broad categories can be divided even more finely, and a variety of concepts bordering two or more areas can be educed.

The human being is the cognitive animal. Human beings know more than other animals, remember more, perceive more complex relationships despite our rather mediocre senses, and think more than other animals. Consequently, psychology, and particularly cognitive psychology, is part of the study of man. However, when we attempt to define exactly what humans know and to understand the basic nature of perception, learning, memory, and thinking, we find that other animals share these basic processes with us. More interesting, we find that animals are not merely inadequate men, but that each animal has its own particular psychological characteristics which may adapt it to its own ecological niche. Many simple animals perceive, develop hypotheses, and learn from past exper-ience, and these processes are as interesting in animals as they are in humans. In fact, our understanding of human cognition comes in large part from an effort to understand cognition in various other animals.

This book, therefore, does not separate human beings from animals but instead approaches the question of the cognitive processes broadly. Descartes handled the problem of mind in animals by asserting that only human beings had souls; animals lacked them. Since animals behaved in complex ways, he came to think of them as exquisitely complex mecha-nisms, whose performance might seem to mimic humanity but must be explained by laws distinctly separate from the theory of human behavior. Whatever the merits of this opinion may be in theology, it is not good psychology. It is far simpler and more natural, as well as more humane, to assume that when an animal writhes, it is in pain; that when it looks at something it sees and pays attention, and that when it performs a learned trick, it expects a reward. Furthermore, from this unified point of view we find that animals can teach us a great deal about human behavior. Human beings are primates, generally related to apes and monkeys, and have many psychological traits in common with the primate order. For example, humans tend to rely on vision and hearing rather than on smell or touch. We tend to explore and manipulate; we live in social groups and communicate with one another; and we are dangerous when threatened. Our young are playful and noisy, stay young a long time, and are terribly helpless during their long childhood. These traits are all very common among the primate order but rare in "lower" animals.

However, other animals have many of the same needs we do. They must have shelter, food, and drink; they procreate and raise their young; and they have interactions with predators, prey, other foods, and other members of their species. In a broad sense, all animals have the same or similar problems and must solve these problems to survive. Therefore, even the ant or the octopus, by demonstrating the skills natural to its station, may throw a helpful light on the problems of humanity.

FUNDAMENTAL CONCEPTS

All behavior can be divided into two broad classes. In the first class are the smooth, repetitive behaviors we may call "habitual" or "instinctive" in everyday language. Habits and reflexes are unconscious in that they demand little conscious attention and are not vividly remembered. When such a smooth behavior is found at birth or appears through maturation and is present in all or most members of the species, we may call it a "reflex," or—if it is more complicated— an "instinct." If it is acquired through practice and depends upon specific past experience, we are more inclined to call it a "habit" or "skill." This general common sense concept will be refined into the concept of a "behavior flow."

The second class consists of inquisitive and erratic behavior, which often appears to be no particular behavior at all. Such behavior has to do with finding out about the world; it will here be called "search." It may be visual (looking around), auditory (listening); it may include manipulating, smelling, and tasting; and it may also include more active mental processes, such as thinking about a situation, generating or changing hypotheses, recalling a past event, and reflecting. In every case, however, the main activity is searching for, encoding, and storing information.

The term "learning" encompasses these two classes of behavior, in two slightly different senses. We say that one "learns to swim," and although the process of learning may involve considerable thrashing about, its final product is clearly a smooth behavior flow. One may say that one "learns about modern art"; here the process is variable and does not lead to any specific form of behavior at all—it is purely a search for information. Learning a skill and learning knowledge are, really, two different things; together they constitute the broader concept of learning in general.

In this text, each behavior process will be described by means of a flowchart. A flowchart is a sequence of boxes, each of which represents an elementary process. These boxes are connected by arrows, and the direction of the arrows indicates the order in which the various events occur (Figure 1).

Even the simplest behavior flow involves at least some sensitivity and some flexibility: the organism may either respond or not respond, depending upon whether the appropriate situation is perceived, or may choose between responses. Therefore, within each flowchart one or more *decision points* are usually found. Each decision point is entered as a box is, but there are always two or more exits from a decision. A decision is symbolized in our flowcharts by a diamond (Figure 2).

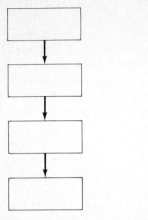

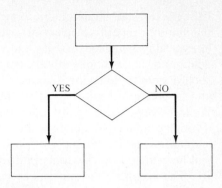

Figure 1 Simple flowchart.

Figure 2 Flowchart with decision
point.

One special kind of event comes from the outside world, instead of being generated by the behavior flow itself: this is called "input." When an input occurs, and what information it contains, depends upon the outside world; and in this way input is different from other processes or events. According to convention, an input box is not rectangular but shaped like a bucket. See Figure 3.

Each diagram begins, at the top, with an entry point, a box that symbolizes the whole structure. From there the flow proceeds step by step through the process. When the flow arrives at a decision diamond, all outgoing ramifications must be explored to see what behavioral possibilities exist. Usually, the several exits are labeled to indicate the nature of alternative possibilities.

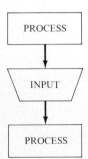

Figure 3 Input box between two
processes in a simple flow.

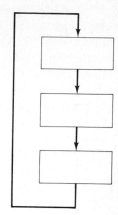

Figure 4 Flowchart of a closed loop.

The basic structure of a behavior flow is the "closed loop." A loop is produced in a flow diagram by having the sequence of events connected so that it returns to a box it has been at before. A simple closed loop contains no decisions, so that it comes back, directly or after some chain of intermediate boxes, to its start (Figure 4). A more complex closed loop may contain some decision points, but all the branches finally return to the same starting box. An open loop contains a decision; one branch from that decision leads into a loop back but another branch does not. Such a system may produce repetitions of the same sequence of events, but not infinitely many (Figure 5).

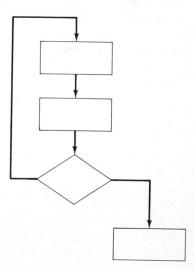

Figure 5 Flowchart of an open loop.

If a flow repeatedly comes back to the decision point, as in an open loop, and then chooses the branch that returns into the loop, it would appear that the flow would remain forever trapped in the loop. There is another "possible" branch from the decision, but that is not the decision made. One of the most common ways such an open loop terminates is through external information. If the loop contains an input bucket, the information that comes in with each trip through the loop may change. If it is also true that the decision depends, in part, on the input information, then the open loop may continue to loop until it gets certain required information and then may branch out to another activity.

The other way out of an open loop is through some development within the behavior flow itself. If the loop consists of repeated searches of memory for some particular past event, the subject may decide after each search whether to quit or to continue searching. This decision may be based on external information, like a glance at one's watch or signs of impatience from the person who asked the question; but internal developments, such as a certain number of consecutive searches with no result, may also result in a decision to quit and leave the loop. The idea of a closed loop is somewhat foreign to psychological thinking, because we do not usually think of behavior as being so extremely repetitive. Instead, conventional psychological thinking has often used another elementary structure, the habit or stimulus-response connection. Such a structure may be diagrammed as a very simple flowchart consisting of just two boxes, the stimulus and the response. Flow is always from the stimulus to the response. Then, theoretically, the system simply stops and awaits another stimulus. Each response of the organism, conceived in this way, must be instigated by some stimulus, either internal or external; when the organism is not so moved, it merely exists without behaving (Figure 6).

The difficulty with the stimulus-response (abbreviated "S-R") theory is that its element of behavior is very small and passive. It has become more and more difficult to specify, in useful detail, how habits or S-R

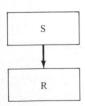

Figure 6 Flowchart of a simple S-R habit.

structures could ever be assembled into the great behavioral systems such as, for example, human language.

The question is, How do simple stimulus-response structures hang together? One way to answer is that a response itself can be perceived by the organism responding. Therefore, each response gives rise to a new stimulus; this situation is symbolized by $R \rightsquigarrow S$. Here, the wavy arrow signifies that S is the stimulus property of response R. Then a stimulus-response chain can be constructed:

$$S_1 \rightarrow R_2 \rightsquigarrow S_2 \rightarrow R_3 \rightsquigarrow S_3$$

Some authors have used this chain as a prototype of thinking. It might be argued that this chain is a model for reasoning, that "All men are mortal" corresponds to the association "$S_{man} \rightarrow R_{mortal}$" and "Socrates is a man" corresponds to the association "$S_{Socrates} \rightarrow R_{man}$." Now, given the obvious $R_{man} \rightsquigarrow S_{man}$, the chain becomes

$$S_{Socrates} \rightarrow R_{man} \rightsquigarrow S_{man} \rightarrow R_{mortal}$$

so that if the thought process is turned loose, when it is started with $S_{Socrates}$, it yields R_{mortal}, just as the syllogism leads to "Socrates is mortal." The problem is that this same S-R structure would yield the following: "Snow is white" corresponds to $S_{snow} \rightarrow R_{white}$, and the strong association "white-black" would be $S_{white} \rightarrow R_{black}$. Then, since $R_{white} \rightsquigarrow S_{white}$, we build the chain

$$S_{snow} \rightarrow R_{white} \rightsquigarrow S_{white} \rightarrow R_{black}$$

from which the thought process, unleashed, leaps to the conclusion that snow is black. Since opposites tend to be strongly associated, the stimulus-response chaining theory will enable the mind to deduce almost all falsehoods and absurdities.

This logical difficulty is not, in itself, enough to defeat an S-R theorist, whose first defense might well be that men are, in truth, illogical and absurd. However, the way the example was constructed does indicate the weakness of the S-R model—namely, its having only one mode of connection, the arrow, between its elements. It has no decision points. Now, if the stimuli had only one association each, each to a unique response, it would be possible to draw a coherent graph of the association structure. In fact, however, most stimuli have more than one association response. The diagram is therefore an expanding network from which almost any number and variety of responses might issue forth. The S-R formula actually imposes little structure or constraint upon the possibilities of behavior, and it is therefore no theory at all.

The element I have chosen to focus on in this book, the behavior flow, is not itself a complete or satisfactory description of all psychological events. However, a simple behavior flow is a useful basic concept, in that it is both genuinely psychological and genuinely simple. Psychology is the study of behavior, and a simple behavior flow describes a whole course of behavior—if you will, a whole biography of the organism, a whole lifetime of behavior. Within a simple behavior flow can be placed a variety of events, including expectations, analyses of stimuli, discriminations, decisions, and responses. However, a simple behavior flow consists of a closed loop, and therefore is simple in that it specifies a particularly monotonous life history. This book begins with an organism that behaves all the time but is too repetitive, too "habit-bound," to be realistic. The theory is expanded by putting more and more decision points within the flowchart, to represent a more flexible and variable life history. To keep the flowcharts reasonably simple, it will often be expedient to present one flowchart as an element of another, larger structure; thus more complex and more realistic behavioral structures can be described.

Chapter 1

The Simple Behavior Flow

The simplest conceivable behavior flow would consist of a closed loop representing an organism doing the same thing over and over throughout its whole life. The simplest flow we need consider, however, contains one decision: one branch from the decision leads to a characteristic response, and the other does not. That is, we consider that the simplest kind of psychological structure is a response which can be either made or withheld, depending upon something in the environment.

The simple mollusc, the scallop, consists of a matching pair of fluted shells, held together by a strong muscle; within is the simple digestive system, and in the mantle at the opening of the shells are several sense organs, including a row of several hundred blue eyes. When light falls steadily upon these eyes, practically nothing happens: the scallop lies on the sand, calmly circulating water through its digestive system and screening out tiny organisms on which it feeds. However, if the light to the eyes is suddenly cut off, then a few seconds later the scallop executes a complex motion of closing its shell and at the same time ejecting a violent jet of water sufficient to send it skittering away. This is clearly a coordinated defense reaction. The nature of the stimulus—the cutting off of light—is appropriate, since the scallop's natural enemy is the starfish, which slowly climbs on top of the scallop and enfolds it. The scallop, in response, coordinates the two actions appropriate to the situation— spitting out a jet of water, to break the grasp of the starfish and to escape; and closing its shell, so that if escape is impossible, the scallop can at least take advantage of its tough shell as a defense.

This defensive reaction of the scallop is a good example of an extremely simple behavior flow. It contains a particular response; and the response is optional, depending upon the particular stimulus situation. Furthermore, the scallop is a relatively simpleminded animal; we can easily imagine it lying in a sunny pool in a continuous state of readiness to escape any marauding starfish that might appear.

ELEMENTS OF THE BEHAVIOR FLOW

The first element of the behavior flow is an expectancy for a particular stimulus configuration. In the case of the scallop, the stimulus expected is a fairly sudden interruption of light to the eyes. The second element is some stimulus input; for the scallop, this input consists of visual information presented to the eyes in its mantle. The third element is an analysis of the information. In the case of the scallop, the color of the illumination is ignored, as are various images that might flash on the eye and very brief shadows such as would be cast by fish swimming by. In this simple case, the only event that is significant is a sharp reduction of illumination, lasting for about 5 seconds. The fourth element is a decision. When the stimulus information is analyzed, it either does or does not meet the criterion "danger": that is, it does or does not match the expectancy. If it does not—if there is no reduction of light—then the system can loop back and pick up another sample of stimulus information. If the information does meet the criterion—if it consists of darkening for 5 seconds— then the animal exhibits its escape response. If the response is successful, the scallop will return to its original state, and again take in a stimulus input.

Such a system, therefore, always returns to its initial state—either immediately, after noting that the stimulus input is not dangerous, or later, after responding to a dangerous situation. A diagram of such a simple behavior flow is shown in Figure 1.1.

To read the flowchart in Figure 1.1, the reader should begin at the first box "expectancy (of danger)," and follow the arrow. The next element is "stimulus input," which is a bucket-shaped box. The bucket

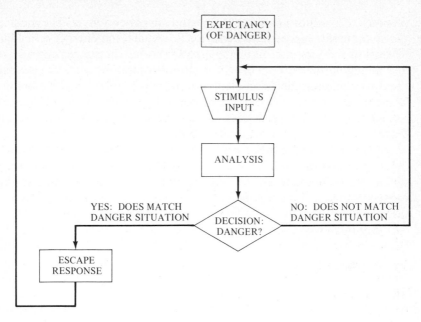

Figure 1.1 Simple behavior flow.

shape indicates that this is an input, not a process generated within the behavior flow: the nature of the input depends upon the outside world; in our example, it depends on whether or not a starfish has climbed onto the scallop. Following the arrow, the reader will arrive at "analysis," the process by which certain information is extracted from the stimulus input. The next stage is a decision diamond labeled "decision: danger?" At this point there are two possible arrows to follow. The reader should first follow the arrow labeled "no: does not match danger situation." Notice that the flow returns to "expectancy (of danger)," then takes another stimulus input, returns again to "analysis," and then returns to the decision diamond, in a loop. From this the reader can see that whenever an analyzed input fails to match the expectancy, the process will simply loop and get new stimulus inputs, doing this over and over. Next, the reader should take the opposite branch from the decision diamond, the branch labeled "yes: does match danger situation." Notice that in this situation the next process is "escape response," after which the flow returns to its original expectancy of danger and takes a new stimulus input. Therefore, the behavior flow is a closed loop: it always returns to the same expectancy of danger. Also, the system continuously resamples the stimulus input and always analyzes it. On each trip through the behavior loop, either the flow finds a match and makes an escape response, or it does not find a match and simply continues its expectancy.

In general, in reading a behavior flowchart, the correct procedure is to start at the top and follow the arrows, noting the succession of events and taking particular note of where stimulus-input buckets are located. If the flow contains a decision diamond, there will be at least two arrows or branches leading away from the diamond. The reader should first take one branch and see where it goes, exploring the pathways until he either leaves the behavior flow or returns to the same decision diamond; then he should investigate the other branch of the decision diamond and follow it out to the end or until it loops back. If there is more than one decision diamond, the procedure is to explore all branches of all diamonds in the most systematic way possible. In this way, the full significance of the flowchart is revealed.

Although we describe the simple behavior flow as having parts which occur in order, it should be clear that we are talking about a unified psychological pattern. To a scallop, the essential thing to expect is the signal of a starfish. We may consider that the rudimentary control system of this mollusc has in constant readiness a kind of expectation or template,[1] to which various stimulus situations might be matched. It also has receptors (the eyes) which can provide information to be matched with the expectancy; and it is capable of some sort of analysis to single out the important aspect of the visual information, namely, the darkening.[2] Finally, it has some way of deciding whether the analyzed information does or does not match its expectancy and of releasing the necessary response if the match is made. No one of these parts makes any real sense except in conjunction with all the others; division of behavior into smaller units would, therefore, result in pieces with no psychological reality.

TYPES OF BEHAVIOR FLOWS

There are infinitely many different behavior flows to be found in the behavior of animals, and most animals have many different flows. Behavior flows differ in the expectancies involved, in the stimulus inputs used, in the modes of analysis, and in the particular decisions and responses involved. However, all behavior flows are formally the same except for the relation of the response to the decision possibilities.

One type of flow entails a matching of stimulus and expectancy. The scallop makes its escape response when the stimulus matches the expectancy. The same is true of a fox hunting a rabbit: when hunting, a fox establishes an expectancy based upon the scent and appearance of a

---

[1] A template is a pattern or mold that serves as a gauge or guide in mechanical work. Here the word is used by analogy: expectancy is to the stimulus that it fits as a template is to the object it fits.

[2] Notice that stimulus *information* is not stimulus *energy;* in this example, darkening is a reduction of energy.

rabbit. The fox expects one patch of grass to move separately from others; it expects to see the flick of an ear, or to catch the scent of a rabbit, a rabbits' nest, or fresh-cut greenery, or to hear the sound of a rabbit moving or eating. When a stimulus input is analyzed and found to match that expectancy, the attack response is released. If the stimulus does not match the expectancy, the fox does not release his attack but merely continues to take in sensory information about the environment. Structurally, this attack response operates like the escape response of the scallop, for the response is released when the stimulus *matches* the expectancy.

Another form of behavior flow is "corrective" or "constructive," like driving a nail or ironing a handkerchief. In driving a nail, one's expectancy consists of the nail hammered flush with the surface. If the nail sticks out, then the hammer is used for another stroke. This form of behavior flow attaches the response to the mismatch. Generally speaking, such flows describe "plans" (Miller, Galanter, & Pribram, 1957), behavior flows that seem directed toward a specific goal. The "goal" is the expectancy of the behavior flow, and the analysis of stimulus input determines what aspects of the goal are significant. The behavior flow continues, and corrective responses are directed at the discrepancy until the stimulus input is brought into agreement with the expectancy. When a match is found, the responses end. The flowchart for such a flow is shown in Figure 1.2.

There are many examples of constructive behavior flows. Obviously, nest building in the bird, dam building in the beaver, or home building in the human will also contain behavior flows of this class, as will house-

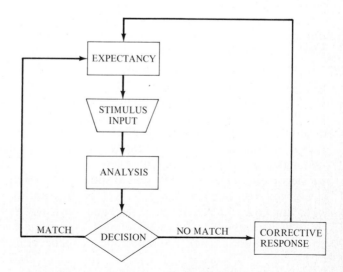

Figure 1.2   Flowchart of a corrective behavior flow.

keeping and repair. A factory worker inspecting manufactured parts for flaws will execute a corrective behavior flow. So will a cautious wolf approaching its den after a night's hunting, for he will have a detailed expectancy of how the area should look, smell, and sound, and will either attack or retreat from anything amiss. In each case, the expectancy is of a perfect or normal state, and the organism responds only to mismatches between the expectancy and what he perceives.

Is it possible for a behavior flow to have two different responses, one after a match and the other after a mismatch? Such structures are difficult to imagine at the lowest level of behavior, but they often appear at higher levels. For example, consider a bluejay pecking at corn kernels on the porch of a farmhouse. The bird will frequently raise its head and look around for a prowling cat or other danger. If it sees danger (that is, if there is a match with this expectancy), the bird will fly away. If it does not see danger, it will return and eat some more corn. Actually, what this seems to be is a behavior flow switching between two rather general motivational systems, fear and hunger; but in such a situation there is one definite response, flight, after a match; and another definite response, eating, after a mismatch.

IMPORTANT CHARACTERISTICS OF BEHAVIOR FLOWS

The simple behavior flow is a description of a stable, closed behavior pattern. In reality, most of what a man or animal does cannot be accomplished by a single spasm of effort but instead requires repeated applications of the same class of response, each adjusted to the changing situation. Only this whole stream of behavior can be thought to constitute a complete, purposive act. However, the whole stream of behavior, as laid out in time, is enormously complicated to list and describe. We see a child eating a candy bar and wish to make a behavioral analysis of this act. We do not want to write out the whole process, bite by bite and chew by chew. But if we used stimulus-response theory, in which the element is the single response, then a complete description of the act of eating a candy bar would have to include such a list. The behavior flow, in contrast, specifies a closed, continuous behavior pattern. The behavior flow is symbolized by a flowchart which clearly delineates its structure and makes all its parts apparent. Then, the fact that the flow loops back to its start over and over is sufficient to specify the repetition of the behavior whenever it is needed. Since there is a decision point within a simple behavior flow, the repetition of the behavior is not mere perseverance or blind habit; rather, it takes account of the appropriateness of the behavior to the situation. Since an expectancy can be complex, a great many responses of great variety can all be controlled within a single behavior flow.

Despite all this, there is a certain rigidity to a simple behavior flow. Since nothing that happens can change the way in which input information is analyzed and nothing can change the expectancy, an organism using a single given behavior flow will always behave the same way in the same situation. This is appropriate and helpful to an animal living in a stable environment to which it is adapted. So long as the scallop's main enemy is the starfish, it has the appropriate defensive behavior; but when humans begin preying on scallops using scoops and nets, the scallop's behavior flow is largely irrelevant, and it has no defense. A fox that has learned to recognize and chase squirrels may be much less efficient hunting rabbits and may find that its methods of approach, well adapted to woods and thickets, are ineffective in open pastures. The encroachment of agriculture has disrupted the lives of many animals because these animals may have fixed patterns of action and simple, unchangeable behavior flows. A change in the environment may turn a skill into a meaningless ritual.

Strictly speaking, it is not really possible for an animal to have only a single behavior pattern, unless it has only one need and meets that need with a single system of complex, coordinated behavior. One might find a one-celled animalcule that does nothing but eat, having no defensive behaviors and no courtship and finding no shelter. But such an animal would be atypical and interesting mainly as a curiosity. Most animals have, as minimal equipment, several behavior flows to take care of several bodily functions.

An interesting contrast between two behavior flows occurs in the female herring gull, who responds to equivalent stimuli (herring-gull eggs) in two different ways. When a gull mother is on her nest or returns to it, she cares for the eggs and broods them. Herring gulls make low nests of stones and twigs right on the ground, and it often happens that eggs roll out of the nest. The gull shows a characteristic behavior pattern in retrieving such eggs, scooping them awkwardly with her beak and drawing them under her into the nest.

Ethologists—students of the behavior of animals—have performed many experiments in the field to learn more about this behavior flow. One thing they have done is to scatter the gull's eggs while she is away fishing or hunting so that they can see how rapidly she finds the eggs, which eggs she will return to the nest first, and so forth. In later studies, imitation eggs were substituted for the gull's real eggs, and it was found that she would retrieve the imitation eggs as well as her own. Further study showed that she would always retrieve a larger egg before a smaller one, even when the larger egg was ridiculously large: she would pull in an object the size of a tennis ball before her own egg. Furthermore, if an imitation egg was speckled with very dark spots on a very light background, it would be retrieved before the gull's own brown-on-yellow egg. The studies also determined that in picking out an egg to retrieve the herring gull pays no attention to shape: she would struggle bravely to drag in a brick painted white with dark spots, leaving her own eggs strewn about. The egg-retrieving behavior flow, then, depends upon analyzing the visual pattern of the egg according to size and speckling, and choosing the object greater in size and with more vivid speckling.

As it happens, the herring gull is a rapacious hunter and considers the eggs of other herring gulls to be good food. When a mother gull goes out hunting, she is dealing with eggs just like those in her own nest, but now she analyzes them in another way. Studies of the egg-hunting behavior of gulls have shown that the gull will attack only an egg that is egg-shaped: shape is a most important variable in selecting which egg to attack. The size of the egg is fairly important but hunting gulls prefer eggs of small size—about the size of their own eggs, or smaller. In hunting, it is not true that the larger egg is better. Finally, when hunting, the herring gull completely ignore speckling; she neither prefers nor avoids eggs with speckling as compared with solid-colored eggs.

The maladaptive retrieving behavior of the mother gull illustrates the difficulties that may be caused by rigidity of behavior flows. Such rigidity is particularly characteristic of birds and other lower animals and would not appear in the same form in humans or other primates. But, in all fairness, it must be admitted that the herring gull's retrieval behavior was quite satisfactory until her environment was altered by the entrance of the ethologist with his painted bricks.

This example also demonstrates the importance of the analysis of the stimulus input and the expectancy. The behavior flow determines what the animal is looking for, what expectancy it will match or mismatch, and what properties of the stimulus input are delivered to the decision-making stage.

Finally, it should be noted that the responses made are often not mere muscle twitches, but are complex adjustments to the immediate situation. Retrieving an egg, for a herring gull, can be a protracted effort, since the beak is better designed for tearing flesh than for dragging an egg, and the technique is inefficient. The task is a little like trying to drag a football up an inclined driveway with a billiard cue, and it is obvious that each response must be finely attuned to the position and movement of the egg and the obstructions around it. Similarly, the spider spinning its web, or the fox chasing a rabbit, must adjust its behavior in a complex and sensitive way to the problem before it.

ENDING AND CHANGING BEHAVIOR FLOWS

In the real behavior of animals, a single simple behavior flow does not exist totally alone, and an animal does not go through its life making only one response to a single need. However, the flowcharts in Figures 1.1 and 1.2 are closed loops; and the implication is that if the animal gets into a behavior flow, there is no way he can ever get out of it. To correct this theoretical absurdity, at least some of the conditions that terminate or interrupt a behavior flow must now be specified.

First, of course, the behavior flow may end because it reaches its object. For example, the fox will stop chasing a rabbit when he catches it. The gull stops retrieving eggs when there are none left outside the nest. In each case the behavior flow has an object, a situation that it is attempting to accomplish. When that goal is attained, the animal naturally goes into another behavior flow. When the fox has caught his rabbit, he kills it, carries it to a safe place, and eats it. When the gull has all her eggs in the nest, she broods them and may also turn her attention to repairing the nest.

This way of terminating a behavior flow implies that there is some larger structure, a higher-order behavior flow, of which the particular behavior flow is merely a part. The higher-order expectancy has as its main function the job of deciding which of several simple behavior flows should be used. A higher-order behavior flow has the usual expectancy, stimulus input, and stimulus analysis. However, the "responses" are not simple: each consists of a whole behavior flow of lower order. Functionally, a higher-order behavior flow makes a decision as to which of two lower-order behavior flows is to begin next. The component behavior flows themselves are just like ordinary simple behavior flows except that they loop back not only to their own lower-level expectancy but also to the higher-level expectancy which controls them.

A predator requires two quite different behavior flows—one to chase its prey, and the second to kill it. Each of these behavior flows may control a protracted effort; but the chase ends at capture, and there the fighting and killing begin. Before the prey is captured, the predator uses a behavior flow with a pursuit response resulting from a match between expectancy (of a fleeing prey) and input. After capture, the predator may use what can be described as a "corrective" behavior flow, in which the expectancy is of a dead prey and any sign of life is attacked. Finally, when the prey is killed, the predator will proceed to some other activity, such as hiding its victim or eating. In the flowchart, this shift to an entirely new activity will be represented by the term "exit." This term signifies that the diagram is incomplete, but for the moment the organism is leaving the stage of our theoretical attention; see Figure 1.3.

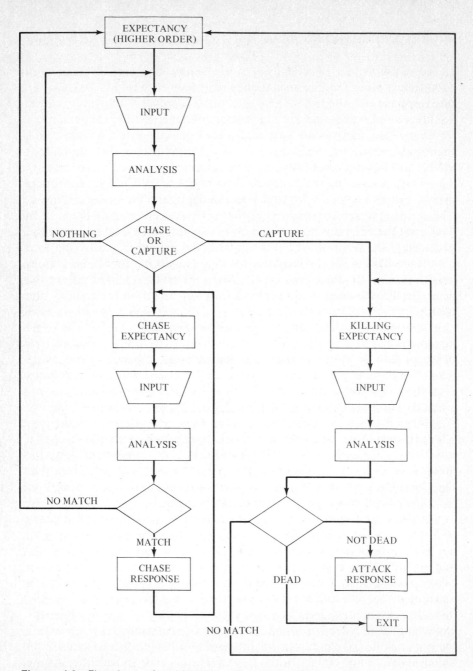

Figure 1.3 Flowchart of a hierarchy of behavior flows, with a higher-order complex hunting behavior flow controlling two lower-order flows, chasing and killing.

Figure 1.3 shows a hierarchy of behavior flows. The "higher-order" expectancy is of a normal behavior flow except that the responses, instead of being simple responses as in Figures 1.1 and 1.2, now are new behavior flows. Furthermore, whenever one of the lower-order expectancies does not produce a match, the system, instead of returning to the lower-order entry point, goes back to the higher-order expectancy.

Consider the fox who is hunting. While chasing, he may just chase, remaining within one behavior flow. After each unsuccessful search for a rabbit, or after any disruption of his process of chasing one, the fox must be prepared to shift to the behavior flow of killing. Therefore, constant decisions must be made as to whether to continue the behavior flow of chasing or shift to the flow of killing. That fact is depicted in Figure 1.3 by going back, after each "no match," to the higher-order expectancy, where a decision is made to look, chase, or kill.

Notice in Figure 1.3 that the whole complex behavior flow must stop when the rabbit is dead, since neither chasing nor killing is now appropriate. Obviously, to be more precise we should somehow have another branch to take the system eventually to another simple behavior flow of hiding or eating, and the branch marked "exit" would lead to the new behavior structure. In fact, such behavior might be controlled by a behavior flow of a still higher order, which decides between the chasing-and-killing structure and a later storing-and-eating structure. Because including this would further complicate the picture, the expedient has been used of merely marking a termination point as an exit from the present flow, even though we must understand that every such exit must go somewhere in a proper and complete account of the behavior.

Another example of a behavior flow made of smaller flows is a bird building a nest. One component of the act is the constructive behavior flow described earlier, by which the bird responds to any lack of completeness or any fault in the structure. However, quite often the bird must leave the nest to get string, grass, or twigs as building material.

The diagram of this more complex behavior flow may be simplified by the use of a block diagram which is like a flowchart except that major subunits (the two component behavior flows) are not diagrammed completely but instead are represented by single boxes; see Figure 1.4. The system in Figure 1.4 is interesting in that the two lower-level component behavior flows are clearly of the two different classes. When the bird is seeking a bit of string she searches all over with the expectancy of a bit of string, and once a match is made she makes the associated response: that is, she picks it up. This is a typical hunting-type behavior flow. At this time the higher-order system takes over, and she flies back to the nest and begins the repair work. The repair job is handled by a typical constructive

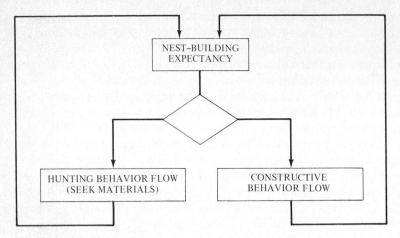

Figure 1.4 Simplified block diagram of a behavior pattern built from two simple behavior flows.

behavior flow, in which the bird has an expectancy of a perfect nest and responds when she finds a mismatch between the actual nest and her concept.

The above paragraphs show how we can understand the process by which an animal shifts from one behavior flow to another; and we have seen that these behavior flows may all be parts of a larger structure, still of the same type. The behavior flow gives a picture of organized, habitual, coordinated behavior systems. However, within this framework the only way one behavior flow can stop is for control to be switched to another behavior flow. Sometimes, it appears, a behavior flow just stops, being finished or interrupted; and on one occasion it has been necessary to use the idea of an exit from a behavior flow without saying where the organism goes.

A classic problem in behavior psychology has been the definition of the response. At one extreme, Guthrie expressed a preference for "muscle twitches"—that is, relatively small responses. At the other extreme, Tolman preferred to deal with "purposive behavior," which turned out to include responses like "looking for restaurant." When animal behavior (or human behavior) is to be used as the index of all interesting psychological events, it is important that the concept of a response be well defined: however, this has not been done adequately in most theories of learning.

Within the present approach, notice that higher-order behavior flows have, as their responses, other behavior flows. Now imagine the possible fine-grain analysis of a complex act—for example, a bird landing on a twig. At the highest level, the decision may be whether to land (responding to fatigue) or to abort the landing (responding to unfavorable wind conditions, fear of a predator, etc.). If the decision is to land, this does not control a simple response but instead integrates a new behavior flow that may involve a downwind approach, turning into a base leg, and then again turning into an upwind approach to the twig. At a certain time the bird may decide that within its approach behavior flow it is time to go into the final landing. This decision in turn initiates a behavior flow that results in reducing forward speed and increasing lift for the landing; and this in turn requires increasing the angle of attack of the wings, dropping the tail as a brake, and perhaps making backward flying movements to maintain lift while reducing speed. Of these parts, dropping the tail as a brake requires several muscular adjustments, including spreading the tail feathers, bending the lower backbone, etc. Each of these major muscular adjustments can in turn be thought of as contractions of certain muscle fibers, and those contractions are controlled by specific nerve impulses through the spinal cord and into the muscle controls. These actions can in turn be analyzed as specific combinations of emissions of chemicals at the contact points (synapses) and the propagation of electrical disturbances through the motor nerves, and specific chemical and physical actions in the muscles.

At every level the behavior flow is controlled by a higher-level structure and itself controls a response that can be analyzed as a lower-level behavior flow. There is no "correct definition of a response," in an absolute sense.

This means that the definitions of "behavior flow," as a whole system, and "response," as a part of that system, are relative to one another. Relative to the decision to land, turning upwind toward the twig is a response. Relative to turning upwind, banking the wings is a response, and the turn is a behavior flow. Any particular item of behavior is a response relative to a more inclusive, higher-level behavior flow and a behavior flow relative to lower-level, more detailed items of behavior.

Chapter 2 deals with another aspect of the mental life of organisms, namely, what they do when they are not doing anything in particular. Most conventional theories of behavior have been satisfied with trying to explain purposeful, organized, and somewhat stereotyped behavior. It is this kind of behavior, after all, that ensures the organism's success and survival. Or does it? What role is played by curiosity and inquisitiveness and the ability to retain information? Is this just an extension of the idea of a behavior flow, or is it something else? These are the questions discussed in Chapter 2.

Learning and Memory

Although behavior is controlled by behavior flows, this does not mean that the higher animals are limited to rigid, unchanging structures. The primates, and especially human beings, have extensive structures of higher-order control systems, so that any particular behavior they perform can always be changed by a suitable shift in a higher-order strategy, motivation, or belief. Laboratory researchers have barely begun to understand the complexities of behavioral control exhibited even by such lower mammals as the white rat.

Obviously, any behavior flow at any level is influenced by the stimulus input. If a nursing puppy's tail is stepped on by a clumsy human, the puppy at once shifts from sucking milk to crying and scrambling. This shift in behavior is directly related to the stimulation from the compressed tail. However, an adult higher animal may also shape his flow of behavior as a result of stimulus inputs that have occurred in the past. If the puppy, when it is a few weeks older, has a history of having its tail caught in a swinging screen door, it will adjust its locomotor pattern as it scampers through the doorway, running with tail between legs. This adjustment is made not to a stimulus that occurs contemporaneously with the response but to a repeating pattern of coincidence between a slamming door and a pinched tail. The puppy has *learned*, we say, and possibly it remembers certain past events.

This type of learned behavior flow is extended over a fairly long period of time—at least several days. That is, events which occur on Saturday help determine the form of responses made on the following Tuesday, so that understanding the pattern of behavior exhibited on Tuesday requires some reference to earlier events. The brain of a higher animal can integrate, or bring together, information acquired over a long span of time, and this ability greatly increases the animal's effectiveness in dealing with the environment.

THEORETICAL APPROACHES TO LEARNING AND MEMORY

How shall the process of learning be conceived? There are a variety of standard theoretical approaches which serve to give an account of learning and memory. Each such analysis emphasizes certain questions about learning and suggests certain answers. This book cannot undertake to give a complete historical and philosophical recounting of this enormous problem; sketching a few approaches, however, will be helpful in indicating the nature of the theory used in this book.

Classical

First, the *classical approach* distinguishes clearly between contemporaneous events and influences, occurring at the same time as the behavior, and past events and experiences. This is the distinction between perception and memory: between thinking about what is not present and seeing what is present. The content of perception, according to this classical approach, is to be understood by analyzing the sense organs, the energy falling upon the sense organs, and the neural networks that transmit such information from the eye, the ear, the skin, or some other organ to the brain. The general concept is rather like a telephone network. If a person or animal reacts to a stimulus that is no longer present, this experience cannot be explained by reference to sense organs; the information must be "stored" when it is received, so that it can be used later. This distinction between memory of past events and perception of present events is deeply ingrained in the commonsense philosophy of western civilization. The reader surely understands this distinction—what he will have to do is question the distinction.

It is interesting to see how this approach handles responses to stimuli that have not yet occurred—events in the future. If the past is remembered, and the present is perceived, what is done to the future? It is expected, imagined, "foreseen" (a word that is either a self-contradiction or a circular definition, depending on your point of view), or predicted. Generally speaking, scientists are not enamored of teleological theories, that is, of theories which consider the present to be controlled by the future. An example of a teleological theory would be an explanation of history as a path toward universal salvation, the dictatorship of the proletariat, or final total dissolution and entropy. In one sense the psychologist is totally willing to agree that an event cannot have consequences that occur before it in time—except for the psychological event of anticipation of a future event. When such anticipation exists, it can have consequences before the event anticipated actually does occur. Since anticipations seem, sometimes, to be powerful organizers of behavior, in this sense the study of psychology is often strongly involved with future events, expectancies, and anticipations.

The first concept of learning and memory, then, arises from simply classifying all time into past, present, and future. Control of behavior from the past is then attributed to memory; control from the present, to perception; and control from the future, to expectancy or imagination. In this classical view, memory, perception, and imagination become "faculties" of the mind. Since people obviously can deal with the past, present, and future, these capacities can confidently be attributed to the mind.

Behavioral

This general classical position was challenged by a second concept, the systematic *behavior theories* that arose during the 1930s and 1940s. Behaviorists were concerned with the evidence that could be used to support various claims about psychology, and they took the position that the only evidence we can use is behavior. The rat is shown to learn if and only if its behavior shows a systematic change over trials. The human is said to remember, not because he has the experience of a past event, but because he can recount it (in "verbal behavior"), answer questions about it, or otherwise pass some objective test. Correctly interpreted, behaviorism does not question the importance of experiences of all sorts, but merely says that the experiences themselves are not the kind of data psychology can use—that an experimenter must always find some external, objective, observable behavior of the subject which discloses the inner state. Naturally, because behaviorists thought that everything must be shown by behavior, they soon found little profit in talking about the inner states of experience at all, and discussions of inner experience by behaviorists gradually decreased.

The most influential form of behaviorism has been the stimulus-response school. According to this approach, any element of behavior is thought of as a response to a stimulus. To say that a response is made *to* a certain stimulus seems to imply that the stimulus and response exist at the same time, or at least that the response occurs immediately after the stimulus. But if a mother calls her child in for dinner (stimulus), and the child answers a minute after the call (response), there is some question whether the answer can be thought of as a response *to* the call. This question is debatable. Suppose that a rat, by running through a maze many times, learns to find food; then, after a week has elapsed, the rat is put back into the starting box of the maze. A behaviorist will not agree that the rat now runs through the maze correctly as a response to the food stimuli given a week ago. The food stimuli of a week ago are not the stimuli which evoke the present running response. Other stimuli, now present in the maze, must be specified to give a proper S-R account of running the maze: the visual appearance of the inside of the maze, stimulation from the ceiling of the room that may serve to orient the animal, odors (which people cannot detect but which the rat can), rough patches on the floor of the maze alley, localized sounds, etc. (Restle, 1957). Each such element is present at about the time the animal responds and can thus be thought to be a stimulus.

The role of previous events, in S-R learning theory, is to modify or change the set of S-R connections the animal uses. Most of S-R theory, consequently, has been concerned with the gradual accumulation of, or change in, S-R *habits*.

A habit resembles the kind of behavior flow discussed in Chapter 1. A standard learning theory would hold that subjects learn (strengthen or acquire) some behavior flows and unlearn, or extinguish, others. Why? One major learning theory attributes learning or strengthening to some sort of specific reward system, that is, to reinforcement. If a habit or behavior is used and the result is the satisfaction of some need or want (as when a certain bar-pressing behavior flow results in food), then the response is strengthened. If, on the other hand, repeated use of a habit does not result in any satisfaction, the habit will weaken in strength, and very probably some competing, incompatible habit will become stronger. According to such a theory, past experiences change the relationship between stimuli and responses.

This approach has a considerable advantage over the classical memory theory. When we realize that any human, and indeed almost any laboratory animal, has a long and complex history of actual past events, the possible content of its memory is too voluminous and complicated to imagine. As a result, classical theory is able to make hardly any definite predictions about behavior. A classical theory has somewhat the role of newspaper around a fish—it wraps facts in words without changing or improving them very much. S-R theory, by narrowing the possible range of effects of past stimuli, greatly simplifies the theoretical problem of explanation. Unfortunately, however, simplification in one area is paid for by great complication in another.

It is not sufficient to know what S-R habits (or behavior flows) an animal has and how they are organized; one must also know how strong each such structure is. Furthermore, since every experience may strengthen or weaken one or more habits, during the lifetime of an animal these various strengths increase and decrease, independently of one another. This makes the psychologists' task quite difficult. The worst difficulty is that the strengths of the habits at a given time serve in part to determine the animal's responses, and these responses, in turn, by affecting the animal's experiences, have an effect on what it will learn and therefore on what the new response strengths will be. There is a "feedback" feature in this theory, so that what the animal happens to know affects what he will learn. The result is a well-defined but impenetrable mathematical morass.[1]

BEHAVIOR FLOWS IN TIME: LEARNING AND REMEMBERING

A behavior flow is extended in time and space: it takes some time to perform or complete such a process, and the animal performing it may move around in its environment during the course of the behavior. When we think of a dog chasing a rabbit, we have no great difficulty in seeing that chasing in one place is part of the same behavior flow as chasing in another place. It is still one behavior flow, even though different specific muscles may be used or the behavior may be adjusted to a different setting. Similarly, a behavior flow extends over time, and it should not be difficult to think of it in this way.

Conventional thinking divides time into past, present, and future, and thereby may cut a single extended event into artificial parts. When divided into these three parts, time is boxed into a particular and usually erroneous frame of reference. Think of a fish just in the process of

---

[1]The simplest form of this kind of theory, the "linear model" has been used in a wide variety of applications; Bush & Mosteller's *Stochastic Models for Learning* (1955), in its discussion of "experimenter-subject controlled events," clearly shows the difficulty of this approach. See also Restle, 1959, page 418.

starting to jump out of a pond. It would be wrong to say that its head is an air animal, its lower body is a water animal, and one part of its gills constitutes a surface animal—it is one fish. Similarly, a behavior flow is not partly a past event (in memory), partly a future event (anticipated), and partly a present event (being perceived)—it is one event extended in time.

Naturally, when a person discusses the effects of past events on behavior he will refer to memory for those events. It is when this memory is thought of as a separate thing, faculty, place, or process, and is separated from perception and anticipation, that the theoretical error creeps in. Terms like "the content of memory," "placing items in memory," and "the structure of memory," are useful in general or informal discourse, but can be troublesome if one is trying to understand exactly what psychological processes occur.

An example of such theoretical troubles is the concept of multiple memories. Experimental work (Sperling, 1960) has identified a "sensory buffer" in which information is stored in raw form (like the image of the letter "A") for very short times, perhaps 200 milliseconds (2/10 second; 1 millisecond = 1/1,000 second). Then the information in that image is translated into a name or is otherwise interpreted, and this information goes into "short-term storage," where it may be retained through cyclic rehearsal. Finally, the information may then be transferred to "long-term storage," a relatively permanent repository. These two types of storage can be further subdivided, according to how long information is held, what particular kind of information is held (images, names, concepts, etc.), and what methods are used to retrieve information from storage. However, the proliferation of different kinds of storages has gradually produced difficulties in deciding how different kinds of memory are related. Is information passed from one storage to another by a process like an old-fashioned bucket brigade at a fire? Does it enter a sensory buffer, rest there, move to short-term memory, recirculate there, and then finally move out into permanent memory? When a picture or an object is named, the process of naming it seems to involve retrieving information from long-term memory. Thus, a picture of your sister might enter a sensory buffer, and then her name might be put into short-term memory for storage—but her name surely came from long-term memory. Furthermore, the content of all memories is influenced by the kind of situation the subject is in and his strategy for remembering. It is not even clear that strategies for remembering reside in memory at all; and if they do, it is still unclear where, in what memory, they may be found.

To avoid this difficulty, this book will concentrate on how behavior flows are distributed over time. The purpose is not to ignore or question the importance of memory, but instead to give a coherent account of memory without introducing complicated mechanisms.

In the simple behavior flows discussed in Chapter 1, the subject set up an expectancy, received an information input, analyzed it, immediately matched the result against the expectancy, and took action. In one manner of speaking, the information in the stimulus input was immediately consumed in the process of deciding whether or not a match was made. Once the response has been made, the stimulus input has ended, and the subject will then take in a new stimulus input in going through the behavior flow again.

If a behavior flow is distributed over a significant span of time, the animal will find itself using old information, making decisions upon the basis of events that occurred a relatively long time ago. This means that the information in those old inputs was not consumed immediately, but instead was stored for later use.

When an animal is not engaged in a specific behavior flow, it may explore its surroundings, gathering information to be stored and used later. Whatever stimuli become inputs are first stored for 200 milliseconds. This process may be thought of as a storage within the input process itself. The information is then analyzed, and some attributes of the input are selected. This process of analysis may take very little time to be completed—perhaps less than a second, perhaps a little longer. The process depends on the subject's expectancies, for analysis depends on the expectancy involved. A behavior flow, initiated or sustained by a stimulus input, may remain active for a considerable while, perhaps by a process like "rehearsal" in the human. The continuous exercise of this behavior flow serves to maintain the effects of the stimulus—the subject "remembers," in the sense that he responds after the stimulus just as he would have responded at the time of the stimulus. If information is to be retained for use after the original behavior flow has been left, it must be suitably analyzed, recoded, and prepared for storage.

Consider a rat in a maze. If there is always food at the end of the maze, the rat will soon learn to take a direct pathway to the food. There are two possible explanations for this. One is reinforcement theory: that the animal at first blunders around but finally reaches the food by chance; response is reinforced by finding the food. In the next trial, when the rat approaches the goal box, the correct last turn is well learned; the rat moves directly to the food, and therefore its next-to-last correct response is also reinforced. In this way the rat learns, working backwards from the end of the maze.

The second kind of explanation of maze learning is that the rat explores its environment—especially if it is hungry, but also from curiosity. During its exploration, the rat takes in considerable information, from which it extracts the locations of parts of the maze relative to one another. The rat will establish landmarks: windows, rat cages along the wall, sounds, odors from within the maze, and so forth. Its cognitive structure concentrates on locations and therefore is like a cognitive map (in contrast, say, to a cognitive list of places, or an association of what sound goes with what odor). Of course, the food is localized in this map, and the hungry rat's approach to food (its typical food-getting behavior flow) soon eliminates all blind alleys.

Which of these interpretations is correct? One test is to see whether a rat will form a cognitive map without reinforcement. This is not a new idea—an experiment to test it was performed in 1930 by E. C. Tolman, the early cognitive theorist, and his student Honzik.

Cognitive Maps in Rats

In Tolman's experiment, rats ran a maze for ten days with reward (one control group) or without reward (the experimental group and the other control group). On the eleventh day, reward was introduced for the experimental group. If a rat had learned the maze by extracting information and forming a cognitive map, the trials it had spent simply exploring the maze would enable it to form long-term memory traces of the various parts of the maze and also to connect various adjacent parts. This complex structure could quite easily be attached to a food-oriented behavior flow, as soon as the animal happened to find food at a known location within the maze. We should, then, expect that the animal would learn as much while exploring the maze as it would while running the maze for food. Before that knowledge is connected to a behavior flow, we cannot expect any very great change in the path taken by the rat. But when food is introduced, the rat will be able to use its knowledge to find a direct path through the maze.

In the experiment, the control group who found reward every day would learn to run the maze with fewer and fewer errors, as they developed a cognitive map and attached it to their food-getting behavior flow. The control group who never received reward should be expected to display much less reduction in errors, since they would simply continue exploring; it is possible, however, that as these animals learned the location of blind alleys, they would be less inclined to explore them, because blind alleys contain less new information than alleys that continue on. The experimental group, finding no food for the first ten days, would simply explore, like the second control group. When food is introduced, however, these animals should quite rapidly connect their

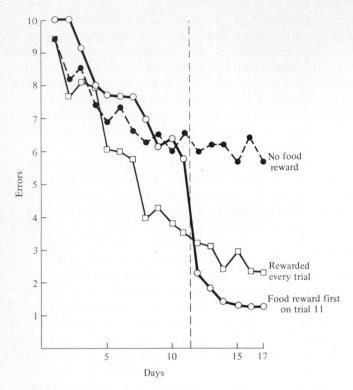

Figure 2.1 Evidence for latent learning. Notice that the experimental group improves slowly without food but immediately improves when given food, showing it had learned on nonrewarded trials. *(Tolman & Honzik, 1930.)*

cognitive map of the maze to the food-getting behavior flow, so that they would perform about as well as the animals who had received food on every trial, the first control group.

The results were as follows: (1) On the first ten days, rewarded rats made fewer errors than unrewarded rats. (2) Even for the groups without reward, there was some improvement in running the maze. (3) The introduction of reward on the eleventh day of the experiment led to an immediate decrease in the number of errors. This last observation is direct evidence for "latent learning." The rats in the experimental group knew considerably more about the maze than their previous behavior had indicated. All that was required to make them show their knowledge was an adequate incentive. The original experimental results are shown in Figure 2.1.

The key question in an experiment of this type is "What did the animal learn?" The animals who merely explored without reward cannot be said to have learned a habit or acquired a smooth behavior flow. However, since they could very quickly learn the correct path when given rewards, they had surely learned something that permitted them to get through the maze. In the human, this would be called "knowledge" of the maze, and could no doubt consist of memories of various parts of the maze and connected memories of adjacent parts of the maze. It might even include the ability to recall various parts of the maze; and it would certainly include the ability to recognize landmarks. The experimental evidence is that rats exploring a maze collect and store information and organize it so that it can be useful in running the maze to a given goal.

It is easy to see why an animal such as a rat would benefit from having the ability to form cognitive maps by exploration and observation. If a rat could learn only from finding food, it would have less chance of learning about places where food might later be found. Hunting and predatory animals, especially, need to know the lay of the land in order to locate and trap or capture their prey. Similarly, herbivores that travel over long distances to find or follow food (like the great herds of antelope and zebras in Africa) may locate waterholes, passes, paths, and areas of vegetation that are not used immediately but can be important later. The ability to gain information and store it without any reward is of great value. We do not know all we should like to about what information can be stored by what species of animal at what age, and following what past experience. Our discussion here is in relatively general terms and must be supplemented by more intensive studies. It is to be hoped that future years will complete our understanding of how and when animals collect information.

PROCESSES OF MEMORY

If information is to be used later, then it follows logically that the information must be stored and must be available at a later time. There is no value in collecting information if it is immediately discarded, like an unread letter. The information consumed in making decisions in a behavior flow may not be stored, but it is still useful. However, if information is not used when gathered, and if it is not stored or is not retrievable, then it is worthless.

The processes of memory are three: encoding, storage, and retrieval. First, the information as gathered must be classified and arranged so that it can be stored. This is the process of encoding. Second, information must produce some trace or other permanent (or semipermanent) change in the brain, which will remain until the information is needed. This is the process of storage. Storage may be short-term or long-term. Finally, when it is needed (as, in latent learning, when the rat first finds food at the end of the maze), the information must be retrieved. Retrieval is a process acting upon the stored trace that arouses a suitable behavior flow based on the stored information.

Encoding

For short-term storage, the first process or stage, *encoding,* consists mainly of a process of "identifying" the stimulus. In the human, this process may be accompanied by naming the stimulus, and short-term memory for words or numbers can often be supplemented by a process of verbal rehearsal, in which the subject repeatedly remembers the item and says it to himself. It also appears that visual situations can be imagined and thereby held for a fairly long time in short-term storage. Encoding into long-term storage appears to be a much more radical reworking of the information, for long-term storage requires that a meaningful pattern be extracted from the information. When college students are instructed to memorize meaningless information, they often supplement it with something more meaningful. For example, when required to associate the pair of nonsense syllables MEK-ZOG, the subject may come up with a construction like "MEK-make-make a cake-soggy-ZOG," thereby placing the impoverished syllables within a larger context from which a meaningful, or at least memorable, pattern can be extracted (Woodworth, 1938, p. 34).

It has often seemed mysterious to psychologists that when a subject is asked merely to remember a few pairs of nonsense syllables, he will go through an enormously more complicated process of invention to try to develop a mnemonic device. The reason people do this is to find a meaningful pattern. The reason it has surprised psychologists is that memories were usually thought of as if they were photographs of past events that could be filed and later found when needed. Instead, it appears that long-term memory can hold only information that fits into a pattern. Thus, when the experimenter (or the environment) asks a subject to learn meaningless material from which no pattern emerges, the subject is forced to exercise enough imagination to form some pattern.

What do we mean by a "meaningful pattern"? The term sounds acceptable, but we often do not know what is and what is not meaningful to a friend, a child, or an animal. Is meaning a property of the pattern itself? If stimuli are made up at random, then surely as a whole they do not form a meaningful pattern. Many lists of psychological materials like nonsense syllables are, in this sense, strictly meaningless. To be meaningful, a pattern must be regular—that is, governed by rules or regularities. Of course, if these rules are completely foreign to the subject's knowledge or to his behavior flow, then the pattern will not be meaningful. If the pattern is to be meaningful to the subject in question, it must correspond to a system in the subject of higher-order expectancies and behavior flows. *Encoding,* therefore, is a process of analyzing the input and selecting properties appropriate to higher-order behavior flows.

Storage

The second stage or process of memory is *storage.* Current studies of memory distinguish between short-term storage, of information which is available only briefly and must remain continuously circulating, and long-term storage, of information that is well integrated and can be retrieved after a relatively long period.

It is sometimes necessary to make a distinction between short-term *storage* and short-term *memory.* If a person or animal remembers something after a short period of time, say 10 seconds, then surely this must be considered short-term memory. However, the information might have been in short-term storage, so that it would soon have been forgotten, or it might have been in long-term storage, so that it would have been available a long time later. There is no way to know, since it was tested so soon. Short-term memory—the ability to perform at 10 seconds—can be divided into components: one component is the information in short-term storage, which rapidly dissipates; the other component is in long-term storage. The way to estimate the amount of information in each storage is to make measurements at several brief intervals—say, 5, 10, 15, and 20 seconds. Suppose that subjects can remember .80 of the material at 5 seconds, .50 at 10 seconds, .43 at 15 seconds, and .40 at 20 seconds. It appears that this "forgetting curve" is leveling out at approximately .35; the point where it levels out represents the ability based on long-term storage. At 5 seconds, when the subject remembers with a probability of .80, we can attribute .35 of this to long-term storage and the remaining .45 to short-term storage.

It appears that the short-term memory of college students can hold only a few independent items, somewhere between four and ten. The actual amount of information that can be stored may be much larger than this if information is efficiently encoded, for four or five items can be expanded into a great deal of specific information during the process of recall. However, it is in short-term memory that this complaint holds true: "If I could only forget my telephone number, I could remember one more fact." The evidence suggests that if short-term storage is full, then if one more item is to be put in, some other item must be dropped out. Only a few lower-order flows can remain active at the same time (Miller, 1956).

In long-term storage, there is evidently no limit on capacity. The information in long-term storage has been related to higher-order behavior flows which are not consciously active all the time. The conscious cognitive process may operate at lower levels of the hierarchy, at lower-level behavior flows, for a long time without requiring any decisions at the higher levels. These higher-level behavior flows, though available to direct behavior, are actually quiescent. Information affecting this structure may be absorbed at many different levels and parts of the cognitive hierarchy, and there is no limit on the number of items held except the complexity and the appropriateness of the whole structure.

Retrieval

The third process is *retrieval.* Retrieval from short-term memory is relatively direct, since the relevant lower-order behavior flows are continuously active. Two major facts should be pointed out: (1) Remembering one item is quite likely to cause other items in short-term to be lost, so that a person can rarely retrieve everything in short-term storage. Apparently, making the overt response of one behavior flow tends to disrupt the rehearsal of the others. (2) Scanning of short-term storage to see whether or not a particular item is stored there is a remarkably rapid process. For example, the search for a single letter or number takes about .036 second. Such a search apparently does not involve making each response but instead is a pure "rehearsal" of the set. Little information is available about the process of scanning (Sternberg, 1966).

Retrieval is a major problem in long-term memory because items in long-term storage do not remain active and therefore must be searched for and found. The ability to find information in long-term storage depends upon having a clear idea of what one is looking for, so as to be able to establish a small and relevant "search set."[2] This in turn requires that the information be stored in relatively orderly and coherent fashion and that the search process be organized in a fashion compatible with the storage system. Suppose, for example, that someone asks you to recall your maternal grandmother's maiden name and that you have to search for it. You might begin a systematic search through your family tree, recalling other surnames. Alternatively, you might remember that it was an uncommon German name, and then try to come at it by its sound or by

[2]A "search set" is a collection of memories or possible memories through which the mind searches when seeking some specific item of memory information. Obviously, this is a higher-order behavior flow that controls, at the next lower lever, a certain set of possible flows. If a flow at much too high a level is activated, the search set is too large. If a wrong branch is activated, the resulting search set is inappropriate (Shiffrin, 1970).

searching your mind for names of that type. If names are not arranged by sound in your memory storage, then there is no way you could establish a set of similar-sounding names to search. Thus, if encoding has not prepared the way, recall cannot follow—at least, it cannot be produced by a systematic and efficient search. The proper arrangement of memories and a process of discerning important and memorable properties are necessary for rapid recall of needed information from suitable, compact, and relevant search sets.

SHORT-TERM STORAGE

There are obvious difficulties in studying the properties of short-term storage. Basically, it is investigated by studying short-term memory—that is, by presenting some information to a subject and testing his knowledge of it within a few seconds. But the subject may respond successfully not by using short-term storage but by using long-term storage. Most of the experimental methods for study of short-term storage have as their main purpose separating it from long-term storage. Another problem, particularly when we study animals, is that in a totally familiar situation subjects tend to respond not on the basis of memory at all, but on the basis of some well-established behavior flow which uses immediately available input rather than old information.

To measure what an animal remembers, we must have some response from him. If this response is to be steady and reliable enough for exact measurement, it will accompany some behavior flow. How, then, do we measure short-term memory?

In animal research, an important method is the study of what is called the "delayed reaction." For example, a monkey sits looking through glass at a tray that contains two shallow food wells side by side. The experimenter places a raisin in one of the food wells, letting the monkey watch, and then covers the two wells with two objects. He waits the "delay period" and then raises the glass and lets the animal push aside just one of the two objects. If the monkey chooses the correct object, he gets the raisin; otherwise, the window is dropped and he has to wait for the next trial. This delayed response is, of course, integrated into the food-getting behavior flow of the animal; but in this experiment the behavior flow must be directed by one key fact, the actual location of the food. This fact changes from trial to trial. The only way the animal can consistently get the food is to remember, over the intervening period, where he saw the food placed.

In 1912, W. S. Hunter wrote the classical monograph on the subject of delayed responses. The essential principle of Hunter's experiment is to

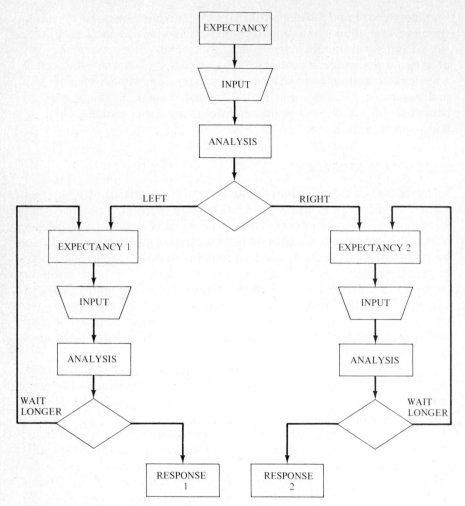

Figure 2.2 Behavior flow system to control delayed-reaction responses. Notice loops, labeled "wait longer," in lower-order behavior flows.

present an animal with a stimulus to which it habitually or instinctively
reacts, and then to withdraw the stimulus and allow the animal to make
the response in its absence. Since the stimulus is absent at the moment of
reaction, the animal must be reacting to some substitute for that stimulus—a memory or representation. Because the information is presented
only once and then changed for the next trial, long-term storage of the
information is not really relevant to the task. The behavior flow is
extended over time. The subject need not store or extend the input, since
only the location and perhaps some general description of the stimulus is

needed. Therefore, one can think of the subject as setting up a complex behavior flow in which it "loops," waiting for an opportunity to respond. (Figure 2.2.)

In studies of short-term memory in rats, Hunter used a three-choice apparatus, as shown in Figure 2.3. In this particular experiment, light was used as the stimulus. First, the rat was taught to go to the lighted door to find food. Any one of the three doors might be lighted on a given trial, and food was found only at the lighted opening. When this was learned, a light at one of the openings was turned on and then off while the animal was still confined in the release cage. After the controlled delay interval had elapsed, the rat was released. If it remembered where the light had last been shown, it could go to the correct opening and find the food. The doors were lit up in random order so that the animal could not react correctly by always going to a certain position or by following any other pattern. In this experiment, Hunter found that the maximum delay a rat could tolerate was about 10 seconds. This is the rat's span of short-term memory for a light that it has seen.

Honzik, in 1931, did a similar experiment, but with important modifications. He used a white curtain and a black curtain, placing the

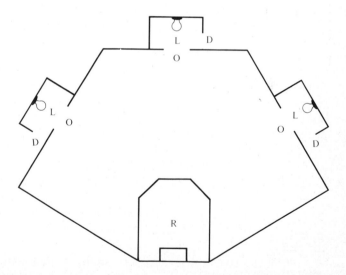

Figure 2.3 Simplified ground plan of delayed-reaction apparatus used by hunter. A light L may be made to shine through any of the openings O. When the animal goes through the lighted opening, he will find food at position D. The animal is inserted in box R, which has glass sides so that he can see which opening is lighted. If the animal attempts to go through an opening that was not lighted, he will find his path obstructed by movable blocks (not shown here).

food behind the door with the white curtain. The rat would run up to the curtain but could not get through because of a wooden block behind the doorway. Then a screen was lowered to separate the rat from the curtains, and a black curtain was substituted for the white one, so that both curtains looked alike. At the end of the delay period the screen was raised. If the animal could in some way remember where it had last seen the white curtain, it would be able to make the correct choice. These rats could tolerate a delay of at least 45 seconds, much longer than the delay the rats in Hunter's original experiment could tolerate. Honzik's opinion was that since he let the rat run up to the curtain, he was sure that it really saw the stimulus it had to remember; he also felt that approaching the stimulus strengthened the stimulus and thereby enhanced the animal's ability, after the delay, to remember where it had been.

It is somewhat dangerous to interpret these results without very careful study. The rat has an extremely sensitive sense of smell and under these circumstances would probably respond to the odor of the stimuli. If the black curtain in front of the wrong door were not changed, rats might solve the problem by always avoiding that "wrong-smelling" door, without using memory at all.

In Hunter's experiments, the rats and dogs were kept pointed toward the food during the delay intervals, and when released they followed their noses to the correct box. If this orientation was disturbed, the animals were unable to react correctly. Raccoons and children, on the other hand, did not need to maintain the orientation to react correctly. Apes and monkeys rarely, if ever, maintain orientation during the period of delay. In more recent studies, Honzik and others have shown that even rats can remember a stimulus for an appreciable time without maintaining their body orientation. Therefore, short-term memory in these animals consists of more than pointing toward the place and then remaining still.

Since the problems just described require only a choice between two or three places in quite different directions, it is conceivable that the direction of the test object is stored, not by gross bodily orientation, but by some pattern of muscular tension. However, Loucks (1931) gave his rats a general anaesthetic during the period of delay, which would certainly destroy any muscular tension, and his rats could still respond correctly.

If short-term storage depends upon continuous activation of low-level behavior flows, it appears that even the lowly rat does not have to hold its body in a given orientation to "rehearse" a location. It is quite possible that a general "intention" to go to a certain place could be maintained for a while despite being turned around, doped, etc. It is not known whether animals can perform an interfering choice response, return to a delayed reaction, and remember where the food is.

Monkeys are quite good at delayed response and can remember which of two objects was baited for quite a while. In one large experiment the forgetting curve (which results from plotting percent correct as a function of the length of delay) was nearly flat. Placing an opaque screen between the monkey and the objects increased the number of errors by 50 percent. When the two objects were dissimilar, there were 25 percent fewer errors than when the two objects were identical. It seems that monkeys do these problems by remembering which object was rewarded, and that viewing the objects and reviewing them serves as a rehearsal to help hold the information in some sort of short-term storage. It should be emphasized that the usual laboratory monkey, the macacque, seems in many ways to be a very "visual" animal, especially in contrast to the rat, which is not at all visual and instead leans heavily upon olfaction (sense of smell).

Monkeys and chimpanzees remember the nature as well as the location of food, as was shown by Tinklepaugh's substitution test. He baited the correct container with a banana, and during the delay interval substituted a less preferred food—lettuce for the monkeys and a carrot or an orange for the chimpanzees. Surprise, disappointment, and resentment were indicated by facial expression, bodily attitude, and vocalizations. The monkeys completely refused to eat the lettuce, though the chimpanzees would take the carrot or orange away and eat it at their leisure. This experiment supports the position that these experiments are studies of memory, rather than merely studies of some sort of short-term habit. Primates clearly remember things and events, not merely a readiness to act. This suggests the kind of higher-order behavior flows, remote from overt behavior, that seem to exist in humans. Such expectancies may also exist in birds and lower mammals, but the evidence is at best inconclusive.

Rapid forgetting is found in studies of human short-term memory when the subject learns a nonsense syllable and is then required to count backwards rapidly by threes during the forgetting period. Under these conditions, the subject's ability to recall the nonsense syllable decreases by about 15 percent per second, so that the material is almost completely forgotten after 10 seconds of counting backwards (Peterson & Peterson, 1959).

Information can be stored longer in short-term memory if it is rehearsed. A common example is the procedure of reading a telephone number from the directory and then saying it over to oneself up to and during the period of dialing the number. Obviously, one limitation of rehearsal is the risk that it may be interrupted, as when someone asks, "Is this the fourteenth?" and you say "Yes," and then have to go back to the telephone book.

When a person has to retrieve letters from short-term memory a great many times, he makes a few mistakes. Conrad (1954) studied these mistakes carefully. In his task the letters were presented to the eye of the subject, in a display, and had later to be retrieved from short-term memory. Some errors were made, and a careful analysis showed that the letters most often confused were those with similar sounds, like "T" (tee) and "D" (dee) or "S" (ess) and "F" (eff), rather than letters that look similar like "R" and "P" or "O" and "Q". This leads to the hypothesis that short-term storage contains items which have already been encoded from visual forms into the auditory-articulatory names given to those forms. This study, at least, warns us that the contents of short-term storage may not directly resemble the stimuli given but may be the result of recoding into another system. The low-level behavior flows used in Conrad's experiment probably used the speech mechanisms, for these mechanisms are well adapted to generating and maintaining several letters. The visual system can "rehearse" letters by imagery, but the process is relatively slow and apparently depends on the verbal system. Weber (1970) found that the average person can generate the twenty-six letters of the alphabet, "speaking to himself," in about 6 seconds but takes about 15 seconds to generate visual images of the twenty-six letters as written.

LONG-TERM STORAGE

When an animal has thoroughly mastered a task, such as running a certain maze, and is then returned to its living area, it will remember the learned task almost indefinitely. For many years there was essentially no study on long-term memory in animals because it appeared that their memory under experimental conditions was essentially perfect. Of course, in such experiments there is very little interference between living in the home area and the habit or skill learned.

Actually, when an animal's memory is tested, the procedure usually consists of retraining it on the task originally learned, and comparing its time of reacquisition with the time it took for original acquisition of the skill. In these terms, memory is excellent; but it often does take one or two trials to reinstate the memory.

When humans are tested on retrieval from long-term storage, it is found that most of their forgetting can be attributed, in general terms, to "interference." That is, if a human learns an isolated item of information or a simple skill, and then for a long time has no experiences that are similar to what he has learned, his memory will be essentially perfect. But if during the retention interval the subject learns or studies material that conflicts with what he has learned, or adopts conflicting behavior—especially if the interpolated material is superficially similar but structurally somewhat different from the test material—then forgetting may be rapid and apparently complete.

The content of long-term memory has several characteristics that may explain why it can be so stable compared with short-term memory. Basically, information in long-term memory has been incorporated into unique and stable structures.

For example, the nonsense syllable MEK is relatively easy to confuse and difficult to remember. If it is recoded into a sentence, such as "Mabel eats kale," or into a modified work (MÉEK with one letter deleted), it then belongs to a more meaningful and distinct structure. Sometimes, subjects select cues that are distinctive and learn to respond on the basis of such features. Given a list of nonsense syllables like MEK, ZOG, XOJ, YIZ, etc., they are likely to pay relatively little attention to the vowel in the middle of the word and will try to remember each syllable on the basis of the first letter, which is relatively prominent and usually unique in the list. Since the alphabet has only five vowels, in a typical list of twelve syllables several must share the same vowels; therefore, vowels are not reliable distinctive cues. One aspect of encoding information into long-term memory is to find highly distinctive and unique features to go with each item that must be discriminated.

The other main attribute of long-term memory is that its contents are organized. For example, material to be learned may be made part of an ongoing story or some other progression. Items may also be classified and cross-classified into a meaningful system that is relatively simple to learn. Complex musical pieces, poems, and the like are in part remembered by discerning their inner structure and logic and thereby becoming able to generate parts upon demand.

In long-term memory, retrieval becomes very important. If a memory has lain unused for a length of time, then it is natural that one will have some difficulty and may take a long time in retrieving it. Retrieval involves a process of search of memory, and some recent research indicates that the process of retrieval may be both protracted and of utmost importance in memory.

A common experience is to have a name or word "on the tip of your tongue" and be unable to think of it. An experimental technique for producing this phenomenon often enough so that it could be studied was devised by Brown and McNeill (1966). First, they give a definition of a relatively infrequent word and ask the subject to name it. If he answers correctly right away, then the experimenter goes on to the next definition. If he does not give the word right away, then a set of inquiries are made to determine what partial information he has. A few typical definitions for such a study are these:

1 A navigational instrument used in measuring angular distances, especially the altitude of sun, moon, and stars at sea.

2 The practice of showing special favor to nephews (or other relatives) in conferring office; unfair preference of relatives over other qualified persons.

3 A semicircular or polygonal recess, arched or with a domed roof, in a building, especially at the nave of a church.

If the subject cannot give the word right away, the kind of questions asked would include the following:

1 How many syllables does the word have?
2 What is the first letter of the word?
3 What words come to mind?
4 Separate the words that come to mind into two groups: first, those you believe to be similar to the target word in sound; second, those you believe to be similar to it in meaning.

The results of this study included analysis of 360 cases of the "tip of the tongue" phenomenon. The number of syllables guessed, though sometimes wrong, was closely correlated with the actual number of syllables in the word. That is, guesses regarding short words were usually that there were few syllables, and guesses regarding polysyllables were usually that there were many syllables. The first letter of the word was guessed correctly 57 percent of the time; considering that there are twenty-six letters in the alphabet, this figure is very high. (Of course, in evaluating the figure, one should take into account that there are many more words starting with S than with X.)

Apparently, giving the subject a definition defines a search set for him, and within that set he attempts to discover a memory trace of the word itself. At a certain point, the subject actually discovers the word, or at least retrieves enough attributes of it to be able to give the word—that is, to pronounce or spell it.

This suggests that the ability to retrieve a word depends not only on the word itself and how prominent it may be in memory, but also upon the search set within which it may be embedded. For example, if you ask one subject to give you, as fast as he can, the names of all cities in the world, and another to give you the names of all cities in his home state, which he would know well, you often find that cities within the state are given more quickly than cities in general. This is quite illogical, for, since any city in one's home state is also a city in the world, there is no answer to the second question that is not also an answer to the first. Surely, then, one knows more cities in the world than cities in his home state; and it should therefore be easier to give cities in general. However, when one tries to give cities in his home state, he is working within a smaller search set and therefore is able to retrieve faster and with less effort than when searching cities in general, which involves searching a very large search set.

The process of retrieval amounts to activating a particular level in the hierarchy of behavior flows.[3] If a person is in the wrong part of his cognitive structure, he cannot remember the item at all. This may lead him to go still higher in the tree, seeking at least to encompass the desired memory. If he finds himself in the right part of the cognitive structure but at too high and abstract a level, then he may be able to give some information about the desired item, generating properties or other items in the structure, without specifically finding the item sought. If the structure is specified and organized well enough, then the subject soon arrives at approximately the proper part and level of his cognitive hierarchy and can generate a small search set containing the item desired.

[3]It is not entirely satisfactory to use the term "behavior flow" for the higher-order structures that have other behavior flows as responses, because the term "behavior flow" implies direct control of an overt response, and the elementary examples given in the first chapter are of the direct control of action in the world. When the subject is a human being or another primate, some of these expectancy-analysis-decision structures are quite remote from any direct action; it would be more natural to call them "cognitive structures" or "motivational systems." However, the form of such structures always involves some expectancy, some kind of input, analysis, and matching of the expectancy with the outcome of the analysis to control a decision. It is helpful to use a single word for a single structure. When the context seems to demand another word, like "cognitive structure," I shall use it. But the theoretical position is intended to remain clear and definite; all such mental or behavioral control systems have the same basic structure.

Chapter 3

Classical Conditioning

About 1900, the famous Russian physiologist Ivan Pavlov discovered that a dog would salivate before receiving food, just because the experimenter came near. Pavlov had been studying the process of digestion, but this discovery turned his attention to the more psychological problems of learning, memory, and expectancy. From the accidental discovery of "psychic secretions" Pavlov developed and exploited his famous method of salivary conditioning in dogs, a method which was the foundation of what is now called "classical conditioning." Pavlov's methods are not followed directly in many American laboratories, but many modifications of them, especially conditioning of eyelid responses and general sweating responses, are studied actively.

The basic phenomena are simple and dramatic. Dogs do not normally salivate when a bell rings. They do salivate copiously when acetic acid (vinegar) is squirted into their mouths. If an experimenter repeatedly sounds a bell and then follows it within a few seconds by a squirt of vinegar, after a while the dog will salivate when the bell rings. White domestic rabbits do not normally blink when a tone is sounded. But if such a tone is paired with the administration of a puff of air to the cornea of the rabbit's eye (which causes a reflex blink), after a while the rabbit will blink when the tone is sounded. College students do not normally exhibit sweating in the palms of the hands when a small white light is turned on. They do show a strong change in electrical conductivity of the palms (the galvanic skin response, GSR, associated with sweating) when a painful electric shock is administered. If the white light is paired with the electric shock, after a while the same college students will show a strong GSR to the small white light.

In each such case, the experimenter uses two stimuli. One is a weak, originally neutral stimulus like a bell, tone, or small light. This is called the "conditioned stimulus," abbreviated CS. The second stimulus is stronger and produces a definite response of its own; examples are the vinegar in the mouth, the puff of air to the eye, and the electric shock. This is called the "unconditioned stimulus," abbreviated UCS or US. (This opaque terminology comes from some unfortunate translations of the early Russian literature. Better translations would be "*conditional* and *unconditional* stimuli," reflecting the fact that the response is made unconditionally to the UCS: that is, the response is not conditional on any special training or psychological developments. Response to the conditional stimulus, on the other hand, depends upon its having been used in an experiment. However, since the bad translations have become standard terminology, there is really no choice but to use them.)

Common sense would suggest that in such an experiment, since the CS is regularly followed by the UCS, the subject comes to expect the UCS whenever the CS is received. The reason the dog salivates to the bell is that it expects acid, and its natural response when it expects acid is to salivate. Similarly, the rabbit expects a puff of air, and naturally blinks its eye; the college student expects the shock, and therefore sweats. This is the germ of what is called the "cognitive" interpretation of classical conditioning.

Pavlov and other scientists of the early twentieth century were engaged in a serious effort to make a natural science of psychology. Most psychological discussions talked about a variety of mental events—sensations, percepts, memories, images, sentiments, intentions, expectancies, and so forth. There was, in the main, no dependable experimental method for answering questions about these mental events, and many scientists were especially interested in getting solid experimental findings upon which to base their psychological theories. One thing they did was either to work within the concepts of physiology or to concern themselves entirely with events they could see and count—namely, stimuli and responses. Conditioning was looked upon as a godsend because it tied learning into a well-studied physiological system of digestion and required only that the experimenter administer stimuli (CS and UCS) and observe when the animal made its response.

The response to the UCS is, in every case, a well established reflex response, like salivating when vinegar is administered. This is called the "unconditioned response," abbreviated UCR or UR. When an animal learns a conditioned response, it makes this same reflex response, or a similar one, to the CS. The dog salivates to the bell; the student sweats when the light comes on. This response, occurring before the UCS is presented, is called a "conditioned response," abbreviated CR. If there were no UCR, then there would be no way to know if the subject has made any connection between the CS and the UCS.

The S-R theory of conditioning is that the conditioned stimulus (e.g., the bell) becomes associated with the unconditioned response (UCR). In Pavlov's thinking, the CS would set up a weak center of excitation in the brain, and the UCS-UCR event (like acid and salivation) would involve a strong center of activity. When one center of excitation precedes the other in time, the weaker center becomes integrated with or drawn into the stronger activity, and a pathway of some sort develops in the brain. At that time, presentation of the CS initiates the activity of the UCS-UCR complex, and the animal makes the UCR. The outstanding characteristic of this theory is that it eschews any mention of what the animal expects; instead, it simply states that the response originally made to the UCS becomes associated with the CS, and that what is learned is a CS-CR bond of some kind, an S-R structure.

One major thrust of research on classical conditioning is the attempt to decide whether these procedures lead the subject to form expectancies or whether they develop S-R associations.

An essential characteristic of classical conditioning is that a CS occurs, then a UCS. The two must occur in reasonably close order, separated only by a small amount of time. Also, of course, the trials must be separated from one another. These time relationships are basic to the training process and are also of theoretical importance. An expectancy theory might say that it is not very important how closely a UCS follows a CS, but that it is important for the CS to be a predictor of the UCS. Consequently, a second major part of the study of classical conditioning is the attempt to determine the best time relationships to use, and to find out why particular temporal arrangements are effective or not.

A third major development of research in classical conditioning has to do with the techniques necessary to obtain and measure classical conditioning. More things can go wrong with such a conditioning experiment than the novice would imagine. Learning about possible pitfalls, and the control procedures necessary to avoid them, will give the reader some insight into the experimental process and permit him to evaluate the importance of classical conditioning as a typical example of learning.

METHODS OF STUDYING CLASSICAL CONDITIONING

Variations

Many variations of classical conditioning have been described, investigated, and named.

The first variation has to do with the time relationship between CS and UCS. Delay conditioning is the most common of the variations and is very effective, with short delays (about half a second) being best for most types of experiments. Trace conditioning is difficult to establish, particularly if there are long waits between CS and UCS. A basic finding is that contiguity is important. Simultaneous conditioning is difficult to observe, since the UCR occurs with or before the CR. To discover which response is which, the experimenter is forced to use "test" trials in which he presents the CS and omits the UCS to see if the subject will make the CR uncontaminated by the UCR. Backward conditioning is mostly unsuccessful. Temporal conditioning is fairly effective, though obviously the subject may have difficulty timing the onset of the UCS unless he has a timepiece. The various kinds of conditioning are shown in Figure 3.1.

Another source of variations of classifying classical conditioning is the kind of UCS used. Some unconditioned stimuli have the nature of rewards (e.g., food powder blown into the mouth); others are aversive (e.g., an electric shock and puff of air in the eye). The former type produce what is called "reward conditioning," and the latter produce "defense conditioning."

Two additional kinds of conditioning experiments, although different from the usual type, are usually studied with regular classical conditioning. One is the "sensory preconditioning" experiment, in which two different neutral conditioned stimuli, CS_1 and CS_2, are used. During the sensory preconditioning period, CS_1 and CS_2 are presented together as in conditioning, but of course no conditioned response is usually observed. Later, CS_1 is used as the conditioned stimulus and is paired with some UCS until a conditioned response is obtained. Finally, CS_2 is presented. If the subject makes the conditioned response he had learned to make to CS_1, then sensory preconditioning has been demonstrated.

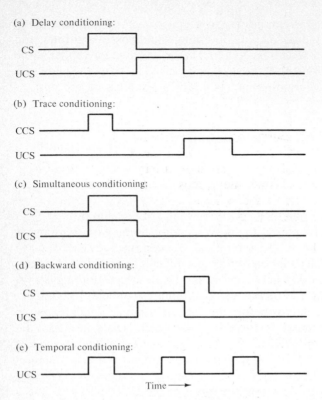

(a) Delay conditioning:

CS

UCS

(b) Trace conditioning:

CCS

UCS

(c) Simultaneous conditioning:

CS

UCS

(d) Backward conditioning:

CS

UCS

(e) Temporal conditioning:

UCS

Time ⟶

Figure 3.1 Types of classical conditoning. Time reads from left to right. An upward deflection means that the stimulus is turned on; a drop back to the baseline means that it is turned off.

The "conditioned emotional response," abbreviated CER, is a less direct way of assessing an animal's expectancies or measuring diffuse conditioned responses. The animal is trained (see Chapter 4) to press a bar for food, or to perform some other easily measurable task. Then the experimenter takes an extraneous stimulus as CS—say, a tone—and pairs it with an electric shock. The animal's response to the tone may be difficult to measure, for it may consist mainly of "freezing." However, the experimenter has the animal perform its bar-press response for food, and then suddenly sounds the tone that has been the CS. Often, the animal will stop pressing the bar while the tone is on. The tone, a signal for shock, will thus be shown to suppress another response. This procedure was originally interpreted to mean that the CR to the tone was a diffuse "emotional response," and its tendency to suppress bar pressing was merely a technique of measurement.

Measurement

The experimenter must not merely produce a conditioned response; he must also measure it. Pavlov developed complex operations to observe the process of salivation, running a tube from the salivary gland of the dog out through the cheek and finally to some sort of flow meter. The GSR is usually measured by placing two electrodes on the palm of the subject's hand and electrically measuring the conductance between them; this conductance increases as a complex function of the condition of the skin but is generally correlated with emotional disturbance, surprise, electric shock, etc. In an eyeblink experiment, it is common to attach a light marker to the eyelid and make a continuous record of its motion.

Whatever means of measuring responses is used, both the UCR and the CR should be measured. What aspects of the response will be recorded? Generally, the experimenter records the probability of (detectable) responses, the amplitude of responses (if that is appropriate), and sometimes the latency of the responses—that is, the time from the start of the CS until the start of the CR. In early work it was said that a probable, large, fast response was "strong," with the implication that the three measurements were all measures of the same thing, "strength." More recent work has begun to show that different properties of a response may have different significance.

The fact that a rabbit begins to blink to a tone is not in itself sufficient to prove that the rabbit has formed a CR. For one thing, an occasional eyeblink may be a reflex response to the tone. This is called an "a-response," and it occurs particularly when GSR, eyeblinks, cardiac responses, vascular responses, or other various "observing responses" are used, for such responses are made as a reflex to almost any stimulus. The proper control method is to test the frequency of such responses to a CS given alone, without conditioning.

Sometimes, presenting a UCS (like a puff of air) may increase the probability of a-responses without actually producing conditioning. This is called "pseudoconditioning." The usual method for dealing with this is to have a control group which receives CS and UCS on different trials, never paired together. The level of response to the CS is a measure of pseudoconditioning and can then be subtracted from the level of conditioned responses.

Sometimes a subject will make responses of the CR type even without a CS—these "spontaneous" responses can be a considerable problem in eyeblink and GSR research. The level of such responses can be assessed by inserting blank trials, with neither CS nor UCS, and observing the frequency of appropriate responses.

Stimuli

Years of research have told us something about what stimuli can and should be used in classical conditioning experiments. Tones, lights, bells, buzzers, etc., have all been used successfully as CSs; research has shown that compound stimuli lead to better responding than simple stimuli (a tone plus a light will be better than the tone alone), that intermittent stimuli (flashing lights, buzzers, etc.) are better than pure ones (steady lights, constant tones, etc.), possibly because a pure stimulus excites the eye or ear only at its onset, whereas an intermittent stimulus keeps the receptor organ working. Russian work includes stimulation of many internal organs, including bladder and pancreas, by applying electric currents and touch stimuli, by distending the organs with a small balloon, by cooling the organs, etc. It is interesting that subjects in such research often show conditioning without being able to express any awareness of the CS.

What unconditioned stimuli can be used? Here the range of possibilities is very limited, because there are only a few stimuli which produce reliable, measurable reflex responses. GSR can be produced by almost any strong stimulus, but electric shock is usually chosen because it will keep producing GSR responses for a long time; other stimuli, like loud sounds, soon lose their ability to produce GSR by becoming "habituated." Salivation can be produced by acid, alkali, and meat powder. Salivation has the advantage of being very persistent, so that salivary conditioning experiments can continue for many weeks or months. Many other reflex responses will soon disappear after being elicited a few dozen times, and then the experiment must stop.

Generally, the UCS must be strong enough to produce a UCR and to keep producing it for a long time; but it must not be too strong, for if the UCS is too strong, the subject becomes excited and restless, and animal subjects may begin to take the apparatus apart.

TEMPORAL CONDITIONS OF TRAINING

Generally speaking, for good conditioning to occur, the CS should begin about half a second before the UCS. For more precise response systems, like eyeblinks, the best delay is more like 200 to 250 milliseconds, about a quarter of a second.

It is possible to establish a conditioned response using a short interval between CS and UCS and then gradually increase the interval without disrupting the CR. As the delay becomes long, or as the experiment shifts into "delay" conditioning, however, changes take place in the behavior. The responses, which had earlier occurred right after the onset of the CS, are now found spread out in time between CS and UCS. It appears that the subjects stop making immediate responses at the onset of CS and replace them with delayed responses which may not differ much in amplitude. If the intertrial interval (ITI) becomes long enough, the subject may actually stop responding immediately after the CS, showing a kind of "inhibition" of the response during that period.

What is happening? First the subject is dealing with an environment in which very little happens over time. Once in a while a tone sounds, and a puff of air strikes the eye. Under what circumstances will these two be connected so that the subject begins to expect the puff of air when he hears the tone? Obviously, there is very little connection between the CS and the UCS; they are not similar and do not come from the same place. Consequently, it is natural that the subject may not easily make any connection. If the two events occur close in time, this seems to lead the subject to expect the puff of air immediately when he hears the tone. The result is a rapid eyeblink response, the response to anticipation of a puff of air in the eye.

Once the tone becomes integrated into the defense behavior flow including the eyeblink, a slight temporal spacing between the two does not destroy the expectancy. However, if there is a substantial delay between tone and puff on each trial, the subject comes to expect the puff, not right after the tone, but later—and this expectancy naturally conforms to the pattern of events in time. When this happens, the subject has actually connected the tone and the puff, but this does not mean that he expects the puff immediately; rather, he comes to expect the puff approximately when it occurs and makes his eyeblink responses when he expects the puff. Actually, we may believe that a rather complicated control system may develop, in which the tone initiates a special behavior flow which then loops, asking at every point if enough time has elapsed for the puff to be expected.

The experimental evidence on delayed and trace conditioning supports the idea that the subject must form some expectancy that CS will be followed by UCS, and this learning occurs most quickly when the two events occur close together in time. Then, if delays occur, the subject modifies this expectancy accordingly (though not very accurately in time).

In simultaneous conditioning, when CS and UCS are presented at once, or if the UCS is presented first, subjects do not seem to come to anticipate UCS when CS is presented alone. There are several possible reasons for this. The UCS is usually a stronger stimulus, well connected with a behavior flow; when it occurs, it takes control of the situation and itself begins the behavior flow. There is really no opportunity for the weak and initially meaningless CS to have much effect on the subject.

Another temporal variable, which at first seems unimportant, is the time between trials. Pavlov allowed long periods to elapse between trials because he was studying the slow salivary response and wanted his animals to recover from any physiological changes brought about by food powder, acid, etc., in the mouth. He also was able to use long intervals between CS and UCS, often as long as 20 seconds. American investigators, using quicker UCRs, from which subjects quickly recover, tend to space trials more closely in time. Thereby, of course, they can make more trials per hour. Several experiments, however, have shown that the longer the interval between trials, the more quickly subjects learn the conditioned response and the more reliably they perform.

At first, this seems surprising, because experiments of this sort at best are rather uneventful and at worst must be frightfully boring to the subjects. The subject is usually restrained in a harness or some other apparatus, with almost no stimulation of any kind except for the rare occurrence of a CS, a UCS, or both. One would think that the subject's attention would surely wander during long intervals between trials, so that it could not pay attention to the CS and UCS when they finally were presented. Indeed, the subject's falling asleep should be, and is, a serious problem to the experimenter. Why, then, are long periods between trials helpful? (It should be mentioned here that in most experiments the trials are not evenly spaced in time but instead occur at variable intervals, perhaps 5 minutes between trial 1 and trial 2, then 2 minutes between trial 2 and trial 3, etc.)

One hypothesis is that when trials are spaced widely in time, some sort of inhibition or fatigue has time to dissipate and that this dissipation has a beneficial effect on performance. But if this were true, then subjects should perform better after a long interval between trials than after a short interval, and such short-term variations in performance have not been found.

A second hypothesis is that with short waits between trials the subject's state of mind is about the same from one trial to the next, with the result that the subject conditions the CR to essentially the same stimulus elements. If more time is given between trials, the subject's state of mind will have time to change gradually and spontaneously, and the CR will be conditioned to a wider variety of stimulus elements. Thus, spaced training gives the subject an opportunity to condition the response to various stimuli, producing better overall performance. If this is so, then

Table 3-1 The events that occur during a simple conditioning experiment.
(The lower right-hand corner represents the events during intervals between trials.)

	CS occurs	No CS
UCS occurs	X	
No UCS		X

after a short pause between two trials the subject deals with almost the same stimulus elements on the second trial as on the first and should therefore be able to perform quite well; after a longer pause, on the other hand, the stimulus elements will have fluctuated, and performance might therefore be expected to deteriorate. This prediction directly contradicts the prediction of the inhibition theory. In fact, however, neither prediction is correct: performance after short waits within a single session is just about the same as performance after long waits. The interval between any two trials simply has no effect. However, if the *average* interval is long, performance is better than if the *average* interval is short.

To understand this effect, we must again consider the whole sequence of events to which the subject is responding. In a pure conditioning experiment, there are times when a CS is presented and immediately followed by a UCS. At other times, there is no CS and there has not been one for a while, and there also is no UCS. Four possibilities exist, as shown in Table 3-1. In a pure conditioning experiment, however, only two of those conditions ever occur.

From this point of view, the contingency between CS and UCS is a result both of "trials," in which both CS and UCS occur, and "spaces" during which neither occurs. By increasing the intervals between trials, the experimenter adds examples of the fact that without the CS there will be no UCS. Experimentally, such time is not counted, and therefore the results are normally interpreted as if each trial were more effective because of the longer interval between trials. But in fact, one may say that the interval is part of the training, part of the information given to the subject; increasing the amount of time is actually adding to the training the subject is given.

This approach also makes it clear that contingency, not mere pairing, gives rise to conditioning. Rescorla (1967) showed that if a subject is given

Table 3-2 The events that occur during a conditioning experiment in which UCSs are administered without a CS
(Notice that UCS is now much less predictable by CS.)

	CS occurs	No CS
UCS occurs	X	X
No UCS		X

UCS trials with no CS, this will greatly retard his formation of the conditioned response. Table 3.2 shows what has happened when these "free" UCSs are introduced: the contingency is greatly reduced.

The subject, after receiving a UCS without CS, may begin looking for some way to predict the UCS. This would naturally draw attention away from the CS.

Suppose that an experimenter wants to evaluate the effects of the UCS on responses to the CS—that is, he wants to evaluate "pseudoconditioning." To do so, he administers CS and UCS from time to time but never pairs them. His presentations are as shown in Table 3.3 which develops a negative contingency between CS and UCS. In effect, in such a procedure, the CS may become a signal that there will not be a UCS for a while. If the UCS is shock, the CS may become a "safe" signal, producing the opposite of the CR.

INHIBITION

When the temporal contingencies are disturbed, conditioning may be severely affected. The most important change is called "experimental extinction." In this procedure, the experimenter stops giving the UCS

Table 3-3 The events that occur during a control test for "pseudoconditioning" in which UCSs and CSs are administered but never paired

	CS occurs	No CS
UCS occurs		X
No UCS	X	X

altogether but continues to administer the CS. A dog may be salivating readily to a tone which has been followed by acid; but if the acid is suddenly stopped and the tone continues to sound, after a while salivation as a response to the tone will disappear. The response is not suppressed in an obvious way, as might occur if the dog were spanked for salivating; rather, it appears that the response slowly loses its original strength.

A simple hypothesis is that the CS simply becomes unstuck from its response and the subject returns to its original state, in which it made no connection between CS and UCS. Pavlov, however, disproved this by discovering "spontaneous recovery." He would first condition a dog to salivate to a tone. Then he would present the tone alone often enough to eliminate the response. After this, he would leave the dog alone for a while, perhaps for a few days. Finally, he would return the dog to the laboratory and at this time the animal would again salivate to the tone—perhaps not very much, but enough to show that the conditioned response had at least partly recovered. The original extinction, then, had *not* returned the animal to its initial state.

Pavlov's interpretation of this phenomenon was as follows: When the CS is presented without the UCS, some "inhibition" builds up—an active process, like conditioning but with the opposite effect. In fact, Pavlov believed as a general principle that whenever anything happens in the brain, a corresponding and opposite condition of inhibition is established. In conditioning, the excitatory tendency which makes the CS give rise to the CR is stronger than its opposite; but when the UCS is removed, the inhibitory process continues, or may even become stronger, and the excitatory process drops away. When extinction is finished, inhibition is stronger than excitation, so that there is no salivation. Now, if the animal is allowed to rest without being exposed to the tone, the inhibitory effect in turn drops away, and eventually the excitation will be stronger than inhibition, and the response will spontaneously recover. The hypothetical course of excitation and inhibition, during conditioning and extinction, is shown in Figure 3.2.

Another theory of extinction and spontaneous recovery, mentioned earlier in this chapter, deals with the spontaneous fluctuation of stimulus elements (Estes, 1955). During conditioning spaced over several weeks, a subject conditions its response to a fairly wide variety of stimulus elements, which have changed from time to time in a random way. Extinction is often "massed," occurring, say, in a single concentrated session which continues until the response no longer occurs. At that time, those stimulus elements present during extinction have lost the power to produce the conditioned response. However, if we wait a day or so, the stimulus elements will again fluctuate. During that time, the animal may

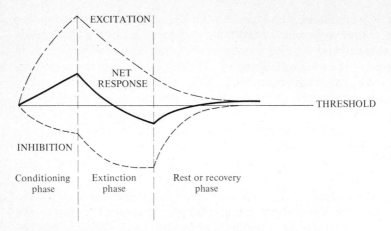

Figure 3.2 Diagram of the Pavlovian explanation of spontaneous recovery as brought about by dissipation of inhibition. Whenever the net response, excitation minus inhibition, is above threshold, conditioned responses will be made.

reinstate some old stimulus elements that occurred at some time during conditioning but were not present during extinction. These elements might still be conditioned to the response and therefore would produce spontaneous recovery. Gradual fluctuation of the stimulus takes the place of the gradual dissipation of inhibition which Pavlov proposed.

A third approach is more cognitive and depends on the contingencies developed during conditioning and extinction. Table 3.4 shows the contingencies during both conditioning and extinction.

Notice that the two situations, conditioning and extinction, are not totally dissimilar. Both have intervals between trials in which neither CS nor UCS is presented, and both have intermittent presentations of CS. They differ as to whether UCS accompanies the CS. In neither case does UCS occur without CS.

When extinction occurs, the subject must form a new expectancy: that when CS occurs, there will be no UCS. This expectancy conflicts with the expectancy formed during conditioning. However, it seems possible that the two expectancies might coexist if the subject made a time discrimination. That is, the behavior flow might be under the control of a higher-level system that decides whether to expect the UCS.

This same principle of contingency can be used to produce an inhibiting stimulus. Suppose that a dog receives food powder occasionally, except that after a buzzer sounds there is a period of 20 minutes during which food powder is never given. Or suppose that a rat cannot predict shocks which occur fairly frequently; when a tone comes on, however, no

Table 3-4 Contingencies in conditioning and in experimental extinction, and the contingency a subject would remember if it did not discriminate between the conditioning and extinction histories.

Conditioning

	CS	No CS
UCS	X	
No UCS		X

Extinction

	CS	No CS
UCS		
No UCS	X	X

Mixture of the two

	CS	No CS
UCS	X	
No UCS	X	XX

Table 3-5 Contingencies for inhibitory conditioning

	CS	No CS
UCS		X
No UCS	X	X

shock is ever administered. The contingency in both cases is shown in Table 3.5.

The effect of such training is that the anticipatory response, like salivation to food or GSR to shock, is notably absent during the CS. In effect, the animal displays a behavior flow like that in Figure 3.3, in which a match of input with the CS causes a branch *away* from the expectancy of the UCS.

S-R theories from Pavlov on have postulated "inhibition," a force like association but opposite in its effects. This section has emphasized, rather, the subject's expectancy that UCS will not occur. Is there evidence that will let us decide between the two theories? Moore and Gormezano (1963) trained two groups of rabbits to blink and then set out to extinguish the response. One group received no more puffs of air; this

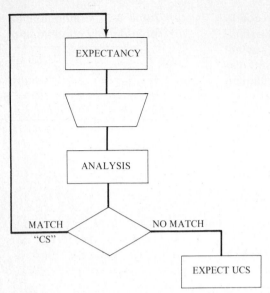

Figure 3.3 Partial behavior flow of conditioned inhibition. Here "CS" is the stimulus that signals that UCS will not occur—the "conditioned inhibitor."

is the usual extinction procedure. The other group continued to receive puffs of air, but these were presented long after CS. If there is such a thing as inhibition, both groups should develop some; but the delayed reinforcements should somewhat counteract the inhibition, so that regular extinction should be more efficient than the method of delayed UCS. However, with *delay* of the UCS, the CS actually becomes a "safe" signal, marking a definite if brief period during which the UCS will not occur. The CS could turn into a conditioned inhibitor, becoming a cue to the absence of the puff of air. If this is so, delay of the UCS should remove the CR faster than regular extinction. The results obtained by Moore and Gormezano show that delaying the UCS removes a CR faster than extinction. These results do not support the inhibition theory; on the contrary, they support the idea that subjects learn to expect that UCS will not occur.

STIMULUS CONDITIONS AND ANALYSIS OF INPUT

The S-R theory of conditioning centers attention on stimuli and responses. To maintain its principle of objectivity, this S-R theory must be able to identify the stimuli used. However, when the CS or UCS is changed slightly, the conditioned response is still made. It is wrong to think that training affects only the specific stimulus used during training. In fact, much of what researchers learn in conditioning experiments they learn by varying stimuli.

First, the stronger the UCS is, the more rapid and complete is conditioning. This has been established mainly in studies of eyelid conditioning in humans. One is not surprised to learn that strong puffs of air in the eye produce more and sharper anticipatory eyeblinks than weak puffs. The subject surely has a more vigorous response (UCR) to stronger puffs, and it is natural that the CR is stronger in anticipation of the stronger puff.

If the experimenter shifts from a strong to a weak UCS, will there be any aftereffect of the strong UCS? One possibility is that the weak puff would be so mild in contrast to what the subject had experienced that the CR would extinguish. Alternatively, it is possible that the reaction to the strong puff, once learned, would be retained. An experiment was performed to compare subjects shifted from strong to weak puffs of air with other subjects who always received weak puffs. Those who had received a strong puff blinked more; this shows that learning to expect a strong puff and blink sharply was fairly well maintained, and that the subjects did not show a "contrast" effect and disregard the weak puff (Trapold and Spence, 1960).

What about the CS? Early studies showed that stronger CSs led to faster conditioning; and the first interpretation of this finding was that more stimulus *energy* led to better conditioning. Then it was shown that turning off a loud tone was about as effective as turning it on, which meant that the crucial variable is not energy in the CS but the amount of change occurring at the time of the CS. An intermittent stimulus, like a flashing light or metronome, is more effective as a CS than a "smooth" stimulus, like a constant tone or a steady light. This may be because an intermittent stimulus consists of a whole sequence of changes.

It is surprising that a group of subjects trained with a weak CS often eventually respond as much as subjects trained with a strong CS. One possibility is that the strength of the CS makes very little difference. Another possibility is that the subject adjusts his process of analysis to fit whatever stimuli are available. Grice (1960) showed that if the same subject was given both strong and weak CSs, it would respond much more to the strong CS than to the weak one. However, if a subject gets only strong CSs or only weak CSs, it responds at a given level, which does not depend much on the strength of the CS. This shows a fact which will be seen many times in the study of learning—that the process of stimulus analysis is flexible and enables the organism to use almost any level of energy as a stimulus.

When the CS is changed after a conditioned response has been learned, there is (on the average) a reduction in the frequency and strength of conditioned responses. Since a response learned to one stimulus is also made to others, this is often called "stimulus generalization." Of course, we do not know whether the subject is truly abstracting a general feature and generalizing its past experience or simply failing to discriminate between stimuli—the phenomenon could be called either "generalization" or "confusion."

If the experimenter uses only one CS in training—say, a pure tone[1]—and keeps the environment quiet and uneventful between trials, the subject can acquire a CS based on almost any analysis of the tone. One subject might respond to the onset and would respond to the onset of anything, even a light. Another subject might respond to the frequency and would generalize to a much noisier stimulus of about the same frequency. Another might respond to the purity of the tone and would generalize to a different frequency.

If the experimenter wants to know what analysis his subject is using, he can require discrimination. A discrimination uses two neutral stimuli; CS[+] is followed by the UCS, and CS[-] is never followed by the UCS. For example, the experimenter can use a 1,000-hertz (or cycles per second) tone as CS[+] and always follow it with a UCS. On other trials he can use, say, a 1,600-hertz tone as the CS[-] and never follow it with the UCS. When the subject responds to CS[+] and not to CS[-], the experimenter knows that the analysis does not accept stimuli common to CS[+] and CS[-]; the subject must be responding to frequency, or to some other property that differentiates CS[+] from CS[-]. When CS[+] and CS[-] are alike except for one property, the experimenter (if he obtains discrimination) knows that the subject is using that one property for analysis.

Do subjects actually analyze stimuli, singling out parts of their environment, or do they tend to absorb all available information? In one type of experiment, a certain stimulus A is used as CS, and a CR is learned. Then a second stimulus X is paired with A; and for many trials the combination A + X is used as the CS, paired with the same UCS. In this experiment, the subject could analyze out the properties of A and ignore X or shift its analysis and gain information about X. When tested after such a regimen, the subject will show very little response to X, the redundant stimulus. Thus, it seems that subjects do adopt a rather narrow analysis, and so long as their expectancies are met, they do not change the analysis to learn new stimuli. Of course, we do not know what would happen if a subject were put through a whole series of A, A + X

---

[1]A "pure" tone is a simple sine wave, all energy at one frequency.

sequences; the subject might begin to pick up the X stimuli during the middle of the A + X training (Gormezano and Moore, 1969).

Changes in CS^+ produce "generalization" or transfer of the conditioned response to stimuli similar to CS^+. Suppose that a stimulus CS^- has become a "conditioned inhibitor," i.e., a signal that UCS is not to be expected. Does this "inhibition" generalize to other stimuli similar to CS^-? Yes, of course (Hearst, 1972).

If a conditioned response is developed to a CS, this could mean (as has been argued in this chapter) that the subject has come to *expect* the UCS and makes the appropriate anticipatory response, or it could mean (as the S-R theory holds) that the response, a UCR to the UCS, has become attached to the CS.

One way to separate the two possibilities is by use of novel stimuli to which no particular response has been attached. A novel stimulus given with the CS serves to inhibit the response (Pavlov's "external inhibition"); but this does not tell us anything about expectancy as opposed to association. However, it is possible to separate the two theories by using novel UCSs. Grings (1960) taught college students that if they moved a lever in one direction they would receive a tone stimulus and that if they moved the same lever in the opposite direction they would receive a bright light. After four to ten trials the subjects were administered a test series containing disparity trials that reversed tone and light. The subjects showed a much greater GSR response to these disparities than they had before the reversal. The tone and light do not, themselves, produce a GSR, so the GSR is not an unconditioned response. In fact, the more the subject expected a stimulus, the weaker was the GSR when the stimulus appeared. However, when one stimulus was expected and the other appeared, a GSR was made. The only possible explanation seems to be that an expectancy had appeared; no S-R explanation has been proposed.

HIGHER-ORDER CONTROL OF CONDITIONING

Theoretically, classical conditioning presents two different questions. First, given that the subject has no idea of the nature of the experiment, how does the conditioned response get started in the first place? Second, once the learning has taken place, what are the factors in maintaining a high level of responding?

The first question, that having to do with learning, is primarily a matter of perception of events over time. Factors which cause the CS and UCS to stand out from other events over time and to be grouped together will increase the probability of forming the new expectancy. The subject's success will depend, in part, on whether it is working under a higher-order behavior flow that causes it to seek "predictors" for important events. Since the ability to predict is so valuable to higher animals, it is quite possible that dogs, monkeys, cats, humans, and other higher animals will actively seek such information. The structure for this would be a complex behavior flow in which the subject's general expectancy is of a successful prediction. When using this behavior flow, the subject would inspect various incoming stimuli and analyze them, and then briefly hold this result to see if the UCS occurred. If it did not, then the next input would be analyzed differently, and again the subject would wait for the UCS. When the UCS occurred, if the subject had some stimulus analysis stored in memory, it would at once set up the appropriate subsidiary behavior flow using the possible CS as a predictor. A sketch of such a higher-order "learning" behavior flow is given in Figure 3.4.

There are several general observations which suggest that the concept in Figure 3.4 may be correct. One is that animal subjects, if they have already learned a number of conditioned responses, become easier and easier to train and show an enhanced ability to form new connections. In fact, this generalized "ability to learn" seems to grow in almost every kind of learning experiment. If the formation of a conditioned response were entirely "automatic" or involuntary, it is difficult to see why the ability should grow as it does. A second fact, limited to work with humans, and mainly to eyelid conditioning, is that instructions have a great effect on how the subject learns. Instructions generally do not tell the subject what the CS will be, but if they suggest that a connection can be made and that it would be permissable for subjects to make it, they accelerate learning and improve performance. It is also interesting that certain CS-UCS pairings are relatively easy to learn whereas others are difficult. It is possible that a subject is very unlikely to try the "hypothesis" that a sweet taste at one time would be connected with an electric shock later, and that it is more likely that the animal would connect a buzzer with the shock. In that case, the two kinds of conditioning would have different probabilities of occurring, because the "natural" CS candidates would be accepted and stored by the animal's higher-order behavior flow, whereas "unlikely" ones would not.

SUMMARY

If a UCS is made contingent on a CS, so that the UCS occurs if and only if the CS has just occurred, then the CS comes to be a predictor: when the CS occurs, the subject expects the UCS. If the expectancy of the UCS is enough to initiate observable responses, these responses emerge as "conditioned responses," made when the CS occurs. A new conditioned

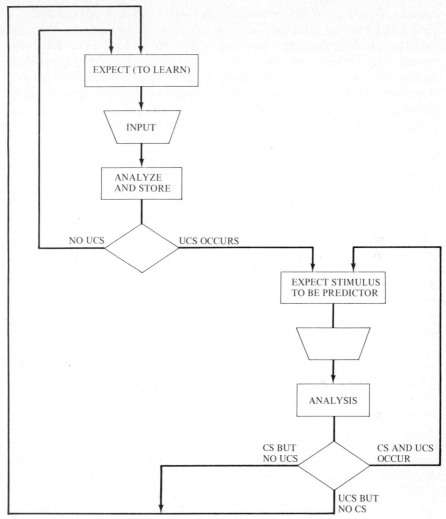

Figure 3.4 Behavior flowchart indicating how subject may look for connections and ways of predicting UCS.

response is formed when the CS-UCS pairs stand out in time. This results in a new behavior flow with the complete structure of expectancy, input, analysis, decision, and response.

Inhibitors are stimuli that predict the absence of the UCS. When a conditioned response is put on "experimental extinction" (no UCS is given), the CS gradually becomes an inhibitor. When UCS is sufficiently *delayed,* then CS actually becomes a sign that UCS will not occur (for a while) and a strong inhibitor.

The conditioning experiment is a way to provide a subject with specific expectancies and then to assess these expectancies by measuring special anticipatory responses. Because only such natural, anticipatory responses will appear, classical conditioning is very limited as a model of learning; but since many CSs can be used, the procedure of classical conditioning is a good method of studying perception in animals.

Chapter 4

Learning and
Behavior Control

How do you teach an animal a trick or a useful skill? Children are often
frustrated in trying to train their animal pets because they cannot transmit
their wishes by words; the animal does not understand. Actually, in the
child's own world, behavior is controlled by obedience: the child is told
what to do and is scolded or punished for disobedience. When this basic
approach is applied to the family dog, it leads to great difficulties because
the dog does not understand. For example, when the dog fails to sit on
command, the child may stand very erect, frown fiercely, and repeat the
command in a deep and threatening tone. This will no doubt impress the
dog but is not likely to cause it to sit. The child will probably then punish
the dog, at first by scolding it and later by spanking it with a newspaper.
This makes the dog obviously unhappy but still may not reliably produce
the desired behavior. At some point the child becomes uncontrollably
frustrated and concludes that the dog has no brain at all and cannot be
trained. Some children, who have a knack for working with animals, may
by kindness and patience develop a few tricks, and then may even be able

to train the dog to a variety of interesting forms of behavior. At best, however, except in the hands of a few experts, obedience training of animals is an uncertain and difficult process.

OBEDIENCE TRAINING

It is natural for a child to use the same procedures in training his dog that his parents have used in trying to control his own behavior. But it is not at all surprising that these methods fail to have the desired effect on the dog. What is more, any parent will admit (unless all his children are very docile) that these training methods are also rather unsatisfactory in shaping the behavior of children. Telling the child what to do is likely to be unproductive if the child does not understand, or understands only vaguely, what is wanted, or if what is wanted is somehow beyond his abilities. As part of instilling good table manners, you may tell a 10-year-old to hold a fork at the end. What gradually develops is a strong tendency to hold a fork at the end *when told to do so.* When the child is more interested in the food or in the table conversation, however, the hand will slip toward the tines to compensate for the relative weakness and poor coordination of the immature hand. Repetition may eventually solve this problem, but it sometimes seems that to demand such behavior is to anticipate maturity.

What is the "commonsense" theory of learning? How does the average parent, pet owner, foreman in a factory, or schoolteacher conceive of the problem of teaching good and useful behavior? Although there is no reason to suppose that ordinary people use any formal or scientific theory, it is possible to get a general idea of the principles underlying their methods.

Obedience Procedures

First, "behavior" is defined in moral terms. When a parent tells a child to "behave," he means that the child should display good behavior, and "good" means "morally good." That is, the desired form of behavior is one that conforms to the social norms suitable for the learner. In practice, the teacher is often rather unclear as to the specific behavior desired but relatively clear as to the general situation he is trying to produce—a well-behaved and obedient pet or child; an efficient and smooth-running shop; a quiet schoolroom with attentive children.

Ideally, such teaching does not produce a single stereotyped response but instead produces what may be called "obedience." A teacher can direct the performance of an obedient learner in various ways; and having established obedience, one can teach a variety of other skills and forms of behavior.

Obedience is measured by the degree to which the learner conforms to the wishes of the teacher. In order to conform, the learner must somehow know the wishes of the teacher. These wishes are formed by the teacher in response to the general social situation. A learner who can pick up the same cues from the situation can truly be obedient. For example, when guests come into a house it is important that the house appear very quiet and that adults have an opportunity to converse in their quiet way, without interruption. At that time (though perhaps not at other times) parents want their children to be quiet and to stay out of the way. A cooperative child will learn that his usual demands for attention, which may be well received at playtime, will be rejected when guests are in the house. At first, the parent may have to tell the child this; the mother, for example may tell the child to be quiet, then perhaps scold him, then physically restrain him, and finally—often enough—retire to the bedroom and join him in a screaming and crying match. In this instance, the mother is reacting to the child as "disobedient," which is the appropriate response within this theory of learning based upon obedience.

Of course, most parents come to realize that even a "good" child does not always behave properly, especially in unfamiliar circumstances. Children may require some instruction. Such instruction is usually spoken, and it is assumed that the child will understand what he is being told. Often, the child will not only be told what to do but will receive rather lengthy explanations and justifications. This procedure is presumably based on the assumption that it is more important to develop the moral context than to give specific instructions as to behavioral forms.

If the child, having been instructed as to the moral significance of the situation, still does not do what is wanted, the next step is to conclude that the child is being uncooperative. That is, the child understands most of the situation but is not assuming the appropriate subordinate role—he is doing what he wants rather than what his parents want. This situation is corrected by the social means of enforcement: the child is ordered to do what he has been told to do; the voice of the parent assumes a note of authority; and the parent shifts into the imperative mode—"Do it, and right now!"

Normally, the threatening posture of the parent—who is, after all, larger than the child—will produce at the very least a cowering and withdrawing response, though it may produce defiance. It may also, of course, produce the desired behavior. This is particularly likely if, in our example, the child is told to go to his bedroom, since that is exactly what he wants to do to escape so threatening a situation. Similarly, if the child can meet the demands of the social and moral situation merely by showing signs of submission and remaining quiet, this is a probable result of strong authority. However, if in our example the desired behavior included approaching the guests, speaking to them, performing, or otherwise entering actively into the social situation, then the natural response to a brusque order might interfere with the desired behavior. Here is another example of such a conflict: "Look at me when I'm talking to you!" Averting the eyes is a common sign of submission; thus the command conflicts with the natural response to it.

If the child is young and the situation has deteriorated, as it so often does in a normal household, the child may begin crying, screaming, kicking, and otherwise having a tantrum. At this point, even the most severely worded and forceful orders are unlikely to terminate the powerful behavior flow. The child is not only disobedient at this point but actually intransigent. Worse, his behavior, which earlier may have been merely irritating, has by now reached such proportions that it totally wrecks the desired social situation—the parents are mortified, and the guests are paralyzed. Commonsense behavior theory now concludes that the reason for the child's misbehavior is complete insubordination. The parents have no recourse but to use physical punishment and restraint— the child is picked up bodily, carried kicking and screaming to the farthest corner of the house, and spanked soundly.

In summary, the stages of discipline are as follows: The child should behave correctly to fit the situation. If he does not, this may be because he does not notice the cues in the situation. Such cues are then supplemented by the parent: "Be quiet now; we have guests." If this does not produce the proper social behavior, it may be because the child does not understand the significance of the situation. This, too, may be explained to the child: "When we have guests in, Mommy and Daddy want to talk with them, and children should be seen and not heard." Depending upon the age of the child, such explanations may be fairly long and involved. If the explanation does not succeed, it must be assumed that the child understands but does not obey; and this situation is handled by giving direct orders. If the orders do not produce what is desired, physical punishment must be used.

Notice that this commonsense system of behavioral control proceeds by a series of operations, each of which is initiated by the failure of the previous one. If the parent is in a hurry, or does not expect the child to behave well, or is under great social stress and dare not risk a prolonged session with the child, various stages of the system may be skipped. In a dangerous or tense situation (an example of a few years ago might be a Negro mother with several children in the waiting room of a white lawyer or doctor, or otherwise alone in a threatening white social environment), the parent may resort almost instantly to physical punishment, without any intervening cues, explanations, or orders. Since parental discipline is so intimately connected with other social factors, including the community standing of the family and the various members of it, the particular methods used by parents to correct behavior depend not only on the child's behavior but also on the social context within which it occurs.

Obedience Theory

We may summarize obedience theory by saying that people (or animals being trained) can be either good or bad. If they are good, they may be either cooperative or merely obedient. If they are cooperative, either they may understand the situation or they may not. If the trainer has time and consideration for the organism being trained—and particularly if the learner is a child and a member of the family—it is assumed that the child is cooperative and understanding. In our examples, a cooperative and understanding child would stay away from the guests, merely shaking hands politely and then withdrawing. If this docs not happen, the parents first assume that the child is cooperative but does not understand the situation. The situation is explained to the child. If he still does not do what is wanted, then the only possible conclusion is that he is not cooperative. The parents then assume that the child, though not cooperative, is good, and therefore will be obedient. Consequently, the parent issues an imperative, which if obeyed will solve the behavioral problem. If the child persists in unwanted behavior, then all other possibilities are exhausted, and it is concluded that the child is bad. It may be possible to produce satisfactory behavior by dominating, forcing the child into submission and therefore into a state in which it will obey. If that is not successful, then physical punishment or restraint is employed to enforce obedience, or at least to punish the child for being bad. Of course, in more elaborate moral systems, such as religions, there are various kinds and gradations of badness, and punishments suitable for each.

REINFORCEMENT TRAINING

Chapter 3 showed how animals and humans can learn new expectancies through classical conditioning. However, the conditioned response is severely limited as a method for training animals and children. The only responses that can be taught by conditioning are those that are an intrinsic part of another behavior flow—for example, salivation as part of eating, or withdrawal of a leg as part of a defensive response to electric shock. A psychological system for training should be far more general and capable of teaching all sorts of responses and behaviors.

Behaviorism and reinforcement theory provide a general procedure for training. This approach has been developed mainly from laboratory studies in experimental psychology rather than from experience and social custom; and it has been applied only in relatively few cases and only in recent years. Despite these limitations, reinforcement theory does provide a consistent and relatively complete theory of how training can be carried out and offers a new approach to such problems as animal training and child rearing.

Almost all the research on reinforcement theory has been done with animal subjects; it is natural, therefore, that the best evidence and support for the theory come from accomplishments in training animals. It is now commonplace in psychology laboratory courses for freshmen students to conduct routine experiments with white rats or pigeons, training these animals to make such special responses as pressing bars or pecking at a panel, and controlling the rate of responding, investigating the disappearance of responses through "experimental extinction," teaching stimulus discriminations, and so forth. No teacher will use an uncertain experimental technique as the basis of a laboratory course; it is a fair guess that experiments with rats, in the introductory psychology laboratory, have as high a rate of success as typical experiments in an introductory chemistry laboratory.

A good idea of the reliability and generality of these methods is given by a report, published in 1951, of a business established to mass-produce learned behavior in animals. Keller and Marian Breland (Breland & Breland, 1951) trained various farm animals to perform unusual and novel behavior patterns, mainly for the purpose of advertising exhibits for General Mills, Inc. Their first acts used 2-year-old hens who were trained and then exhibited at county fairs in the Midwest. One hen played a five-note tune on a small piano; another performed a tap dance in costume and shoes; and a third "laid" wooden eggs from a nest box—the eggs rolled down a trough into a basket, and if the audience called out any number of eggs, up to eight, the hen would lay that number, nonstop.

According to Breland and Breland, the basic operation in all these acts was reinforcement at the proper moment in the behavior chain, by giving the chicken a chance to eat a small amount of grain from a hopper. During the training period, successive approximation of the desired behavior pattern, and component parts of the final pattern, were reinforced. During performances, long strings of responses or highly elaborate completed patterns were reinforced.

The acts proved to be unprecedented crowd-stoppers at the fairs where they played, showing to as many as 5,000 people in a day. The success of these acts led to the developement of a trained pig show, "Priscilla the Fastidious Pig." Priscilla's routine included turning on a radio, eating breakfast at a table, picking up dirty clothes and putting them in a hamper, running a vacuum cleaner, picking out her favorite feed from those of her competitors, and taking part in a quiz program, answering "yes" or "no" to questions put by the audience by lighting up the appropriate signs.

Other displays mentioned by the Brelands include a continuous display with small chicks: each chick ran up an incline, pushed the preceding chick off a platform, grabbed a little feed, and was then pushed off by the next chick. In this display, a continuous circle of chicks perform until they become sleepy and then are replaced by a second group. More than 2,500 chicks have been trained for this display over several years. A calf, a turkey, and other grown chickens have been trained, and a couple of nonpsychologists (humans) were taught to train animals and instruct the handlers at the fairs.

Reinforcement Procedures

Reinforcement theory provides a systematic method for training animals that produces highly reliable behavior. It can be used in the laboratory to develop special responses, for studying animal perception, motivation, response to drugs, and many other matters. It can be used, as was described above, to train animal displays. Furthermore, it is not an arcane craft but, quite the contrary, can readily be taught—for example, to "an average male high school graduate, whose only speciality had been radio repair work" (Breland & Breland, 1951, p. 203).

How does reinforcement training differ from obedience training, the "commonsense" approach to child-rearing and social control? It differs in several respects—particularly, in its definition of the goals of training, in the way it develops a new response and continues an old one, in its methods of removing unwanted behavior, and in its criterion of success.

First, reinforcement training defines its goals as specifically as possible in terms of the actions of the learner. In reinforcement theory, a "response" is a movement (perhaps accompanied by glandular secretions, etc.) or system of movements that can be observed and recorded by the teacher. A response may be defined very narrowly (twitching a given muscle in the arm) or very broadly (walking to a restaurant). A certain amount of change or substitution of movements may be allowed within a given response, but such variations must not affect the ability to identify whether the response has or has not been made. In the Skinner box, the response desired from a rat is to press a bar far enough to make an electrical contact that is then recorded. The rat can depress the bar with both forefeet, one forefoot, or the nose, or in the course of biting the bar, or even by jumping up in the air and landing on the bar. What is recorded is the electrical contact; thus all the various activities that result in a depression of the bar are classified together, and that category of behavior is called "the response."

In some experiments and many applications of the theory, the experimenter actually wants a whole sequence of specific responses, in a particular order. This would be true, for example, in the case of the hen playing a tune on its piano, which requires that five different pecks be made in the right order. The particular posture of the hen, the angle of attack of the beak, etc., are immaterial if the correct key is struck with approximately the correct force. Thus, each of the pecks is a "response" and the final total behavior is a "chain."

The goal of reinforcement training is to establish or to remove some particular response or chain. Consider the problem of a young child who approaches guests, monopolizes their attention, and is generally a pest. From the perspective of a reinforcement theory, this problem will be solved by either (1) defining exactly what responses or chains are involved in this misbehavior, and removing them, or (2) defining an acceptable alternative response, such as the child's going to his own room, and establishing the chain. Of course, it is quite possible that both procedures may be followed at the same time, since they are quite compatible and even help one another. Although the overall goal may still be to establish a suitable context for adult conversation, reinforcement theory immediately shifts to a much more specific goal—a narrow response class.

To establish a given response, the teacher ordinarily waits for the response to occur. The frequency of a response in the unmodified environment is called its "operant level." If the operant level is very low, then it may be quite difficult to train the subject; but various methods can be used to increase the operant level. For example, if one wants little Linda to go to her room when guests arrive, she may be placed near the room and some enticements may be used to get her to go into the room in the first place.

When the specific response occurs, it is *reinforced*. Generally speaking, this means that it is rewarded, but the concept of reinforcement is more specific and cold-blooded than simply reward. One administers something to the learner that has the effect of increasing the probability of the learner's last response. When Linda goes into her room, she may be played with, or given a candy, or allowed to play with her doll—anything that will reinforce the response of going into her room.

How does one know what will be a reinforcer? This is a difficult and rather awkward question for reinforcement theory. A few examples of reinforcers are known, of course. For most animals (especially the more voracious species, particularly rats), food will serve as a reinforcement, provided only that the animal is partly starved and hungry. Water serves as a reinforcement for a thirsty rat, and sweetened water is still more effective. A comfortable temperature, relief from either excessive stimulation or monotony, and many other events are also known to be reinforcers to some extent.

Obviously, reinforcers are things the learner likes, although it is not the liking but the reinforcing that is essential. However, the general pattern is one of deprivation of some essential life substance, and then its administration at the time of reinforcement.

What about an opportunity to play with the doll—is that a reinforcer for Linda? If the child has previously been deprived of an opportunity to play with the doll, that increases the probability that it will be a reinforcer; but something like a doll might or might not be a reinforcer, and in general we cannot be sure without trying it. According to reinforcement theory, we can test whether the doll is a reinforcer as follows: We could use the doll as a reinforcer for some simple, neutral act like saying "baby." If we give the child the doll every time she says "baby," and if the doll is a reinforcer, then before long the frequency of the word "baby" should increase. This would be an indication that the doll is a reinforcer. To be more sure, we could then have a few sessions in which the doll is not given (extinction), and we should expect that the frequency of the word "baby" would decrease. We can then recondition the child by again giving her the doll whenever she says "baby," and if the response again gains in frequency we are quite sure that the doll is functioning as a reinforcer.

Now if the doll is a reinforcer, we make sure that the child is given the doll as soon as she makes the desired response, that is, as soon as she enters the room. Any delay is very harmful. On the other hand, the response must actually be made. There is no good in giving the child the doll when she does not go into the room, to encourage her. The doll must be *contingent* upon the desired response; that is, the doll must consistently and quickly be given when the child goes into her room, and not otherwise.

By this process, Linda is trained to go into her room. The training is quite straightforward and can easily be managed by either parent, a baby-sitter, or even an older brother or sister who is properly trained. Linda is not punished or coerced; she simply does not get the doll unless she goes into her room. This is a relatively kind, gentle, and peaceful form of training, though it is true that in the early stages Linda may want her doll and express some frustration when she cannot get it without going into her room. However, the trainer need only have patience and resolution to succeed.

This response will continue if it is reinforced all the time. In fact, it will not always be necessary to give Linda her doll; if she never gets the doll otherwise, then she may be given it on only some of the occasions when she goes into her room. For example, on a "ratio" schedule, she might get the doll only every third time she goes to her room. (This does not seem to make much sense with the example of the doll; but if the reinforcer were a piece of candy, then both economics and nutrition would dictate reducing the number of reinforcers to the minimum. It is useful to know that responses can be maintained with only intermittent reinforcement.)

At some stage of training it may be decided that Linda spends too much time in her room, for she often goes there just to get the doll, even when she would be welcome elsewhere. Then the experimenter may introduce "discrimination training." He may give Linda a distinctive cue—for example, by saying, "Linda, go to your room"—and if Linda goes to her room on this cue she is reinforced. If Linda goes to her room without the cue, she is not reinforced. Eventually, Linda will stop going to her room except when she receives the cue, and that cue will now control the response. In this way it is possible to get specific control over the response.

Getting the first few responses to be made, so that reinforcements can be given, may require some tricks. Also, there are sometimes difficulties with reinforcers, for the learner may become satiated (e.g., tired of the doll) and stop performing as desired. However, these difficulties can often be overcome, at least in a practical fashion. The techniques of "shaping" a new response will be discussed later and will serve as a general solution to the problem of a low response level. Satiation with, or failure of, a reinforcer can often be corrected by increasing the time of deprivation; if that does not work, one can shift to a new reinforcer.

If reinforcement theory works as described above, then there simply is no reason to have badly behaved children. If the parents want some particular response from their children, they need only reinforce it, consistently and without error.

One obvious problem is that a learner may not adopt the desired behavior, because he already has some conflicting response at high strength. In the example we have been discussing, one can easily imagine this scene: Linda has been skillfully trained to go to her room. A guest arrives, and she toddles up to him and tries to climb into his lap. She is then told to go to her room; but she finds the guest more interesting than her old doll and begins her old pestering routine. What should the parents do?

At that moment, there is not too much they can do. But they should analyze the situation, defining both the response they do not want and the stimulus which evokes it. Linda toddles toward the guest; this may be called an "approach response." What is the stimulus? The guest—a new adult. It will be worthwhile to discover just what about the guest makes him the stimulus for her approach—his size (will small children also be approached?), the sound of his voice, the parents' response to him?

Now the parents must consider why the child approaches guests. According to reinforcement theory, either this is an instinctive response (in this case unlikely) or it is reinforced. Guests usually play with babies and give them attention. In fact, when Linda climbs onto the guest's lap, she is the center of attention, particularly to her harassed parents. Perhaps this "attention," with approach, touching, verbalization, and other such stimulation, serves as reinforcement to Linda. Few children can resist the limelight.

If this is the diagnosis of the problem, the cure is obvious—this approach response must be extinguished and replaced by the response of going to her own room. The parents should bring in various adults; and when Linda toddles up to them, parents and guests should ignore her completely, giving her none of the reinforcing attention she seeks. This puts the approach response on an extinction schedule, and after a while it should decrease in frequency and drop out. If the child's approach response is extinguished to several guests, it will probably (though not certainly) also be extinguished to guests in general. (The process would be called "generalization of extinction.") If parents combine a program of extinguishing the child's approach to the guest with positive reinforcement for going to her room, they are very likely thereby to solve the problem.

Of course, it is possible that they did not properly diagnose the source of Linda's approach to the guest. Perhaps it was not attention which reinforced her response, but some other element of the situation; and perhaps her parents cannot uncover the source of her motivation. Since she was not taught to climb into laps, we do not know what the reinforcement history may have been, and therefore it can be rather difficult to place such a response on extinction. If so, punishment can be used. When the child approaches a guest, her parents may inflict pain or fear, by slapping the child, speaking very sharply to her, or the like. Most parents will have established a "secondary" means of punishing their children, such as a scolding or just the word "bad." The point is that the stimulus administered, the punishment, must be aversive—the child must turn away from it and try to avoid or escape it. If this aversive stimulus is made contingent upon the response of approaching guests, then that response will be suppressed. When the approach response is suppressed, and the child has been stopped but has no other response to make, it might be a good idea to say "Linda, go to your room"—that is, to bring in the positively reinforced response.

Punishment suppresses a response but is not believed to remove it permanently: if the child somehow finds out that punishment has been discontinued, she will soon recover the response that was punished. However, punishment given after the response has begun sets up a contingency partly under the control of the child. If she does not approach the guest, she is not punished—she has *avoided* the punishment. Of course, when she is not being punished, she has no way of finding out whether she would be punished if she were to approach the guest. She is therefore in a situation in which she will not respond, and she cannot learn whether it is now safe to begin to respond. The result is that she is likely to refrain from approaching guests even after her parents have changed their minds and would admit a certain amount of friendliness.

Another way to develop the response of going to her room, if other motivations fail, is to place Linda in a continuously aversive situation (a continuous scolding, for example) which she can terminate only by going to her room. In such a situation, the mere termination of scolding may be enough reinforcement to control behavior. This is called "negative" reinforcement and may be useful if the child's strongest positive reinforcement is to meet the guest, so that no other available positive reinforcer can steer her to her room. With such a combination of techniques, the parent using reinforcement training is apparently ready for any contingency.

To summarize, reinforcement training begins with a specific, concrete definition of a response, in terms of particular motions or a class of motions that produce a given effect on the environment and can be observed and measured. Second, the desired response is elicited in some way, or the trainer simply waits until it is made. When the response is made, it is reinforced by immediately giving the learner a reward. This reinforcement should increase the frequency of the response, which gives the trainer more opportunities to reinforce it. When the response is sufficiently frequent, the experimenter may omit some of the reinforcements and still maintain the response. If some competing response gets in the way, it can be extinguished by removing its usual source of reinforcement. If the reinforcement for the competing response cannot be discovered and removed, the response can be suppressed by punishing it, that is, by administering an aversive stimulus as soon as it is made. If the learner can avoid the aversive stimulus either by making some avoiding response or by refraining from some bad behavior, such avoidance will eventually be learned and will be difficult to extinguish. Finally, a response can be established by negative reinforcement, which consists of stopping some aversive stimulus when the learner makes the desired response.

If it is true that these methods will teach a pig to keep house, then they are indeed powerful. By such methods, a child can be educated efficiently. By such methods, a whole population can be held in check, and in fact welded into a fantastically efficient social organism. Abnormal behavior can be eradicated and replaced by useful and beneficial responses.

Considering the apparent potential power of this method, it is perhaps surprising that the world is not already dominated by determined behaviorists. And considering what efforts politicians will expend to gain power, it is perhaps surprising that they are not yet converted to behaviorism. It is true that their prejudices and preconceptions may be incompatible with simple behaviorism and may lean more toward obedience training. However, successful politicians display willingness and ability to give up their prejudices in exchange for power.

One possibility is that reinforcement theory simply does not work. Unlike other theories and methods of control, however, it has been investigated in the laboratory, where rats, mice, dogs, cats, monkeys, apes, raccoons, elephants, psychotic children, schizophrenic veterans, and college students have all been studied.

Reinforcement Theory

One of the most influential theories in modern psychology is reinforcement theory. It has been developed by many men; Watson, Thorndike, Hull, Spence, and Skinner are but a few of the famous names. This section will give a brief description of reinforcement theory and the facts supporting it.

Reinforcement theory is part of modern behaviorism, which arose from an effort to make psychology "scientific." This goal may not seem important to us now, but in 1920 there were only a handful of avowed psychologists in the world and they were not universally accepted as scientists. For one thing, common sense, philosophy, and the physical sciences all agreed in dividing the realm of reality into two major parts, the "physical" and the "mental," or "spiritual." Science concerned itself with the physical; the moral sciences, theology, psychology, and aesthetics muddled around with the spiritual. Experimental psychologists interested in pure scientific research and in applications to the world of affairs felt themselves misclassified and struggled to become more scientific. To do this they eschewed mentalism and made their theories as objective and scientific as they could. One branch of this effort was behaviorism, a school of thought which claimed that a psychology could be constructed by referring only to observable events in the physical world; feelings, emotions, experiences, etc., need not enter in any essential way into the theories.

One objective concept used by behaviorism was that of a "stimulus," which consists of physical energy falling on the receptors of the subject—in practice, it is a physical object or event that can be identified by the experimenter and that is available to the subject.

A second objective concept used by behaviorism was that of a "response," which is mainly to be distinguished from experiences, opinions, feelings, and other mental phenomena. A response is an overt act of a subject which the experimenter can see, identify, and record. A response may be what the subject says he sees, but it cannot be his truly private visual experience. Actually, in most experimental situations, the specific details of the response may vary from one instance to another; accordingly, Skinner proposed that a response be thought of as a *class* of acts, all of which are treated as equivalent by the experimenter.

An instance of behavior, on this theory, is a succession consisting of a stimulus followed by a response. In formulations of this theory the stimulus is often called "S" and the response "R"; and the element of behavior is called an "S-R pair," a "reflex," an "association," or a "habit." The subject may have a disposition to make response R to stimulus S, but this disposition is not manifested unless S is presented. Such a disposition is often called a habit or association.

Reinforcement theory introduces a third class of events, called "reinforcers." Sometimes it appears that reinforcers are stimuli, and sometimes they seem to be responses. In fact, they are often stimuli to which the subject makes a specific response. They have a specific important property, however: they can reinforce S-R habits. In this theory, to "reinforce" means to "make stronger"; a reinforcer, then, can strengthen the bond between S and R.

The *basic law of reinforcement* is roughly this: If S is a stimulus, R is a response, and F is a reinforcer, then whenever the succession S-R-F occurs, the bond between S and R is strengthened. As a consequence, other things being equal, if S is presented, the probability or strength of R will be increased. The sequence S-R-F is called a "reinforced trial."

The law is applied in a simple way. Decide what response R is to be made to what stimulus S. The experimenter then presents stimulus S (which may be a constant situation) and tries in one way or another to elicit response R. Whenever R occurs, it is immediately followed by F, the reinforcer, which increases the strength of the S-R bond and makes it easier to elicit the next instance of R. This procedure is repeated, steadily increasing the probability of R, until the sequence S-R-F occurs frequently. At that point, the response is "learned" and behavior has been modified as desired.

Several subsidiary principles are usually invoked. If S-R occurs but F is omitted, this tends to weaken S-R. If a new response R′ is attached to S, this interferes with performance of R. Interfering responses, particularly those produced by aversive and punishing stimuli, are often effective in removing an unwanted R. If a new stimulus S′ is given that is similar to S, the learned response R will often be made to S′ but with a reduced strength—this is called "stimulus generalization."

To give some of the flavor of research on reinforcement theory, it is useful to review what is known about reinforcement itself.

Parameters of Reinforcement   From the point of view of reinforcement theory, the pivot of learning is the concept of reinforcement. What is known about reinforcement?

First, what are some typical reinforcers? Food for a hungry animal, and water for a thirsty one, are two standard examples. In both cases, the animal must be deprived of food or water for a substantial time to make the reinforcer powerful enough for reliable learning. The degree of deprivation affects how vigorously the animal will work for reward. That is, a hungrier animal will run faster, or press a bar harder and more often, for its reward of food. Its final level of performance, after learning is complete, will be higher if it is more hungry. The rate of learning—the speed with which performance changes trial by trial—does not depend on the degree of deprivation, beyond a necessary mimimum that makes the food a reward.

How can this last statement be proved? A typical experiment is that by Hillman, Hunter, and Kimble (1953). Two groups of rats learned a complex maze for a reward of water. One group had had their water bottles removed from their cages two hours before running the maze, and so were on the average only slightly thirsty. The second group had had their water bottles removed 22 hours before the running the maze and were therefore very thirsty. (In fact, they were allowed to drink only for a while after each run through the maze and then were without water all day and all night until the next run.) Naturally, the thirstier rats ran faster. After ten trials in the maze, the very thirsty rats were running it in about

25 seconds, whereas the slightly thirsty rats were running it in about 60 seconds. Before trial 11, the motivational conditions were reversed for half of each group. Half of the rats previously deprived of water for 22 hours were switched to 2 hours' deprivation, and on trial 11 these rats immediately took as long to run the maze as the animals that had always been on 2 hours' deprivation. This indicates that the very thirsty rats had not learned any more than the slightly thirsty ones but had merely worked harder. When less thirsty, they did not take such an interest in water and slowed down. Half of the rats previously deprived of water for 2 hours were switched to 22 hours' deprivation. These rats took only two trials to become just as fast as the rats that had always been on 22 hours' deprivation. The slightly thirsty rats had learned but had not performed very well; as soon as they became very thirsty (which probably took two days of deprivation), they ran as fast as the animals that had always been kept very thirsty. This experiment is typical of studies which indicate that the degree of deprivation affects how hard an animal will work but does not have much effect on learning.

An experimenter can also vary the amount of reinforcement given— e.g., one food pellet or many. Large reinforcements lead to rapid and strong responses, but—like deprivation—they do not lead to more learning. In fact, when you shift an animal from a large reinforcement to a smaller one, it may stop responding altogether. This was shown, for example, by Zeamon (1949), who used 0.5 grams of food as a low-reinforcement condition, and 2.4 grams for a high-reinforcement condition. When an animal had learned to run a runway to 0.5 grams of food, it ran rather slowly; but within two or three trials of 2.4-gram reinforcements the animal speeded up and ran as fast as animals that had learned the runway with 2.4-gram reinforcements. Similarly, a group that had learned the runway for 2.4 grams of food slowed up after having found 0.5 grams on one trial, and in fact these animals stayed slower than animals that had always had 0.5-gram reinforcement.

What about the quality of food used as a reward, independent of amount? To study this question, Guttman (1953) had rats press a bar in a Skinner box for water sweetened to different degrees. He found that rats performed more steadily for sweetened than unsweetened water. Later studies strongly suggest that it is the level of performance, rather than learning itself, which is affected by the quality of food.

A reinforcement should be administered promptly after a response, according to reinforcement theory. Delaying the reward generally makes learning slower or performance poorer, but the results are somewhat complicated. It appears that delays of a few seconds have little effect but that delays of about 10 seconds are harmful. The difficulty in interpreting this is that a delay seems to involve forgetting, but the earlier research on delay of reinforcement did not talk about forgetting or analyze what the animal might be forgetting.

What, Exactly, Is a Reinforcer?   According to Skinner, a reinforcement is simply some event that strengthens a response. The only way to find out if something is a reinforcer is to use it, giving it selectively after a certain response. If the response increases in frequency, then the event is a reinforcer. If the response disappears, the event is aversive.

The obvious reinforcers, like food for a hungry rat and water for a thirsty one, have in common that they reduce a bodily need. The first general theory of reinforcement was that all primary reinforcers reduce bodily needs. Obviously, behavior is shaped by praise and other events that do not actually reduce a need, but such reinforcers are considered "secondary." It is argued that if a neutral, nonreinforcing event (tender words, for example) is consistently followed by a primary reinforcer (mother's milk, for example) then the previously neutral event will become a secondary reinforcer and can reinforce other responses. Experimentally, it is easy to establish a secondary reinforcer (it is merely a signal that the primary reinforcer will soon be forthcoming); but when the primary reinforcer is removed from the situation, the animal soon loses interest in the secondary reinforcer. The theory of secondary reinforcers is very important in all general applications of reinforcement theory (e.g., Skinner, 1972).[1]

Some events that do not reduce any bodily need are nevertheless reinforcers. Saccharine, for example, has no food value, but when added to food or water it increases the reinforcement value of that food. This finding leads to the idea that it is not the actual *need* that is reduced but only a psychological concomitant of need—*drive*. This is the drive-reduction theory of reinforcement. It can survive many experimental tests, partly because the concept of "drive" is defined by the psychologist, and it is sometimes difficult to establish whether or not certain drives exist.

For example, Butler (1953, 1954) showed that a monkey would solve problems merely for the opportunity of looking out of a small window in its box to see what was going on in the laboratory. This finding, that mere inspection of the surroundings is a reinforcer, requires postulating a "curiosity drive" which is reduced. This appears to be the opening of

---

[1]Harlow (1958) has clearly shown that certain maternal characteristics, especially softness, are *not* derived from food but are original instigators of filial love. The concept of "secondary reinforcers" has been used by reinforcement theorists to explain many characteristics of human behavior. However, few of these explanations have ever been proved or even tested empirically.

Pandora's box; as we find new reinforcers, drive-reduction theory evidently will be forced to postulate new drives, and eventually the theory will become meaningless.

A more direct attack on drive-reduction theory comes from an experiment by Sheffield, Wulff, and Backer (1951) on sex behavior in the rat. The copulatory pattern of the male rat consists in a series of intromissions and withdrawals, terminating finally in ejaculation. Sheffield et al. ran male rats down a 32-inch runway to a female, and then stopped their sexual act short of ejaculation. This, they expected, should increase rather than decrease drive and should not be primarily reinforcing. Because young rats with no previous sexual experience were used, there were no previous experiences to make the interrupted coitus secondarily reinforcing. Nevertheless, the rats whose coitus was interrupted ran the runway faster and faster. They soon outstripped rats running to find male rats in the goal box, and outran male rats that did not copulate by an even wider margin. The experimenters concluded that copulatory activity short of ejaculation is reinforcing. This is not in itself a surprising fact, but it seems almost fatal for a drive-reduction theory of reinforcement.

Another kind of reinforcer, found by accident but by now well explored, is stimulation of certain centers in the midbrain. Stimulation of some areas of the midbrain appears to be "pleasant" (Olds, 1955), and rats can be induced to run mazes or press bars until they are physically exhausted for a reward consisting only of such stimulation. Whatever is the precise mechanism of this reinforcement, it is very difficult to attribute it to either a need or a drive. Brain stimulation in the right place is accompanied by behavior that appears alert and inquisitive and may include sniffing or staring at nearby objects.

The discussion so far suggests that some events are reinforcers and others are not. However, recent research by Premack (1965) shows that there is no such thing as a category of reinforcers. Instead, he has shown that a stronger or more likely response will reinforce weaker or less likely responses. We may think of eating as a reinforcement for muscular activity, but it is also possible to use the opportunity for muscular activity as a reinforcement for eating. Johnny eats his spinach because he knows he can go out and play when he has finished. Experimentally, Premack (1965) rigged up an activity wheel (squirrel cage) with a drinking tube just outside. If the wheel was always free and the tube rarely had water, the rat could be taught to run the wheel for water—the conventional reinforcing effect. The tube was arranged so that the wheel had to be turned 10 times to permit a few seconds of drinking water, and the rats speeded up their turning of the wheel. However, the same experiment could be reversed. The wheel was locked most of the time, and water was present. If the rat took five licks of water, the wheel would be released for 10 seconds. This increased drinking time from about 25 seconds per hour to 98 seconds per hour. When the contingency was broken (drinking no longer freed the wheel), the rate of drinking returned to normal.

According to Premack's theory, the stronger of the two responses would reinforce the weaker. By depriving the rat of the opportunity to run the wheel, the experimenter made running a stronger response than drinking. Therefore, according to this theory, running became a reinforcer for drinking, once the contingency was set up.

If Premack's position is correct, there is no class of "reinforcing events"; rather, reinforcement results from the relationship between two responses. We may ask what the relationship is. In practice, there is a contingency—the reinforcer cannot be obtained unless the response is made. The subject is deprived of the reinforcer and cannot have all that he wants unless he increases his performance of the response beyond what he would do anyway.

When can a response be reinforced? Only when it is made advantageous to the subject to increase the frequency of that response. Why should he do so? To obtain something he wants that cannot be obtained otherwise. If the situation prevents a rat from eating all it wants, unless it makes a certain response like pressing a bar more often than it wants, the rat must press the bar at an increased rate to normalize its food consumption. This does not mean that food itself is the reinforcer. If a rat must press a bar to get the opportunity to scratch its back as often as it wants, then it will increase bar pressing in order to get its level of back scratching up to normal.

Allison and Timberlake (1973) have been able to contrast this response-deprivation theory with the theory that one can reinforce a response only with something the subject prefers. Imagine a child who prefers chocolate to vanilla ice cream. When presented with an ample supply of both flavors, the child eats about six times as much chocolate as vanilla. According to Premack's theory, since eating chocolate ice cream is a stronger response than eating vanilla ice cream, it should be possible to increase the rate of eating vanilla. Merely make the child eat five spoonsful of vanilla in order to get two spoonsful of chocolate, and he will eat more vanilla than normal. Premack's explanation is that by making the preferred response (the reinforcer) contingent on the less-preferred response (the ordinary response), the less preferred response is strengthened.

According to Allison and Timberlake, the experiment can be reversed: vanilla (the less-preferred response) can be used to increase the intake of chocolate (the preferred response). The method is as follows: make the child eat (say) eight spoonsful of chocolate to get one spoonful of vanilla. Normally, the child would eat chocolate and vanilla in a ratio of 6 to 1, but you now require a ratio of 8 to 1. In order to keep its intake of vanilla up to normal, the child would have to increase its intake of chocolate above normal. This would appear to be using vanilla as a reinforcement for eating chocolate. Premack's theory, that the preferred response reinforces the other response, would hold that there is no way to reinforce eating chocolate with eating vanilla. However, in an experiment of this type,[2] Allison and Timberlake obtained the result they expected.

This suggests that every response has an operant level and every stimulus intake has a "normal level." If a response is prevented or a stimulus withheld, so that it is below its normal level, then the subject is willing to make some change in its behavior to get up to return to the normal level.

Allison and Timberlake state clearly that their theory merely indicates what an animal or person will do after experience in a given contingency. They do not say how a rat ever comes to know that it must drink more water with 0.4 percent saccharine to get access to water with 0.3 percent saccharine, or how a child would learn that eating extra chocolate ice cream might earn some vanilla ice cream. Simple reinforcement theory speaks of the "strengthening of a response," but Allison and Timberlake's theory merely discusses the arrangements or contingencies in the animal's environment. There is no automatic adjustment the animal must make to this situation—the observed behavior may be a result of the cognitive structures, particularly the expectancies, that arise.

COGNITIVE TRAINING

The behavior-flow theory provides a basis for a third theory of training, which can be contrasted with both the commonsense theory of obedience training and the strict reinforcement theory. However, one should not concentrate too much on contrasting the reinforcement and cognitive theories—each grows out of the other, attempting to clarify it and improve the results obtained. The present cognitive theory is built on the foundation of reinforcement theory.

---

[2]Actually, the subjects of the experiment were rats who licked sweetened water. For "chocolate ice cream" read, in the actual experiment, "water containing 0.4 percent saccharine"; for "vanilla ice cream," read "water containing 0.3 percent saccharine." Each "spoonful" in my fictitious account would correspond to 10 seconds of licking.

Cognitive Procedures

What is the aim of training in cognitive theory? It is defined in terms of the cognitive process of the learner. Recall that obedience training set up its goals in terms of the moral and social needs of the trainer. Reinforcement theory set up its goals in terms of the responses of the learner, making them conform to the motivations of the trainer. Cognitive theory is concerned with the cognitions—the perceptions, expectancies, sensitivities, and decisions—of the learner. For obvious reasons, the learner's behavior must be directed—that is also part of the goal of both obedience training and reinforcement training. But cognitive training makes the learner do the right thing for the right reasons, or at least sets this as its goal.

Basically, in this theory, getting the right behavior means initiating the proper behavior flow. In some cases the observed responses may be very simple and repetitive, as when a child is taught to stand up straight. On the other hand, the behaviors may be extremely complex and organized at a high level of hierarchical structure, as when the child is taught to converse politely. Similarly, a rat may be taught merely to press a single bar in a small box or may learn to run a complicated fourteen-unit T-maze.

Unlike reinforcement theory, however, cognitive theory does not assume that behavior flows can be "strengthened" in any way. The organism has a complex of behavior flows, some relatively independent and others bound into systems, and within this complex it distributes its daily behavior in a fairly regular and predictable way if it is allowed to choose freely from among responses. The trainer can try to get the organism to expect new contingencies in the environment, and thereby may change the behavior flows that follow the occurrence of events. For example, a child may learn to expect danger after the warning "Look out!" The verbal stimulus will not initiate defensive behavior flows at the outset; but as the expectancy develops, the child will more and more consistently duck, look around, and generally initiate defenses when warned. The defensive behavior flow is not itself changed, but it becomes connected to a new situation. This, of course, is very much what the S-R psychologist says when he speaks of connecting an old response to a new stimulus.

In cognitive theory it is important not merely to change overt behavior but to establish correct behavior flows. Recall that in S-R theory a "response" is actually a whole class of behaviors. Now consider a trainer teaching a dog to sit by his side at the command "heel." The dog may sit as part of a submissive behavior flow, responding to the dominance of its trainer; but in that case its posture will be flaccid, its head will be down and its eyes turned up, and generally it will appear defenseless and pitiable. Show judges will rate this performance as poor, even though the animal is "legally" sitting. However, if sitting is integrated into a play structure that has elements of hunting, retrieving, and other canine behavior flows, the animal may sit tensely, slightly off the ground, with eyes bright and ears pointed. To a cognitive theorist, the two "sitting" responses would probably be quite separate, parts of entirely different behavior systems, and the trainer would find it important to make sure that he has installed the right general motivational system before working on details of the sitting posture.

Still, the goals of the cognitive theorist are not general and trainer-oriented, as they are in obedience training. In cognitive theory, as in reinforcement theory, one must have specific goals. In fact, cognitive theory sets more specific goals than reinforcement theory; for instead of specifying the desired response merely by its external appearance, cognitive theorists also specify it by the motivational system or large-scale behavior system of which it is a part. Obedience theory classifies children into categories like "good" and "bad," "obedient" and "cooperative"; but it does not require a close study of the precise capabilities of the child. Reinforcement theory is more sensible in setting as its goal a response that the child can perform. Cognitive theory requires not only a study of specific superficial responses but an understanding of the whole motivational and cognitive structure of the learner.

In ordinary language, obedience training involves moral judgments, in that the concepts of "good" and "bad" are basic to it, and it involves the frequent use of coercion. Since the system is also generally ineffective, and may put the learner in a bind, it often becomes cruel.

Reinforcement training, on the other hand, involves the use of selective reinforcements and generally gives rewards for good behavior. Because it is perfectly neutral about the learner and classifies behavior merely as "wanted" or "unwanted," it is not moralistic. However, though it is not moralistic or cruel, reinforcement training can be said to manipulate the learner, because the learner's motivations are not seriously considered and conforming behavior is established without any consideration for the goals, aims, or other activities of the learner.

Cognitive theory does not classify learners as good or bad, but it is interested in the reasons (that is, the overall behavioral systems) behind specific responses. For that reason the cognitive theorist is more interested in the learner as an individual, in the learner's capacities and the organization of the learner's behavior. It is quite sensible, from the cognitive point of view, to say that a person did the right thing for the wrong reason. This is a moral judgment—not about the individual but about the cognitive underpinning of his activities.

The methods of teaching used by a cognitive theorist are quite complicated, for they involve getting the subject into a particular motivational system, directing his attention to certain cues, impressing on him the contingency between one event and another so as to produce expectancies, and often developing or refining his method of analyzing input so that he will take in the correct and relevant information. Such cognitive teaching procedures are taken up in detail in the chapters which follow. However, the important aspect of cognitive training is how we get a learner to change his behavior in a given situation. In other words, here we should center attention on the cognitive theory of behavioral control.

How would a cognitive theorist handle the problem of Linda and the guest?

First, it would be important to analyze the behavior flows and their relationships. What is the nature of Linda's approach? Is she merely exploring a new person in her environment? If so, this behavior might soon terminate once the person is at all familiar, and the "training" might better not be done at all—one would merely try to make the inspection as comfortable as possible for the guest. Another possibility is that Linda approaches the guest in expectation of some response from him—will he play with her, pay attention to her, flatter her, or give her a present? Such expectancies would presumably initiate a behavior flow of approach. In this case, if the attention, present, or whatever is not forthcoming, it might be rather difficult to get Linda to terminate her behavior, and unpleasantness would follow. If Linda expects attention or a present, then the trainer might be well advised to try to break this expectancy both by preventing guests from giving attention or presents just as they arrive and by giving presents and attention at other times. In other words, one would try to disrupt the contingency, so that Linda would not selectively expect fun when a guest arrives.

This last possibility is very close to the S-R concept that the undesired response has been "reinforced" and that one should find and remove the reinforcements. It is almost the same thing to say that the subject may expect certain rewards in a given situation, that these expectancies will initiate behavior flows we do not want, and that the best thing to do is to change the expectancies.

Second, the cognitive method would select available behavior flows and try to integrate Linda's behavior into them. This is very similar to the reinforcement theorist's use of a competing response. However, according to cognitive theory, this method will be most successful if the behavior flow is readily accessible. The guest may be coming in the evening right after Linda's dinner, for example. Her tendency to approach the guest will be high when her stomach is full and she has her usual burst of energy and exploration just before bedtime. The parents might be able to control the situation merely by withholding Linda's dessert until the guest has arrived and then trying to maintain her dinnertime behavior flow during the first few minutes of the visit. This might lead Linda to ignore the guest; but of course it is open to the danger that when Linda is finished with dessert she may then still be curious, and even stickier than usual. On the other hand, Linda's curiosity may be by far the dominant behavior flow under the conditions, in which case attempts to suppress it will be unavailing and the parents may need some more radical solution, such as leaving Linda with a neighbor for the crucial hours. The cognitive theory specifically does *not* assume that behavior is infinitely modifiable; there are some behavior flows that simply cannot be unseated at a given stage of development and time. As Linda gets older, of course, she will develop a much more complex and differentiated system of social behavior and will learn when to approach and when not to approach a guest. These more complex forms of acceptable social behavior should and must be taught, so that as Linda comes to think of herself as part of her family and society, she will know how to behave. However, young children simply may not have a sufficiently developed and elaborated system of controls to be able to withhold the simple, friendly "approach and climb" response.

Generally speaking, behavior can be changed by environmental modifications. Obviously, if the trainer has sufficient control over his subject, he can prevent certain behavior simply by withholding the opportunity for it to occur. A child will not eat if no food is given or drink if no fluids are available. It cannot play ball without a ball and playmates, and it cannot build without materials. Responses that ordinarily will be made with some frequency can therefore be eliminated if they depend upon external stimulus supports. But how can the frequency of a behavior be increased? Here Allison and Timberlake's analysis of reinforcement will serve our purposes well. Suppose that we want a child to learn to put all his toys into a toybox, and that this response has a very low probability of spontaneous occurrence. The cognitive trainer selects some other response, preferably one which is fairly common in the situation but which requires a behavior support. The behavior support is withheld and made contingent on picking up toys. The child is then "reinforced" for picking up toys by being given his "reinforcement," namely, the opportunity to resume his uninterrupted behavior.

A reinforcement theorist might pick any strong "reinforcer," like eating candy. He would then withhold the candy until the child has put away his toys. When the child has put the toys away, the trainer would then reinforce with some candies. The method would be successful in many cases; but, unfortunately, if the theorist becomes tired of this procedure or feels that the child is too old (or too caried) to be given candy merely for picking up his toys, he will have to begin extinction. What he can do is to put the child on partial reinforcement, giving candy only sometimes for picking up toys and perhaps adding some secondary reinforcement like praise to maintain the behavior indefinitely.

A cognitive theorist would not be satisfied with this result, though he might accept it. He would like instead to integrate the picking up of toys into a stable and meaningful behavioral system. Therefore, he might pick a certain time of day for cleaning up the room, a time which is appropriate and natural for picking up toys. This might be after play (so that the child will not start playing with the toys instead of picking them up), at some time involving a system of related activities. For example, it might be just before the child undresses and washes up to go to bed. Then, the trainer may try to develop a whole routine in which the child would check whether all his toys were picked up, whether all his clothes were in the hamper, whether his face was washed and his teeth were cleaned, etc. If these various activities are regularly scheduled, the the child cannot go on to any activity until he has finished the preceding one. This in turn means that a whole sequence of contingencies can be established so that such low-probability responses as picking up toys are made as frequent as the inescapable response of going to bed. Assuming that it is appropriate for the child to pick up his toys once a day (or, say, twice a day—before the child's nap and then again at bedtime), the behavior can be integrated into a system of contingencies and will thereby gain its necessary frequency.

When Benjamin Franklin (Franklin, 1793) set out to acquire the moral virtues, he planned to acquire them one at a time so as not to be overwhelmed by the task: ". . . As the previous acquisition of some might facilitate the acquisition of certain others, I arrang'd them with that view. . . . Temperance first, as it tends to procure that coolness and clearness of head, which is so necessary where constant vigilance was to be kept up, and guard maintained against the unremitting attractions of ancient habits, and the force of perpetual temptations. This being acquir'd and establish'd, Silence would be more easy." So as to have more time for developing the other virtues, Franklin put "Order" third, defining it as requiring that "every part of my business should have its allotted time." He therefore prepared a daily schedule, arising at five o'clock; planning his day and breakfasting until eight o'clock, working from eight to eleven o'clock; dining, reading, and looking over his accounts until one; working until six; then putting things in their places, having supper and entertainment, and examining the day until ten o'clock; and finally going to bed. By this system he arranged to have plenty of time—except that, as a businessman, he was never able to keep to the schedule, having to attend upon others at their convenience.

This same general principle is a useful guide in training; for by putting each activity into a place, it enables the learner to develop a single unified and organized behavior flow containing needed behaviors and eliminating those that interfere with overall goals. Reinforcement theory correctly suggests that one must look at detailed behavioral goals, and that such behaviors can be acquired by reward or eliminated by removing their reinforcement. What reinforcement theory fails to emphasize is that one cannot successfully attack problems piecemeal but must consider the entire behavioral economy of the individual and develop in him an organized system of behavior, not a mere list of responses.

Cognitive Learning Theory

The cognitive theory of learning and behavior control has three main points: the form of a behavior flow, the role of expectancies, and the systematic organization of behavior.

The idea of a behavior flow was developed in earlier chapters: it includes an expectancy, to start every behavior system; the acceptance of a stimulus input; the analysis of that input; and a decision as to whether the analyzed input does or does not match the expectancy. This system is more complex than an S-R system of reinforcement theory but considerably more specific than the idea of "good behavior" as defined in obedience theory.

Learning, in cognitive theory, does not consist of strengthening a response or an S-R tendency. The S-R tendency is embedded in a behavior flow, and there is no way to strengthen or otherwise modify such a behavior flow by experience. However, experiences, particularly if repeated, may permit the organism to form new expectancies by extending the behavior flow in time or determining more exactly when a given behavior flow can be applied. New expectancies are formed especially when behavioral contingencies (of the kind discussed by Allison and Timberlake) are imposed on the subject.

Third, according to cognitive learning theory, behavior flows do not usually exist independently but instead are parts of larger systems. Recall that the "response" in a behavior flow is often another behavior flow of a lower order in the system. This also implies that a given behavior flow is itself subordinate to a still higher-order behavior flow. For this reason, it is not appropriate to work on a given "response" without determining the larger behavior system of which it is a part. S-R theory taught psychologists how to look at a desired pattern of behavior and analyze it into its component and subordinate parts. Cognitive theory carries this analysis on, but also completes the symmetric thought, pointing out that the desired response itself is no doubt an element of a higher-order and more complex behavior flow.

WHAT IS LEARNED

According to reinforcement theory, what is learned is a stimulus-response bond or habit. This connection, the tendency to make the response, is strengthened by reinforcement. The cognitive position put forward here is that the learner acquires expectancies by observing events that occur together in time and can be connected by the learner. These two ideas are quite different; can they be subjected to experimental tests in the laboratory?

Latent Learning

Obviously, one argument in favor of the idea that what is learned is expectancies has to do with "latent learning" in the maze, which was discussed at length in Chapter 2. The experiment described in Chapter 2 showed that a food reward at the end of the maze was not essential for learning, though it was very helpful in producing fast running. However, we might now decide that when a rat finds a blind alley in the maze, this deprives it of the opportunity to go to a new place, and therefore that merely traversing the maze itself provides a weak form of reinforcement. In other words, even when the rat does not find food, it can be learning the maze by strengthening S-R connections—but when food is introduced, then those connections are greatly energized and the animal runs fast and accurately. If so, then we do not have conclusive proof that learning is of expectancies, not habits.

Autoshaping

Some recent work on the process of acquiring a simple response throws new light on the question of what is learned. We may deal with a rat learning to press a lever or a pigeon learning to peck a plastic key on the wall of its box. These two responses are typical examples of the kinds of responses that can be developed by the use of reinforcement training, and they are archetypes of the kinds of responses used by Breland and Breland in their preparations of commercial animal displays.

In practice, it is not at all convenient to wait for a rat simply to press a bar in its Skinner box and then give a reinforcement. This may be possible, but most experimenters would like a more rapid and sure method. Furthermore, it is possible to teach rats very complicated chains of behavior. A rat can learn, for example, to pull a string and thereby release a marble, which it then picks up, carries across the cage, and drops into a slot; this releases a lever; the rat then presses the lever and gets a pellet to eat, after which the whole behavior chain is begun again. Clearly, the experimenter would not be well advised to sit and watch a rat until it happens to complete that chain of behavior spontaneously, and then give a reinforcement. Instead, following the precepts of reinforcement theory, the trainer uses the method of *shaping*.

The method of shaping begins with some response that the subject is likely to make and does make. If we want to train a rat to press a bar, we may find that at first it simply will not approach the bar at all. Using the technique of shaping, we at first administer food whenever the rat approaches the bar; then we give it only when the rat comes very close to the bar; then only when the rat touches the bar; and finally only when the rat depresses the bar far enough to make a "click" that can be heard and felt.

The process is not as smooth as this description suggests, although it is usually successful even in the hands of undergraduate college students working with their first rats. Quite often, administering the reinforcement actually takes the rat away from what it was doing, and we find the animal waiting around the food tray rather than returning to its original response. When this happens, there often must be a rather protracted period of waiting for the animal to tear itself away from the food tray and return to work near or on the bar. Shaping is not usually done automatically, but instead is performed by a patient and attentive research assistant who carefully observes the animal and laboriously tries to shape the desired behavior by selective reinforcement.

How would this process be described in cognitive terms? First, because of initial training to establish eating, the click of a food pellet dropping into the food mechanism (or some other distinctive sound associated with administering the reward) becomes the cue for a food-eating behavior flow, and that cue immediately establishes an expectancy for food. Whenever that stimulus occurs, the animal enters into its process of eating.

Now, the experimenter's problem is to establish a connection between pressing the bar and hearing the sound of the food pellet. His method usually consists of giving reinforcement whenever the animal approaches the bar, so that the stimuli (olfactory and visual at first; later, tactile stimuli as well) from the bar are often being received at the time that the food pellet drops. Therefore, a contingency between the stimuli from the bar and the cue to eating may finally be perceived by the rat, at which time stimuli from the bar initiate a food expectancy. We might, from a study of Pavlovian conditioning, expect the rat to salivate. The rat does not turn to the food tray, for the cue of the pellet dropping has not yet been received, though of course the animal develops an expectancy for that sound. However, it is now common for the animal to approach the bar, which protrudes into the chamber, and respond to it somewhat as it does to food. That is, the rat may take the bar in its paws, bite it, and lick it, somewhat as it handles a bit of food. Such responses usually depress the bar, with the result that they are reinforced (i.e., followed by the click of a food pellet dropping), and this pattern may readily be detected by the rat. Then the animal runs quickly over to get its food; but it can return and attack the bar, expecting more food. In this way, the bar-pressing response can become integrated with eating behavior. After much further training, the situation is less an expectancy of food and more precisely an expectancy of the sound of food being delivered, so that the biting responses directed to the bar may drop out and a smoother response be established.

From this account, it is not really necessary to be so careful to observe the rat. All that is necessary is to enable the rat to detect a pattern connecting the bar with the sound of a pellet dropping. Suppose that a retractable bar is devised which can be extended into the box or withdrawn. Now, merely introduce the bar and then administer food. While the animal is eating, quietly withdraw the bar. A few minutes later, again introduce the bar, and then give food. This process can be carried on without even noticing anything about the rat; it can, therefore, be automatized.

According to the reinforcement theory, such a procedure should be quite an inefficient way to train rats. In fact, the experimenter would have to call himself lucky if it succeeded at all. The following might happen: The rat might notice the bar coming into the box and go over to explore it. Then the food reinforcement would be administered, strengthening the exploratory response. The next time, the animal would be farther into its exploratory behavior when the food came, and therefore closer to the bar. On each trial, the animal would be closer to the bar at the time of reinforcement, so that there would be a gradual shaping of the response. If, by accident, the rat should press the bar during exploration, this also would be reinforced. Possibly, therefore, there might be a painfully slow and inefficient sort of response shaping just from putting a contingency between the bar and the food.

According to the cognitive theory, on the other hand, this proce-dure—introducing the bar and then giving food—should be a highly efficient way of training. On every trial, the rat sees the bar and then hears the pellet drop and therefore can relatively easily make the connection between the two events. Certainly the environment is more regular than in ordinary shaping, in which reinforcements come not whenever the bar is present or seen but in a mysterious fashion that actually depends upon the experimenter's judgment as to the animal's response.

This procedure, in which the bar is introduced and then food is administered, is called "autoshaping." The term implies that the animal actually shapes itself, or that the response is shaped by itself. In fact, the procedure produces remarkably rapid learning of bar-press responses. Although exact comparative studies have not yet been done on the rat, the impression one gets is that autoshaping is actually more effective than the regular shaping procedure in forming the response.

Now consider teaching a pigeon to peck a key. The key is a translucent piece of plexiglass, approximately 2 inches square and a fraction of an inch thick, which can be illuminated from behind. The key is mounted on the wall of the apparatus, hinged at the top and lying against a microswitch at the bottom, so that if it is pecked by the pigeon the switch is closed and the response can be recorded automatically. In the usual experiment, a hungry pigeon is put into the box and the key is illuminated so that it stands out. Whenever the pigeon approaches it, reinforcement is given. After a while, the animal learns to peck the key by successive approximations.

To "autoshape" the pigeon, one would merely illuminate the key for a little while, then give food. The key would then be left dark awhile, and then illuminated and followed by food. In cognitive terms, the animal should look at the key lighting up and soon afterward hear the food coming and might, in a reasonable number of trials, detect the pattern of coincidence. Then, when the light comes on, the pigeon would expect food. In the pigeon, the pecking response is an important component of the eating behavior flow, and pecking is often directed at any prominent visual stimulus. Therefore, we might expect that if the lighted key comes to elicit the expectation of food, the animal might peck it.

Now, it may be argued that the pecking response is quite frequent to a lighted key—as indeed it is when the animal expects food—and therefore that there may be a number of "accidental" reinforcements of the key-peck response. This would mean that autoshaping is merely an interesting finding that a response may be systematically reinforced even when the experimenter is not looking at it. But Herbert Jenkins (1969) has shown that accidental reinforcements are probably not the reason for autoshaping. He used a very long Skinner box, which was almost a long runway. The light and key were at one end, and food was given at the other end of the runway; and the light always came on just before the pigeon was given food. The result was that when the light came on, the pigeon would trot down to it and begin pecking at it. Then the food would be made available for a few seconds, and the pigeon would have to hop down the long runway to get to the food. By going all the way to the light, the pigeon would actually put itself so far from the food magazine that it could get only a small amount of food at each reinforcement. In this situation, the pigeon would be differentially reinforced for staying near the magazine and waiting for food. Nevertheless, the pigeons chose to "autoshape." Clearly, then, the process must not be caused by accidental reinforcement.

The facts brought out in autoshaping suggest that animals can learn instrumental responses in the Skinner box without any reinforcement for the response. They need only establish an expectancy of food when a given stimulus is detected, and they will make a food-directed response to that stimulus. Bar pressing in the rat, associated as it is with grasping and eating food, is a good example of a "food-directed response" which happens to go along with food expectancy. Similarly, key pecking by the pigeon is an obvious food-directed response that occurs to the key when the key becomes associated with the availability of food.

At this point, the two interpretations are somewhat in balance—the shaping of the animal can be explained systematically by reinforcement theory, and autoshaping is somewhat explained by the cognition-oriented theory of expectancy. The cognitive theory has the advantage with respect to autoshaping, if it is agreed that the results cannot be explained by accidental reinforcement and shaping.

However, the general issue cannot be drawn sharply. The reinforcement theory says that any response which can be made by the animal can be attached, by judicious use of reinforcement, to any stimulus one wishes to use. The cognitive theory says that the only responses you can attach will be responses, directed at the cue, which are part of the food-expectancy pattern of the animal.

Fixed Behavior Flows

Does the commercial animal training done by Breland and Breland (1951) offer practical proof of reinforcement theory? The answer appears in Breland's book (1962). It should be realized that although they were in business, Breland and Breland continued to be scientists and objective students of animal behavior. In the course of their work they used a variety of animals and naturally progressed toward more elaborate behavioral systems—and they ran into trouble. They could still teach a pig to clean house and a chain of chicks to run up an incline, peck food, be pushed off, and return. But a variety of other attempts which should have worked did not. Being scientists, they analyzed their failures to see how they had erred in applying reinforcement theory. Finally, they concluded that it was not that their application of the theory was wrong but that something wrong was with reinforcement theory itself.

For example, Breland and Breland planned to train pigs to press a lever to obtain a token (coin), then carry the token across a small enclosure, place it in a slot, and thereby have an opportunity to eat some of the sponsor's hog feed. The pig's appetite should support such behavior indefinitely, but in fact this display did not work. A pig was successfully trained, but then it began to root around with the token rather than putting it in the correct slot. To increase the effectiveness of the primary food reinforcement, Breland and Breland reduced the animal's food intake so as to make it more hungry. The result was that the pig's trained behavior went completely to pieces: it began vigorous rooting, destroying both the point of the demonstration and the ground on which it stood. The reinforcement contingencies were perfect, but the shaping method collapsed.

They also planned to train a raccoon to earn a token and deposit it in a slot for food. But after a while, the hungry raccoon refused to give up the token and instead would rub it between its "fingers" in just the way raccoons manipulate their food before eating it. Again, no amount of starvation, and no precision and care in training, would get the raccoon to place the token in its slot with any regularity.

The difficulty, in these two cases, was that the experimenters ran afoul of strong food-directed responses already in the repertoire of the animals. Hungry pigs root the ground, and hungry raccoons shred food in their "fingers." These innate responses superseded the responses desired by the experimenters.

What does this prove? Clearly, since systematic efforts to apply reinforcement theory have failed because of such "innate" responses, reinforcement methods do not always work. But what is the general significance of this fact?

One approach would be to return to obedience theory and say that one has simply run into "human nature" (or, in our examples, animal nature). Recall that obedience theory begins with a classification of learners. The fact that certain responses cannot be removed by training would therefore merely be an indication that the animals in question are not obedient with respect to food—they have their own fixed way of responding to food and therefore do not learn an alternative. The difficulty with the obedience approach is that it is ready to deal with general categories of organisms, whereas the difficulties found by Breland and Breland are very specific. Raccoons are not generally disobedient—in fact, they are among the more clever and trainable wild animals—but they specifically do not learn to put tokens in slots for food. Obedience theory may be correct in appealing to the nature of the animal, but the broad categories used by that theory cannot deal with the specific successes and failures of reinforcement methods.

Reinforcement theory can say that though the theory tells us how to strengthen and weaken responses, there are certain instinctive responses of some animals that are not subject to change by reinforcement. Reinforcements will control only "arbitrary" responses but cannot override certain biological imperatives. One possibility is that such imperative, innate responses correspond to "reinforcers" and that reinforcers cannot be themselves modified by reinforcement. However, it should be obvious that such an admission would greatly weaken reinforcement theory. It would be in danger of becoming a theory of how to make trivial changes in superficial behavior, a theory that does not tell one how to modify important or characteristic behavior of the organism. In other words, if reinforcement theory really does not apply to innate responses, then perhaps it can be used only to teach tricks, not as the basis for education, social control, or clinical psychology. Most reinforcement theorists would be dismayed by such a conclusion. Also, of course, applying reinforcement theory would become a much more complicated and chancy process because of the difficulty of deciding in advance which responses can be changed and which are innate. Finally, reinforcement theory has trouble with the nature of the responses that interfere with learning. Why would the raccoon finger and rub the token instead of putting it into the slot? Why is this rather peculiar response so strong and so resistant to modification? If this is the kind of response that can block reinforcement learning, then one cannot localize such difficulties in simple biological functions like eating, hunting, mating, fighting, and running—all sorts of peculiar, low-intensity responses may also defy reinforcement.

Findings like Breland and Breland's have served as part of the basis of modern cognitive theory. Behavior is organized into fixed systems or "behavior flows" rather than consisting of independent responses. This hypothesis of cognitive theory makes it perfectly natural that when an animal is hungry and expects food, it will initiate whatever is its own food-getting behavior flow. The pig will root, and raccoon will "finger" an object—each animal will follow its own peculiar response systems as far as possible. The response of human beings will be similar to that of other primates: primates generally eat both vegetable and animal food but seek concentrates (fruits, roots, meat) and are willing to work to find food. Cows, on the other hand, which spend their summers knee-deep in low-concentrate grass, have quite a different approach to food.

This complex system of behavior flows, appropriate to the animal and its normal wild behavior, is the material that a teacher can use. By setting up contingencies in the world, the teacher can develop new expectancies and thereby connect behavior flows to previously neutral stimuli. However, this does not change the particular responses made by the subject. As is shown in studies of autoshaping, the response may be directed to a new stimulus, as when a pigeon pecks a key or the rat bites a lever. Later chapters in this book will go into more detail about how expectancies can be changed, how the analysis of stimulus input can change, and how the "responses" made after a decision can become more elaborate. However, in this approach, the teacher must always realize that he is working with a given learner, within that learner's capabilities and behavior flows, and that the scope of the learner's accomplishments is limited by the trainer's understanding of his pupil.

SUMMARY

This chapter has dealt with the central topic of learning, how animals and people come to change their behavior, and with procedures one person may use to change the behavior of another. Three general approaches have been discussed. The first, obedience training, represents the conventional wisdom of our time, which is based on a complex classification of people (good or bad, obedient or cooperative, understanding or ignorant). Essentially, the procedures of obedience training consist of steady escalation of conflict, for the trainer goes through a series of stages, progressing to the next stage whenever a given stage fails to have the desired effect. The second approach, reinforcement theory, is the basis of many technical advances in behavior modification. This theory is based on stimuli and responses and the concept of reinforcement and holds that whenever a response is made and then reinforced, it becomes more probable. The procedure involves shaping and maintaining a response through various manipulations of reward and punishment. When complex acts are to be learned, the process may involve stages, but the trainer goes to the next stage only when he has succeeded in the previous stage. The third approach, cognitive theory, stresses the organized interrelations of responses in behavior flows. This theory holds that responses cannot be strengthened but that learners can form new expectancies, so that behavior flows can appear in new parts of the behavior system. However, this theory emphasizes that a given behavior flow is usually subordinate to a higher-order and more complex system; it is not, therefore, possible to make piecemeal changes of one response at a time—instead, it is important to have the learner perform the right response for the right reason.

Animal Work Schedules

To a great extent, the modern industrial world is built upon work. For a psychologist, "work" may be defined as a repeated behavior flow that is not itself intrinsically satisfying or natural but is maintained by extrinsic rewards. When you see trained dogs working in a circus, you may notice the trainers giving the animals tidbits as they complete each part of the act (though of course the lion trainer is less likely to arouse the eating behavior of his lions, for fear that they might eat him). But when a human being works on an assembly line or at a workbench, the management is not seen to slip candy or cigarettes into his mouth after each particular job is finished. In fact, he eats at mealtime whether he works or not, and his only reward is a paycheck at the end of the week.

The obvious difference between humans and animals is that humans can foretell the future, can calculate costs and benefits, and therefore can arrive at the rational decision to work. However, before we congratulate ourselves and blithely accept the economic approach to work, it may be worthwhile to be sure that animals cannot be trained to work as humans do, for delayed rewards. In considering this possibility, we think of feeding the animal for every response (continuous reinforcement) as a special schedule of reinforcement, and we examine alternatives.

In this discussion we are no longer concerned with learning—that is, with the acquisition of a new response or the development of a new expectancy—but with maintaining a pattern of behavior. If you change the conditions under which an animal works, its behavior changes; but if you keep the conditions at the new state for a long time, the animal's pattern of behavior is likely to stabilize. This stabilized performance is what we study now. Stabilized work habits are the basis of a work force capable of operating a modern society. To what extent can analogous work habits be instilled in a rat or pigeon?

CONTINUOUS REINFORCEMENT

Suppose that a rat is fed each time it presses a bar. As soon as the rat presses the bar, a pellet of tasty food is dropped into a small metal food tray within reach of the rat.

The most stable behavior is an alternation between pressing the bar and eating the food. A flowchart of this pattern of behavior is shown in Figure 5.1: notice that there is an overall expectancy such that if the animal remembers pressing the bar, it expects food; but if it does not remember pressing the bar, it does not expect food and instead presses the bar.

If an animal slipped through this behavior flow without any errors, its progress would be as follows. First, suppose that the animal has just finished eating a pellet and enters the expectancy from the long arrow from "eat." The input is the situation of the box, as the animal stands in front of the now-empty food tray. This input is analyzed to determine if the animal has just pressed the bar, probably on the basis of its position. Since it is in front of the tray, the rat decides that it has not pressed the bar (taking the left-hand branch at the first choice) and therefore goes over and presses the bar. It then reenters the expectancy.

The second time through, the animal analyzes its position and short-term memory and this time decides that it has pressed the bar. It takes the right-side branch and expects food. Now the animal, expecting food, approaches the food tray, listening, smelling, and looking at the food tray and reaching for food. If it does not find the food, it will loop, taking in new information (searching the food tray) until it finds the food. Then, of course, it eats the food and returns to the expectancy at the top.

An animal following this procedure would alternately press the bar (B) and eat (F, "food"), in a sequence we can schematize as B-F-B-F-B-, etc.

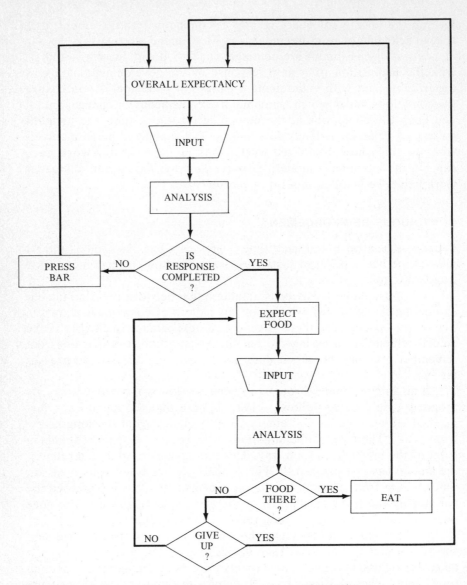

Figure 5.1 Flowchart of behavior based on continuous food reinforcement.

Now suppose that the animal is not so precise and mechanical as the
above analysis indicates and sometimes is confused. What would happen?
First, suppose again that the animal has just finished eating a food
pellet and reenters the expectancy but finds itself positioned halfway

between bar and tray. Since its memory is full of both pressing the bar and eating, it may erroneously think that it has already responded. It takes the right-hand branch at the first decision and expects food. Now the experimenter will not give food, since the bar has not actually been pressed since the last response; the next decision, then, will be that there is no food. The animal is not likely to give up right away, so it will begin looping back for more input, analyzing it, looking for food, and deciding that there is no food. That is, the rat sniffs excitedly all around the food tray, obviously looking for food. Finally it gives up and goes back to its overall expectancy. At this point, since it is just coming from an empty food tray, it is not likely to think that the bar-press response is completed; it will, then, probably press the bar.

This possibility makes us think that one thing the rat will do, instead of performing perfectly, will be to spend too much time sniffing around the empty food tray instead of getting back to the bar. This is exactly what typically happens (Hurwitz, 1956).

The other possible error is for the rat to think it has not pressed the bar when in fact it has. This could happen in several ways. Suppose, for example, that a certain rat uses its own position to decide whether it is time to press the bar or to run to the food tray. Suppose that it finds itself halfway between the two places, after having pressed the bar. Then it does not know what to do next and often will go back and press the bar again. Also, if it has pressed the bar from a slightly unusual position, it may not receive the input usually associated with finishing a depression of the bar. In such cases, one would see the rat press the bar more than once before eating.

This particular error can be more or less frequent, depending upon the amount of noise the pellet makes when it hits the food tray. If this noise is very loud, the rat is almost certain to go over and eat whenever food is dispensed and will almost never press the lever more than once. If the food dispenser is more discreet and quiet, one can expect the rat to make multiple presses many times. If the food dispenser operates automatically at every bar press, the rat can get a whole pile of pellets by a simple burst of responses, and may do so. However, learning of such a technique would be a separate process, not the simple maintenance of a response by continuous reinforcement.

PARTIAL REINFORCEMENT: INTERVAL SCHEDULES

It should be obvious that an experimenter who wants a lot of work out of his rat will not be satisfied with continuous reinforcement. The rat consumes a pellet for each response, which is excessively high wages, and its bar pressing is interrupted so frequently by eating that it has very little time to work. It is as if an office manager rewarded every completed job by sending the worker off for a coffee break—very little work could be completed in a day.

To increase the amount of work and decrease the toll in food pellets, we can try feeding the animal only for some bar presses, not for others. The question we ask here is, What will happen to the bar pressing? Can it be maintained when some bar presses are never reinforced?

Look back at Figure 5.1 and notice what will happen if the food dispenser is disconnected. The rat will press the bar and then take the right-hand branch, expecting food. After he fails to find food and has searched for it thoroughly, he gives up and returns to the overall expectancy. At this time, having just left the empty food tray, the rat is likely to believe that the response has not just been made and will again press the bar. This process can occur repeatedly, though after a while the expectancy of food after bar pressing is bound to be replaced by an expectancy that nothing will follow a bar press. At that point, the response ceases and the animal has shown "experimental extinction."

Now suppose that we do not take the rat all the way to extinction but instead merely turn the dispenser off for a minute or so after each time the rat wins a pellet. That is, after each reinforcement there is a certain fixed interval of time during which the dispenser is disconnected. At the end of that time interval the dispenser is again connected, so that the next bar press (if it is made) will cause the dispenser to operate.

Fixed Interval

A fixed-interval (FI) schedule is like regular wages, in that the animal is given its pellet only at intervals. The food is always given for the bar-press response rather than being automatically handed out at the end of the period, but this seems necessary if the rat is to continue to see any connection between its bar-press response and the food pellets.

Now suppose that the fixed interval is 5 minutes. What will the animal do? Its most efficient behavior would be to do whatever it likes for 5 minutes, then press the bar once and obtain its pellet. In this way it would not waste any bar presses. But since the rat does not have a stopwatch and has no way of knowing when the time interval will be finished it must "guess" when the 5 minutes are up.

The typical behavior of the animal is easy to describe. After each reinforcement, it may fail to respond for a short while. Then it tends to respond quite steadily, placing responses at equal intervals, up until the next reinforcement. The shorter the interval (that is, the more frequent the reinforcements), the faster the overall speed of responding.

In an interval schedule of reinforcement, the basic problem before the animal is to discriminate when food can be expected and when it cannot. From the animal's point of view, food cannot be expected again soon after it has been received; also, food is available only after a bar press.

The process needed to make discriminations in an interval schedule is shown in Figure 5.2. Note that this is a complex flow, consisting of three separate simple behavior flows: the time discrimination, testing of the bar press, and testing for food. The general form is that the time discrimination is made first. If the response has been performed, then the animal checks for food. This may be thought of as a string of simple behavior flows of which the first is the highest-order: that is, the decision in the first determines whether or not the animal goes to the second; then the outcome of the second decides whether the animal goes to the third.

The animal's ability to judge whether the time is up is not very good in this situation, particularly because the actual time between reinforcements is not necessarily fixed at 5 minutes: it may be longer if the animal does not respond promptly at the end of 5 minutes. If its time discrimination were very good, the animal would simply delay until the 5 minutes were up, and then begin responding and continue until it found the food. If its time discrimination were poor, the animal would begin responding early, since it would mistakenly decide that it was "late" and time for food long before the food was actually ready. Of course, responses will tend to be spaced out in time because the animal is actually looping through the whole complex behavior flow, deciding that it is time for food, making a response, and then finding that there is no food.

In some experiments, it is possible to give a pigeon a "clock." One method is to begin with a red light on the key, and gradually, during the 5-minute interval, have a green area encroach upon and take over the illuminated portion of the key. When the key is completely green, the device has "timed out" and food is finally available. Given a "clock" like this, the pigeon can make an accurate time discrimination, withhold its response until the clock times out, and then begin responding vigorously until it finds food.

Without a clock, an animal has difficulties, and we can see that the overall steady responding of the animal in a fixed-interval schedule depends considerably upon its inability to make precise time discriminations. If we consider how a "time discrimination" can be made, we notice that (without an external clock) there really is no stimulus input. The "time since food" is not itself an attribute of the situation that can be directly apprehended through any sense organ. The events of the experimental session are presumably stored in short-term memory, and any

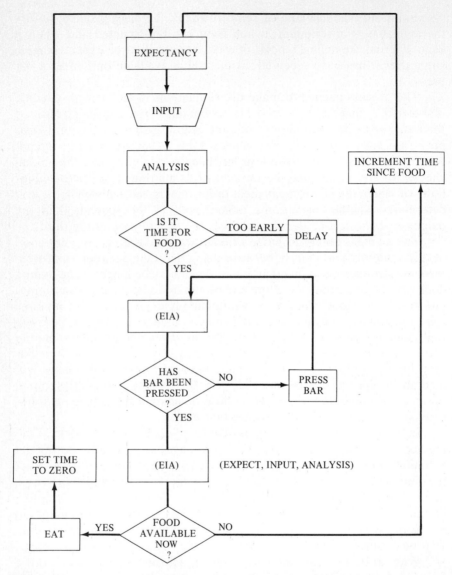

Figure 5.2 Flowchart of behavior based on fixed-interval food reinforcement.

attempt to determine whether the time is up requires that the animal interrogate its short-term memory. It can first decide whether a reinforcement can be found within the contents of short-term memory; and if one can be found, it can attempt to estimate how much has happened since.

This can at best lead to a crude time estimation; yet it requires a symbolic memory and a means of measuring the amount of content in short-term memory since the reinforcement—and therefore it requires that the contents of short-term memory be accessible in their original temporal order. All this may seem natural with respect to our own memories, but it is surprising when we consider the rat or the pigeon.

One final possibility is that the animal might itself generate an "external clock" by itself making a progressive motion, like a dance, that would consume an appropriate amount of time. It is true that such behavior, with an accurate time course, is usually not observed during FI schedules, but then it must also be remembered that animals do not make the time discriminations at all accurately.

In "experimental extinction," the experimenter merely disconnects the food magazine, so that the animal will receive no more reinforcements, and then continues to record behavior. Of course, after a while the animal reaches the point where it is a long time since the last reinforcement. The first decision, then, is always that it is "late"; and thus the animal should continue to respond steadily. After a long time, the continued absence of food will change the expectancy, so that although the animal still decides that the time is up, it ceases to expect food at that time, and its behavior drifts off into some other behavior flows.

Variable Interval

The variable-interval (VI) schedule differs from the fixed-interval schedule in only one way. Whereas in an FI schedule the animal always has to wait some fixed time—say, 5 minutes—in a VI schedule the delay imposed between reinforcements varies from one reinforcement to the next: it might be 10 minutes one time, 2 minutes the next time, etc. Generally speaking, variable-interval schedules have been arranged to give a random time between reinforcements, and the schedule is designated by the average time. For example, VI-5 (variable interval, 5 minutes) means that the time between reinforcements varies, with the average being 5 minutes.

The variable-interval schedule makes it essentially impossible for the animal to make any valid time discrimination. Since there is sometimes a very short interval, the animal may expect food even right after receiving a reinforcement. And since there are some quite long intervals, if the animal has already waited 5 minutes it still has no strong expectancy of food at that time. The animal's level of expectancy for food should therefore be essentially constant over time, but for this very reason the animal really does not expect food with any confidence at any given time.

The animal actually may expect food at some times and not at

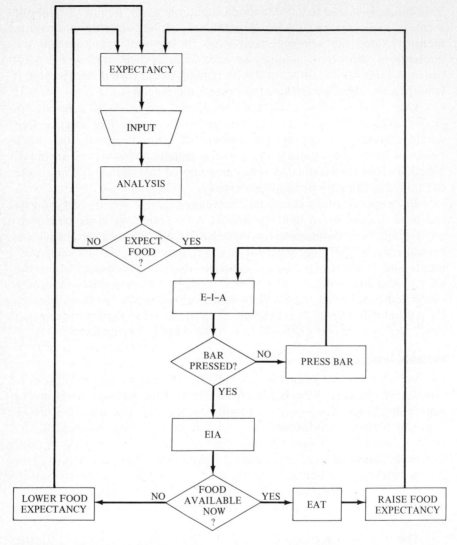

Figure 5.3 Flowchart of behavior based on variable-interval food reinforcement.

others—essentially at random as far as time is concerned. An important series of studies on the expectancy of an event that occurs randomly in time has been done by W. K. Estes and his associates; their main results, relevant here, are very simple. Suppose that a certain event f, such as food, occurs randomly in time with probability $P(f)$. Suppose now that a subject, either human or animal, makes a simple prediction as to whether f

will occur. Let the probability of the expectancy be called *P(E)*. After sufficient experience with the situation, usually a few hundred trials, *P(E)* gradually converges close to *P(f)*, so that the organism predicts the event just about as often as it occurs. This is called the "probability-matching law"; it states that the probability of expecting a random event will converge toward the probability of the event. Of course, since *f* cannot be predicted on every trial, the subject is right only sometimes; but nevertheless he tends to match the frequency of his predictions to the frequency with which they would be true, (Estes, 1964).

Whenever a rat or pigeon "expects" food, it will test whether it has made a response, make the response, and then test for food. This leads to a complex behavior flow like that in Figure 5.3, very similar to the one for the fixed-interval schedule. The only difference is that in a variable-interval schedule the animal is not making a time discrimination but merely making random predictions of an event that occurs at random in time.

With this behavior flow, a response is made every time the animal expects food. The animal eventually will come to expect food just with the same probability as food is delivered; we should, then, expect the rate of responding to be proportional to the rate at which reinforcements are administered. This is exactly what happens, as is shown in Figure 5.4.

There is one further important characteristic of VI schedules. Notice that a given response is reinforced only when (1) the variable interval

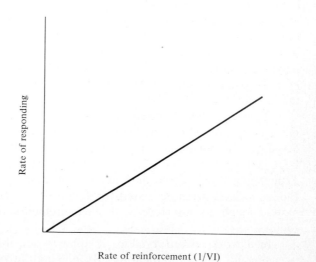

Figure 5.4 Rate of responding as a function of rate of reinforcement in variable-interval schedules.

terminates before the response is made, and (2) no other response has been made since the interval terminated. Now suppose that the animal has just made a response, 2 seconds ago. The probability that another bar press would be reinforced at this instant is very low, for it is very unlikely that the timer would time out within that 2-second interval. But suppose that the animal has not responded for 2 minutes. Now, there is quite a high probability that the next response would be reinforced. This means that the animal will not expect food if he packs his responses close together in time; but if he waits a while, his expectancy of food increases. Apparently the animal can make a discrimination on the basis of how long it has been since its last response, and will tend to space its responses more or less equally in time, like the ticking of a clock, rather than bunching the responses into "bursts" or even distributing them randomly in time. This process can be represented by a slightly more complicated behavior flow, as shown in Figure 5.5.

Since the VI schedule tends to produce very steady responding, it is convenient to use in measuring other factors in the animal's behavior. For example, the experimenter may wish to study the similarity of various hues for the pigeon. He trains the animal to peck at a certain pure color and then wants to know how similar other colors would appear to the training color. Therefore, he replaces the training color with test colors and observes the animal's level of expectancy of food. When the pigeon was originally trained on a VI schedule, the result is dramatic; it has been called the "dial-a-response-rate" experiment. The pure colors are generated by a device called a "monochrometer"; as a dial on the monochrometer is turned, the color changes smoothly. When the experimenter turns the dial on the monochrometer away from the training color, the animal's pecking rate can be heard to slow down; a steady turn of the monochrometer dial may result in "tap-tap-tap tap tap tap-tap tap tap . . .," and so forth.

Another useful characteristic of the VI schedule is that the animal persists in responding for a very long time after being put on extinction. Possibly, one reason is that the animal simply does not notice that it has been a long time since the last reinforcement. The animal's level of expectancy slowly drops as it accumulates many trials without food, but the animal can often be tested for several hours before its rate becomes slow enough to interfere with measurements of other experimental factors.

In a work-reward system, it appears sensible to provide rewards occasionally and unpredictably. By making the rewards infrequent, we rarely interrupt the work for consumption. By making the rewards unpredictable, we avoid "dead spots" when the worker can predict that

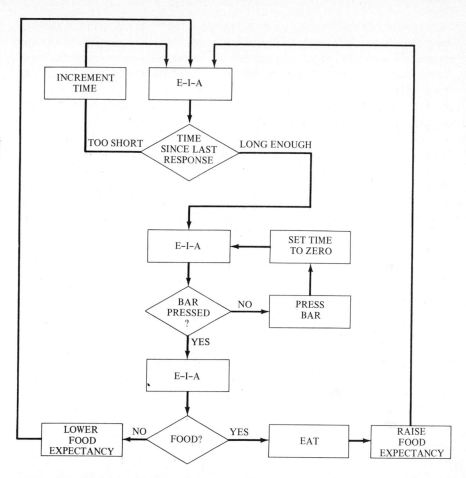

Figure 5.5 Flowchart showing control system that leads to responses equally spaced in time in a VI schedule.

he can receive no reward and therefore might slow down or stop. In general the rate of work will be directly proportional to the frequency of reward, until rewards begin to eat into the working time. This produces steady work, though not the utmost expenditure the organism might put out, and is suitable for routine tasks—like watching a radar scope—which may be maintained by occasional, unpredictable visits from a supervisor.

This theory applies relatively well to simple repetitive behavior in lower animals, involved with some established behavior flow like eating. To apply the same theory and methods to human workers—for example, on an assembly line—might or might not be appropriate. First, it would be sensible to find out what behavior flows the workers have, what the reinforcements really are, and how complex the behavior control system may be. As an obvious example, labor unions exert a complex effect on output of work, and a random payday system might produce countermeasures from organized laborers to the point where it was entirely "counterproductive."

FIXED RATIO: PIECEWORK SYSTEMS

It seems to some employers that the most natural way to pay a worker is to give a certain amount for each unit of work completed. This is called "piecework," or an "incentive" plan. From the point of view of the employer, it motivates workers to increase their productivity—and that, of course, is the employer's goal. It also permits the worker to adjust his pay by varying the energy he expends or the intelligence and skill he may bring to the job. Socially, piecework systems often do not work out well, for various reasons. Such systems often establish stiff competition between workers so that they have no solidarity or feeling of cooperation but instead overwork themselves. If everyone works hard and efficiently, increasing productivity, the employer is strongly motivated to reduce the price paid for each unit of work or to change work standards so as to decrease the effective pay rate. Workers usually suspect that such a change will occur and therefore will often organize to place a ceiling upon productivity. This usually leaves the worker with adequate pay and relieves the pressure for constant increases in productivity.

These complex controls, based upon social organization, communication, and foresight, not to mention deep-rooted mistrust of the managerial class, are not found in the behavior of the rat or the pigeon. In an experiment with rats, the experimenter usually begins with continuous reinforcement and then begins to introduce occasional nonreinforcements. After a while, the animal must make a certain number—say, N—responses before it will receive a single reinforcement. It is then on a "fixed-ratio N" schedule, abbreviated FR-N. Working with food reinforcements and a hungry rat, Skinner was able to establish an FR-192 schedule (192 responses per food pellet) and found that the rat responded rapidly in relatively long "bursts" of responses. The high fixed ratio had to be approached very slowly, by gradually increasing the ratio of responses to reinforcements and letting the animal adjust to each level before thinning the ratio to the next level.

Skinner's analysis of the process of learning a fixed ratio is in terms of the "extinction ratio," which is the number of responses the animal will make before extinction. Suppose that a rat has an extinction ratio of 5 and is put on an FR-6 ratio. It must make six responses to get the next reinforcement, but it will only make five on the way to extinction. This animal will extinguish and completely stop responding before it gets to the next reinforcement and therefore cannot initially be taught such a high ratio. If the experimenter tries too high a ratio, his animal extinguishes the response. At this point the experimenter knows he has made a mistake but is not in a convenient position to rectify it, since the rat has stopped responding. Somehow the animal must be induced to make one more response (perhaps through spontaneous recovery—that is, the experimenter just waits until the rat tries again), and that response is reinforced. Then the animal is put back on continuous reinforcement and slowly shifted to higher and higher ratios.

Why does it help to shift gradually from one ratio to another? If the animal's extinction ratio is 5, there would seem to be no way that it could be trained on FR-6. However, the extinction ratio itself changes when an animal is trained on a fixed ratio. The thinner the ratio schedule, the more responses the animal will make to extinction. Therefore, when an animal has learned a fairly high ratio, its extinction ratio is high enough to permit further thinning out.

Behavior in a ratio schedule is not at all like what is observed in an interval schedule. In both cases a rat can respond whenever it likes; and it receives food only for some of its bar presses, not for others. The animal has no direct information as to whether its food pellets are being withheld for a fixed time (as in fixed-interval schedules) or for a fixed ratio of responses. In an FI schedule, remember, the animal does not respond for a while after reinforcement, and then responds at a fairly slow, very steady rate until it finds food. In an FR schedule, the same animal will also withhold responses for a while after reinforcement, but when it again returns to the bar it will respond in rapid bursts, with pauses between bursts. If put on a high ratio, the rat will respond with a large number of bar presses per minute, and these will appear not in a steady stream but in spurts and stops.

The reason why responses occur in bursts can be seen if we examine the nature of the discrimination the animal is required to make. Suppose that the animal is on an FR-10 schedule and makes a burst of N responses. Suppose further that neither we nor the rat know how many responses it has made since the last reinforcement: anywhere from 0 to 9. What is the probability that its burst of N responses will lead to reinforcement? First, if the burst is of 10 or more responses, then it automatically will lead to reinforcement. If it is a burst of $N = 9$, it will lead to reinforcement unless the previous number of responses was 0. A burst of 8 will lead to reinforcement unless the previous number of responses is 0 or 1.

For simplicity, suppose that the probability of 0 previous responses is

Table 5-1   Probability of reinforcement for a burst of N responses in an FR-10 schedule

N	Number of previous responses										P(reinforcement)
	0	1	2	3	4	5	6	7	8	9	
1	0	0	0	0	0	0	0	0	0	1	.1
2	0	0	0	0	0	0	0	0	1	1	.2
3	0	0	0	0	0	0	0	1	1	1	.3
4	0	0	0	0	0	0	1	1	1	1	.4
5	0	0	0	0	0	1	1	1	1	1	.5
6	0	0	0	0	1	1	1	1	1	1	.6
7	0	0	0	1	1	1	1	1	1	1	.7
8	0	0	1	1	1	1	1	1	1	1	.8
9	0	1	1	1	1	1	1	1	1	1	.9
10	1	1	1	1	1	1	1	1	1	1	1.0

1/10, that the probability of 1 previous response is also 1/10, and generally that the probability of any number M of previous responses is 1/10. Now the probability of reinforcement is as shown in Table 5.1.

Every indication is that the rat eventually becomes able to detect that longer bursts are more likely to be reinforced than shorter bursts, up to bursts of the fixed ratio itself. All long bursts are reinforced, of course. Single and double responses, and very short bursts, tend to extinguish in favor of longer bursts, so that the animal comes to respond more and more in bursts.

Furthermore, as the ratio is increased, the animal comes to establish longer and longer bursts, so that the change that comes about with higher and higher ratios is not only a higher rate of responding but, in particular, the adoption of longer and longer bursts of responses. Somewhat the same kind of result is obtained with pigeons' pecking, except that the behavior is more obvious. Because of the nature of its neck and the reflex system involved in pecking for food, the pigeon can peck at very high rates with what is apparently a ballistic head movement—the head is thrown at the target and "bounces" back. It takes wonderful switches and very fast recording apparatus even to catch responses as fast as they can be made by a pigeon. Some pigeons even learn to make a "wiping" motion with the bill open and can thereby record two responses with a single thrust of the head.

If an animal trained on a high-ratio schedule is placed on an extinction schedule—that is, if food is no longer given—it will continue to respond in long bursts. However, the responding does not continue forever, because gradually the animal loses its expectancy that long bursts of responses will lead to food. During the extinction process, a very large number of responses may be made, in rapid bursts, although the extinction process does not usually take a very long time.

It is possible to establish a variable-ratio schedule, in which the number of responses required of the animal is varied. This is not as effective as might be imagined in smoothing the animal's behavior. The animal is still usually fed during bursts of responses and therefore still shows the erratic performance of responding rapidly, then stopping temporarily, etc., which is shown in a fixed-ratio experiment. The difficulty of a variable-ratio schedule is that some of the ratios are very high; that is, the animal is required to make a very large number of responses to get a reinforcement. Sometimes the animal simply extinguishes while working toward a high ratio and never gets to its goal.

To apply these results to the human situation, one would make the generalization that piecework—paying people for work accomplished—especially if it is carried out by paying for a certain number of units, will result in rapid but sporadic work habits. Of course, the human may instead keep count of his responses and merely time his work to obtain some appropriate number of rewards. However, it is quite possible that usually being rewarded during periods of intense work, and not expecting reward when slacking off, might affect the human worker somewhat as animals are affected. It has been my experience that scientific and professional workers often receive their rewards, which may merely be the satisfaction of solving a problem, during periods of furious work. Also, it seems to me that people with this kind of history are given to working in intense spurts. However, higher control systems in the human can override the simple constraints controlling the rat or pigeon.

SLOWDOWN SCHEDULES AND A MICROMOLAR THEORY

The discussion above shows how an experimenter can use reinforcement schedules to control the behavior of an animal. Behavior can be made even or sporadic by using interval or ratio schedules, and the rate of responding can be controlled by the frequency of reinforcement (in interval schedules) or by the ratio requirements imposed. Since the animal's rate of responding can be increased, is it also possible to establish a very low rate of responding without losing the response entirely?

The attempt to establish controlled slow responding is an effort to study the role of inhibitory and control processes in behavior. It is quite impressive to see a pigeon pecking rapidly at a key for occasional reinforcements. Would it not be even more impressive to see the pigeon return every 5 minutes to the key, give one peck for reinforcement, and then turn away for another 5 minutes? This would demonstrate a kind of restraint that would bring honor both to the bird and to its trainer.

According to one technique, the animal is differentially reinforced for a low rate of responding in the Skinner box. The experimenter uses a timer as follows: When the bar is pressed, this starts the timer. The food magazine will not work until the timer has completed its interval and "timed out." Whenever the animal pecks the key, the timer is reset to its starting value. Of course, if the timer had already timed out, then the bar press would deliver the animal its pellet—but it would still restart the timer.

Now imagine an animal that, having found that bar presses produce food, presses quite consistently at the bar. It keeps resetting the timer without ever letting it time out; and as a result, it never gets any food. This, of course, means that the animal will extinguish and stop pressing the bar. If it stays away for a while, it may then return; and since the timer has now timed out, it will get food. If this is enough to reinstate its earlier behavior of steady rapid responding, it will again get no food and will again extinguish. If it then comes back, after a long pause, it will again find food.

This process of extinction, reconditioning, and reextinction may occur several times, but gradually there will emerge a control system by which the animal comes to expect food only when it has not responded for a long time. Finally, the animal will learn to respond only after a long wait; and as soon as it responds, it will go do something else.

The behavior flow to control this slowdown performance is shown in Figure 5.6. The key discrimination the animal must make is to judge whether it has waited long enough since its last bar press so that the next bar press will be reinforced. This in itself is most difficult, because it is more difficult for the animal to remember its own bar-press responses than to remember reinforcements or other more distinctive stimuli, such as places.

CONCLUSIONS

In this chapter various experiments on animal work schedules have been reviewed. If every response is reinforced in a continuous-reinforcement schedule, the animal alternates between the bar (or key, or whatever) and the food hopper, responds rather slowly, and eats a great deal. The most common irregularity in this behavior occurs when the animal stays at the food tray when it should go back and press the bar again. In interval schedules, the animal must remember how long ago it received reinforce-

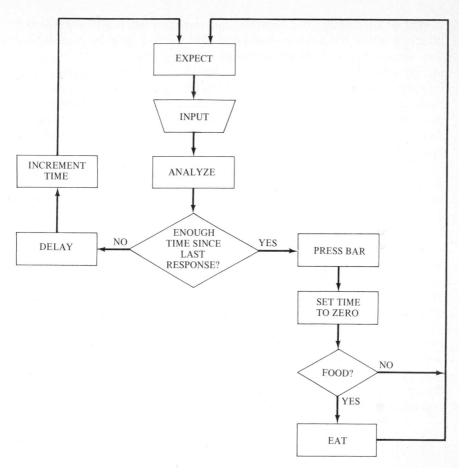

Figure 5.6 Flowchart of behavior in DRL (differential reinforcement for low rate of responding) schedule.

ment and does not expect food right after food. An interval schedule leads the animal to respond steadily but not at a high rate. Because the animal's expectancy of food is highest when it has not responded for a while and lowest when it has just responded, it compromises with a moderate, steady level of responding. During extinction, such an animal will respond for a long time at a slow, decreasing rate. In ratio schedules, the animal must remember the number of responses to food but actually is controlled by the fact that it is usually fed during a burst of responses; therefore, it learns to respond in rapid bursts. In a slowdown schedule, the animal must remember how long it has been since the last response and respond again if that time is long enough.

It is interesting that animals can maintain an artificial response, attached to the food-getting behavior flow, even with quite complicated and unnatural schedules of reinforcement. Clearly, bar pressing is not merely rewarded by food—the behavior structure is considerably more complex. Basically, the animal learns that a bar press produces food and then finally comes to make the bar press when it expects food to be available. The different schedules result in different behavior because the food is actually available under different conditions, and the animal ends up making different discriminations.

It should be remembered that the behavior described in this chapter is "ideal" and is not observed in every animal. Furthermore, it may take many hours in the Skinner box before an animal "solves" a more complicated schedule. However, laboratory experience clearly shows how an animal can learn to gather food or hunt even though most of its attempts meet with limited success. Furthermore, this theory provides some understanding of how human work behavior may be shaped by reinforcements. As we study more of human learning, however, we shall see many higher-order control systems that permit the human to make more flexible responses to some of these reinforcement schedules. Certainly, these ideas of reinforcement are more precise and correct than the conventional ideas of work motivation, especially the usual theory of why men work for wages. Rather than merely saying that the wages are the price the worker exacts for his services, we can arrive at a more detailed and sensitive understanding of why men work at dull and repetitive jobs and what factors may control their work output.

Chapter 6

Simple Discrimination Learning

In conditioning and in the Skinner box, an animal has the choice of responding or not to a given stimulus. In the outside world, however, the situation is more complicated. It is not sufficient to know what responses to make; one must also know the circumstances in which they are to be made. Diving into a pool is a pleasant and fairly safe response if the pool is full of water, but not if it is empty. In this chapter, we study in more detail how external stimuli control behavior.

There are many ways that discrimination learning can be studied in the laboratory. One method is adapted to conditioning and to the Skinner box. An animal is taught to expect food in the presence of one stimulus, S^+, and not in the presence of another, S^-. Only one stimulus is shown at a time, and the animal displays its discrimination by responding to S^+ and not to S^-. A second method is to have the animal approach one stimulus (S^+) and not the other (S^-). In the usual procedure, both stimuli are presented together, side by side, S^+ being on the left in some trials and on the right in other trials, at random. A third method presents only one stimulus but permits the subject two responses. A college student, for example, may be told to use two nonsense syllables, DAX and ZOG, as his responses. When he is shown a square, DAX is the correct response; and when he is shown a rectangle, ZOG is correct.

In the laboratory, a whole series of trials are given to the subject, in which the stimulus arrangement is constantly changed. Correct responses, as described above, always lead to success (food in the case of animal, a verbal reward in the case of human subjects); errors lead to no food or to the verbal feedback that the subject is wrong. The subject usually does not respond with consistent correctness at the beginning; but if the experiment is well controlled, the subject will perform at chance, being correct or wrong about equally often. After extended training, the subject will usually give only—or almost only—correct responses.

DISCRIMINATION CAPABILITIES OF LOWER ANIMALS

To the early behaviorists, who devised many of the standard laboratory methods of training animals, it was quite impressive to see a dumb animal learn a complicated conditioned response or respond appropriately to a schedule of reinforcement. They thought of discriminations as complex behavior systems, far more complicated and difficult than simple conditioning. It would be natural for laymen to think of discrimination learning as quite difficult and to expect only the highest animals—humans, and perhaps apes, monkeys, and a few intelligent domestic animals like dogs and cats—to be capable of it. Therefore, it is perhaps necessary to say at the outset that discrimination learning, complex and difficult as it may be, is not restricted to primates or mammals, or even to vertebrates. There have been many failures to teach animals what seem to be simple discriminations; but as we shall see, these are not failures of the animal but failures of the humans doing the testing.

In recent studies by Jacques Cousteau and his group, discriminations were taught to sharks underwater in the open sea. Learning was so rapid that the animals could master simple visual shape discriminations to a high criterion of success and be tested before they even left the area. Under more controlled conditions, these animals may do worse, because the conditions connected with captivity are often unfavorable; but it has certainly been verified that sharks, animals at the bottom of the vertebrate scale, can learn simple shape discriminations.

A series of studies by Sutherland and others on the Italian octopus are even more remarkable. An octopus is a mollusc, related to clams, oysters, snails, and other creatures not known for mental prowess. The octopus and the squid are predators, and both have good underwater vision. Whereas eyes of mammals develop from brain tissue, eyes of molluscs develop from epithelial (skin) cells. Despite these differences and its extremely primitive brain, the octopus is quite capable of discriminating between rather similar shapes, learning to attack targets of a certain shape for a reward (fish) and ignoring other shapes.

Finally, excellent color discrimination has been shown by an insect, the honeybee. It would seem obvious that bees can see colors and are thus guided to flowers of bright colors, to the benefit of both bee and plant. However, it is another question whether the bee can learn to select one of two colors when the colors are not parts of a flower (to which an instinctive response might be available) but are merely patches of construction paper such as children use. Von Frisch (1954) has demonstrated this sort of discrimination learning in bees, the main technical difficulty being that since the response was learned by a whole hive of workers, he could not usually single out specific subjects. The responses made by the bees were so precise that it was possible to determine that the bee's color vision is rather different from ours, having only two instead of three primaries and reaching out into wavelengths not visible to the human.

The first thing to know about discrimination learning, then, is that it is not limited to the higher animals. The habits and sensory capacities of very simple animals like paramecia (one-celled slipper-shaped animalcules) and planarians (very simple flatworms) are not very well understood, and therefore it is sometimes difficult to demonstrate learning in such animals. However, the indication is that they may be capable of conditioning and also of discrimination learning.

STAGES OF LEARNING

Motivation

Before discrimination training can begin, it is necessary to establish a "motivation." In work with animals, the usual motivation is food: food withheld until the animal earns it by responding correctly. In this way, the desired discrimination becomes attached to the behavior flow of eating. Highly preferred foods that are not usually available are as effective as withholding ordinary food—for example, raisins for monkeys and chocolate candies for young children. Candy and cigarettes have been used with good effect in discrimination training of mental patients in a hospital.

Since the subject must look at the stimuli to solve the problem, the experimenter must attempt to direct the subject's attention. For this purpose, the rewards should be closely associated with the cue objects. With rats, one effective method is to have the visual stimulus painted on a

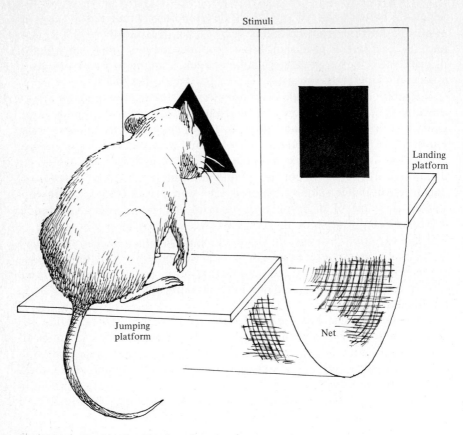

Figure 6.1 Rat in a Lashley jumping stand.

wall of the apparatus and to have a small door in the center of the stimulus that the animal can push its head through to find food. In the standard apparatus used with monkeys and apes, the two stimuli are objects presented side by side on a tray. Under the objects are shallow food wells, and the well under the correct object contains a raisin or peanut. The animal is trained to brush aside one object or the other and is allowed to have the raisin or peanut if it is there. Since college students are relatively quick at these problems, experimenters working with students make relatively little effort to obtain the fastest possible learning. Still, when a reward or the indication of a correct response is associated with the stimulus object, as when a light is illuminated right under the correct stimulus, this accelerates learning.

With the lower animals, it may be difficult to get the subject to stop and look at the cue stimuli. There are many possible reasons, one being that the human, as a large, vision-oriented primate, has a very inaccurate idea of the world of lower animals like the small, odor-oriented rat. However, many of these difficulties can be overcome by skillful handling of the motivational problems. Thinking in terms of a simple reinforcement theory, experimenters might try to force an animal to learn a discrimination by making the motivations very strong—for example, by starving the animal until it either learns or dies. This is a self-defeating approach, however, since if the animal is too hungry it becomes extremely active when it expects food and dashes through the apparatus to the food well without paying much attention to the stimulus objects. To get a rat to learn a visual discrimination fairly quickly, it is necessary to make it stop within view of the stimuli. One apparatus, designed in the 1920s by the master experimenter Karl S. Lashley, is called the "Lashley jumping stand." In this apparatus (shown in Figure 6.1), the rat is placed on a small platform several inches from two stimulus cards. The animal is trained to jump; if it will not jump otherwise, it can be induced to jump by having its tail tapped with a pencil or being given a mild electric shock. If the animal jumps to the correct card, the card falls down easily, and the animal lands on a large, safe platform where it finds food. However, if the animal jumps to the wrong card, the card is fastened and the animal bounces off and falls into a net below. Facing this risk, the rat stops for quite a while and looks carefully at the two stimuli, particularly at those parts of the card near where it will jump. A rat trained on this apparatus can learn to discriminate patterns and complicated forms and will master easy problems in only a few trials.

Familiarization

Once the animal is motivated, the experimenter normally employs a procedure to familiarize the animal with the apparatus and teach it to make the desired response. In the Lashley jumping stand, some rats are quite timid about jumping across a gap, especially after they have fallen, and the process of familiarization may be extended. The stimuli to be used in the actual experiment are not used during familiarization. Unfortunately, familiarization has often meant presenting the animal with an insoluble problem or with a problem that has a very simple answer quite different from the one intended by the experimenter; it may therefore sometimes do more harm than good. When adult human subjects are used, the familiarization period is sometimes forgone in favor of detailed verbal instructions or very simple problems given as practice.

Training Procedure

After familiarization, the actual training of the discrimination begins. In the Lashley jumping stand, for example, two different cards can be presented. One, here called S⁺, is "correct"; the other, here called S⁻, is "incorrect." On each trial, the two cards are presented side by side, and the position of S⁺ is on the left, then S⁻ is on the right.

On every trial, the animal must make a choice, jumping to one or the other of the two cards. To ensure that a response is made on every trial, the experimenter may either merely wait or, if necessary, push the animal along in some way. One simple way is to squeeze the animal off its jumping stand with a sliding wall.

Recall that if the animal jumps to the correct card, S⁺, the card falls down and the animal lands on a safe platform and receives food. After the animal has had time to eat and rest a moment, and after the cards have been positioned for the next trial, it is picked up and returned to the jumping stand.[1]

A trial is a complete response and is scored either correct or wrong. At the beginning, the food is completely hidden from the animal until after it has made its response. Unless there is some failure of control, such as allowing the odor of food to reach the animal, or giving the animal a cue in the form of some sound made by the experimenter, the animal cannot consistently make a correct response. Therefore, initial success must be a matter of chance. If the animal can learn the discrimination, it will eventually choose the correct stimulus consistently, having learned from previous experiences which stimulus is correct.[2]

Actually, it is a fairly simple matter to ensure that an animal is in fact

---

[1]Often rats adopt such tenacious habits that it seems they will never give up jumping to (say) the left. In that case, the experimenter may have a single trial consist of a large number of jumps. When the animal makes an error and falls into the net, the experimenter may pick it up and put it right back on the jumping platform, continuing this procedure until the animal finally makes a correct jump. This is called a "correction procedure" and is intended to help break up very strong response tendencies of the wrong type, particularly position habits, which are very strong in the rat. The correction procedure is also sometimes used with young children and in other experiments in which the subject may adopt a strong habit.

[2]In the 1950s, it is said, the Yerkes Laboratories of Primate Biology in Orange Park, Florida, were put into a turmoil by a chimpanzee with extrasensory perception. This animal could consistently choose the correct one of two objects placed before it, even when the two objects were entirely new and even when they were exactly alike. Since adult chimpanzees are large and fairly dangerous animals, the experimenters did not march the chimp to the laboratory, but instead took a portable laboratory on wheels, somewhat like a wheelbarrow, up to the animal's cage. The experimenter would sit behind a large shield with a supply of raisins, objects to use as stimuli, and data sheets, and would, from that position, bait one of two food wells, put objects over them, and then raise an opaque window and slide the tray within the animal's reach. The chimpanzee's behavior was extraordinary, particularly since this apparatus and procedure had been used for years without any known faults. It was finally discovered (by testing the director of the laboratory, who placed himself in a chimpanzee cage) that the experimenter's stool on this particular apparatus was slightly squeaky and made a sound when the experimenter shifted her weight to bait the left-hand food well, but did not make any sound when the raisin was put in the right-hand food well. The chimpanzee (having little else to occupy its considerable intellectual powers) had noticed this sound and therefore always knew where the food would be, irrespective of the objects used. This is but une of many instances in which experimenters have been surprised (to put it mildly) by their subjects. It is a good example of a failure of experimental control which, if not noticed, might have led to a variety of invalid conclusions.

responding to the stimulus objects intended. The basic control is to present the objects to the left or right (or otherwise alternated) in random order, for if the animal then consistently makes correct responses, one can be sure that it is not using anything, like position, that is not correlated with S^+ and S^-. A most useful control is to introduce new objects from time to time. If two plain white cards are shown to the rat for a few trials (food being positioned alternately right and left as usual) and the rat continues to respond correctly, one would be strongly suspicious that the rat had an unwanted channel of information. If we suspect that the animal is directly sensing the location of the food, we can put the food behind the "incorrect" card and see if the animal then jumps to that card. By the use of such control techniques, an experimenter can be perfectly confident that his animals have solved the discrimination problem he intended.

All-or-None Learning

At the start of training on a discrimination-learning problem, the animal has only chance success, and this level of success often continues for several, perhaps many, trials. During this presolution period, the animal often follows quite regular patterns of responding. In a four-unit discrimination box, for example, rats learned to discriminate black from white. Each unit of the apparatus gave the rat a choice between two doors, one white and one black. A correct response got the rat through to the next unit, and the last unit led to food. Before mastering the problem, rats would often run a trial going always to the left or always to the right, and sometimes alternating. Monkeys, when learning to discriminate between two objects, will often show a preference for one stimulus. For example, they may refuse to touch an object with bristles and insist always on choosing the other object, even if it is never rewarded. A second factor is their tendency to explore; they will sometimes choose the wrong object just to see if there is food under it. College students, before they solve the kind of complicated problems they are given, usually respond systematically, sometimes using the wrong properties of the stimulus object.

Do not think that an animal persists solidly in one kind of behavior before solving the problem. Quite the contrary: the animal is not consistently successful, and as you would expect, it varies its behavior pattern frequently.

There are two ways discrimination learning might progress. It could be that the correct stimulus gains strength through reinforcement, and the correct stimulus slowly becomes aversive. The animal may therefore gradually change its response pattern, beginning at about 0.50 correct responses and gradually shifting until it makes nearly 1.00 correct responses. The alternative is that the animal may try one behavior flow after another until it hits upon the correct solution of the problem. In a well controlled experiment, the animal will perform with 0.50 success until it hits upon the correct answer and then will switch to perfect behavior. Considering all the things that can go wrong in an animal learning experiment, we cannot expect that either theory will be correct as a description of all experiments. However, several facts indicate that pure discrimination learning is an all-or-none process. By "pure" discrimination learning, I mean an idealized experiment in which the animal is perfectly adapted to the experimental apparatus without undue confusion and in which the animal really has to learn only one element of the problem, namely, the nature of the cue that tells which stimulus is correct.

DISCRIMINATION AND THE BEHAVIOR FLOW

The second stage in a behavior flow, after the expectancy itself, is analysis of the situation. In the discussion of analysis in earlier chapters, it appeared that either the animal had only one way of analyzing a situation or, if it had more than one, it chose its analysis on the basis of motivational conditions. But higher animals have many ways of analyzing a given situation and, of course, have to have some way of selecting the proper analysis.

When faced with an unfamiliar situation, the animal either may or may not already have a system for choosing the correct analysis. If it does not already know what analysis to use, it must try one analysis after another until it comes upon a correct one. In discrimination learning, the experimenter constructs an artificial environment in which there is no way for the animal to know what analysis to employ.

The basic principle of discrimination learning is that the animal makes some analysis of the situation and begins responding. If it decides that the analysis it has been using is in error, then it may select a new analysis. The general idea is shown in the flowchart in Figure 6.2.

The exact method of changing analyses can be quite complicated and depends upon cognitive structures. For now, it is enough to think of the animal as having some set of possible ways it might analyze the situation and choosing one of these at random whenever it fails. An animal will consider its response a success if the outcome is as good as it expects and a failure if the outcome is worse than it expects. This leads to many interesting complications; but for the present we can think of the animal as evaluating its response more simply—if it is rewarded, it will consider its response a success, and if it fails to get a reward, it considers its response a failure.

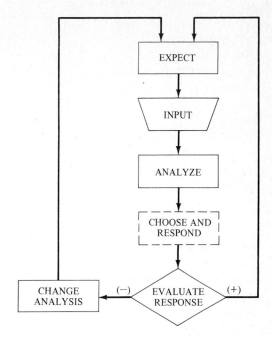

Figure 6.2   Basic structure of discrimination learning.

In the flowchart shown in Figure 6.2, notice that the animal starts with some expectancy, and its input consists of the stimulus display presented. It uses some analysis of that display: for example, it might immediately orient itself and select those properties of the stimulus that help it tell left from right. It would then make some response based on those orienting cues—say, a jump to the left-hand card. If this response is successful and leads to a safe landing and food, then the animal would keep the same analysis and on the next trial would analyze the new situation or input in the same way. Now suppose that it again makes a jump to the left and finds that this is not correct—that is, it hits the card which is fastened and falls into the net after a hard bump. This should lead to the choice of a new mode of analysis, so that when the next trial starts and the subject gets a new input, it may analyze it a different way.

In such a process, the animal might make errors at random for any number of trials while it tries out various analyses that cannot lead to consistent success. The rat might try various orienting cues, odors, or differential characteristics of the visual appearances of the two cards, such as the white area at the bottom of the card. Such analyses will lead to only chance success. For example, if the animal always jumps to the first card it notices that has a white area at the bottom, it would respond

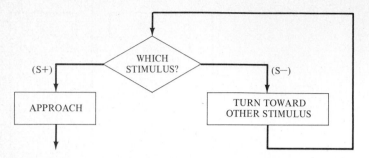

Figure 6.3 Structure of discrimination performance based on approach to correct stimulus as in Lashley jumping stand.

indifferently to either card. It might, of course, happen to jump to the correct card, in which case it would keep its analysis. But before long, it would surely jump toward the wrong card, make an error, and then change its analysis. If a card with vertical bars is S⁻ and a card with a triangle is S⁺, the animal might eventually orient toward one of the acute angles at the base of the triangle, analyze the situation for that property, and jump toward the acute angle. Since there is no such acute angle on S⁻, in this case the rat would always jump toward the correct stimulus. At this point the rat would have solved the problem and would respond consistently to the correct stimulus, S⁺. Notice that from this analysis of the behavior flow, the performance of the animal, as seen by the experimenter, will show "all-or-none" learning. Actually, it is a pure case of trial and error, imposed upon the subject by the structure of the experiment.

In Figure 6.2 there is a box drawn in dotted lines labeled "choose and respond." Depending upon the kind of experiment, this may have slightly different meanings. In the Lashley jumping stand, for example, there are two stimulus cards. After analyzing the situation, the subject has to orient toward one stimulus or the other and then decide whether it is the positive or the negative stimulus. If it is considered positive, the animal approaches it; if it is considered negative, the animal will avoid it and turn its attention toward the other stimulus. The approach response, when finally made, leads to evaluation of the outcome. This is given as a behavior flowchart in Figure 6.3. This same segment, with a slightly different interpretation, applies to experiments on monkeys and chimpanzees using pairs of objects. In this case, "approach" merely means that the animal brushes the object aside and sees the food well beneath it.

In some experiments using the Skinner box for discrimination learning, only one stimulus is presented. For example, an experimenter may decide to teach a pigeon to discriminate between red and green as follows: He will illuminate the key with red for a minute and reinforce all

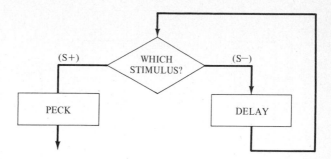

Figure 6.4 Responses in a Skinner box discrimination of the "GO—no GO" type.

responses. Then he will shift the illumination to green and disconnect the feeder, so that the animal is on extinction. This procedure will be repeated until the animal learns to peck the red and not the green key. In this experiment, the animal can either peck a key and get information as to the correctness of its response or decide that it has the negative stimulus and make some delaying response. The difficulty, from the point of view of the animal, is that it cannot find out if it was correct in the latter case. The flowchart is as shown in Figure 6.4.

A serious difficulty with teaching discrimination this way is that the pigeon might learn entirely the wrong discrimination and yet perform quite well. It might merely test the key every now and then; and if it gets food, it might keep responding until the first extinction trial. Then it would stop responding for a while. This would adapt its performance quite well to the experiment and might be mistaken for discrimination, even though the animal might actually not be analyzing the color of the stimuli at all. Suitable controls for this are somewhat complicated to design.

Finally, in a typical experiment using college students as subjects, the subject has two keys or buttons or may be given two alternative verbal responses. The instructions say that one key is correct when stimulus S_A is shown, the other when S_B is shown. Then on test trials the subject is shown one stimulus at a time, makes his response, and is shown or told which response would be correct. This last stage is usually called "feedback," since it is not in the form of a reward or reinforcement but is merely information as to whether the response was correct. This is shown in Figure 6.5.

Evaluation of the Outcome

When the subject has an opportunity to decide whether his response was a success or a failure, this in itself may involve a rather complicated

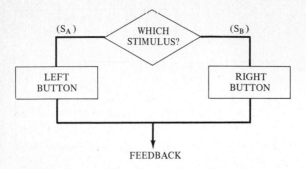

Figure 6.5 Flowchart for a human discrimination experiment with two buttons.

behavior flow. In simple experiments, the rewards for success are relatively high, the punishment for failure is relatively different, and the animal's behavior is very consistent. However, these experiments go on trial after trial, and eventually the animal will have experienced many successes and many failures. It may come to expect about 0.50 successes and 0.50 failures on the average and therefore may not always interpret a wrong response as a failure—the wrong response may be ignored or treated as a neutral outcome. In that case, the subject might well not change its mode of analysis of the stimulus. If this occurs, the subject will "never" learn the problem, at least until there is some major change either in the experimental procedure or in the state of the subject. To overcome such a difficulty, the experimenter might give the subject a very easy problem which can be solved at once and thereby establish in the animal an expectation that reward can be obtained every time. This might serve to reinstate the high level of aspiration which is required if the subject is to interpret every mistaken response as a failure that calls for a change of analysis.

If the magnitude or quality of rewards is changed during an experiment, the result may be a severe disruption of performance. For example, suppose that the experimenter sharply reduces the magnitude or quality of rewards after the animal has mastered a discrimination. What will happen? The animal's level of aspiration will be quite high because it has just finished a sequence of consecutive correct responses with high rewards. The inferior new rewards may be below the level of aspiration and therefore may be classified as "failures." If so, the animal will change its analysis, lose the learned discrimination, and appear totally disrupted.

The Process of Changing Analysis

According to the theory described above a subject will choose a new analysis at random if it finds it has made an error. This might be possible with a lower animal but certainly does not seem plausible for human subjects. Indeed, even in work with animals there is some indication of a more highly organized method of choosing a new hypothesis or method of analysis.

In the example of a rat choosing between two cards, one with vertical bars and the other with a triangle, there are several possible cues the animal might use. First, there are visual versus nonvisual cues; for the rat, the nonvisual cues may have many more important possibilities than the visual. Among the visual cues, there are cues within the apparatus and more distant cues outside the apparatus by which the rat might orient itself. Of the visual stimuli within the apparatus, there are those belonging to the cards and those belonging to the remainder of the apparatus. Of the visual cues on the cards, there are several aspects: for example, total brightness, horizontal and vertical (and oblique) contours, and corners. There are locations on the cards, and stimuli might be identified by position.

After an error, the rat might choose any of the above cues. However, choosing a visual corner on the card is not the same kind or level of hypothesis as choosing a visual stimulus as opposed to an auditory or olfactory stimulus.

Human subjects appear to have a tendency to exhaust a category or level of hypotheses before leaving it. For example, if a college student tries a red stimulus and is told he is wrong, he will choose a green stimulus next. That is, he will not give up the color dimension but will first exhaust it, trying both colors. Then he is likely to change to another dimension somewhat like color—for example, he may try a shape. This is more systematic than random sampling and reduces the chances that the subject will make the same mistake twice.

However, if the various hypotheses are not perfectly organized— divided into neat subsets and with various levels, each nested beneath the one above—the subject cannot gain anything from his attempts to test hypotheses systematically. In fact, it is found that college students doing their first hour's work on such problems are not very systematic, but they become more systematic as they practice at many discrimination learning problems. For most animal studies, particularly with the lower animals, the "random sampling" hypothesis is satisfactory. That is, whenever the animal judges the outcome of its choice to be unsatisfactory, it resamples randomly from its set of possible hypotheses and chooses a new one—but since it does not accurately remember what hypotheses it may have used in the past, it can resample an old hypothesis and try it again.

Chapter 7

Efficiency in Discrimination Learning

Discriminations, although many animals can learn them, are not necessarily easy; in fact, children and even college students often fail to learn a discrimination within 50 or 100 trials of training. Some discrimination problems are very difficult to learn; others are much easier. Furthermore, when the same discrimination is taught to a number of subjects (animal or human) that should be of approximately equal ability, the actual number of trials before they learn the discrimination is not constant but varies widely.

Teaching discriminations, especially fairly complex ones, is often a practical problem. A skilled worker must learn to discriminate very fine differences that determine a perfect result or a reject. A salesman must learn to discriminate slight changes of expression on the face of a prospective buyer. A laboratory technician must learn to discriminate and identify many different bacteria in a slide strewn with debris. A truck driver must discriminate the positions and velocities of oncoming vehicles, to avoid a possible collision. A nurse must discriminate slight changes in the facial color of a patient in intensive care. In each of these examples, the choice of appropriate behavior hinges mainly upon making a suitable discrimination, and the discrimination must be learned.

Much of what we know about the senses of animals is derived from experiments in discrimination learning. That monkeys and apes have color vision just like ours has been established in experiments with them on color discriminations. The hearing of cats is analyzed in detail using discrimination-learning procedures. The similarities between colors as seen by pigeons has been studied using tests after discrimination learning. If you wonder whether a dog can see colors, or whether desert rats have extremely sensitive hearing at high frequencies, or whether a cat with its main body-sense nerves cut can still discriminate roughness of surfaces with its paws, the usual method will be that of discrimination learning. Such investigations are aimed at finding the limits of the animal's sensory capacity, and therefore negative findings are as important as positive. If an animal cannot learn a given discrimination, this may yield basic information regarding its sensory system. However, one would always wonder if the animal had failed to learn the discrimination because it could not sense the necessary cue or for some other reason having nothing to do with perception—inadequate motivation, or inappropriate procedure, or use of an unnatural response, or some form of interference. Therefore, to use the method of discrimination learning in studying the senses of animals, we must have a good understanding of the usual sources of difficulty in discrimination learning.

Fortunately, the main sources of difficulty in discrimination learning, and the best ways to overcome them, are reasonably well understood. Furthermore, we can analyze a situation so that (in an experimental context) it is possible to make quantitative predictions about what an organism will do and how rapidly a problem can be learned.

HYPOTHESIS-SAMPLING THEORY

In Chapter 6 we saw that discrimination learning consists, in the main, of selecting an appropriate analysis of a stimulus input. Actually, each such analysis can be thought of as a "hypothesis," for when the subject chooses to analyze the input in a given way, this is the same as having a hypothesis that this analysis will yield the relevant cue. The difficulty in discrimination learning arises because the subject has not one possible analysis but many. If it had available only one analysis, then it either would not have to learn the discrimination, (already having the correct analysis) or would be incapable of making it. Discrimination learning occurs when the subject has many hypotheses, at least one of which is relevant and at least some of which are irrelevant to the problem.

Figure 7.1   The abstract structure of a typical discrimination-learning problem with four irrelevant hypotheses and one relevant hypothesis.

A typical problem of intermediate difficulty is shown in Figure 7.1. Notice that the subject in this problem has one relevant hypothesis and four irrelevant hypotheses.

Quantitative Prediction of Errors

Now let us consider how many errors, on the average, a subject would make in learning this problem. We shall use the simplest model, assuming that the subject samples one hypothesis at a time each time it makes an error, and keeps trying until it happens to hit a relevant hypothesis. Let R be the number of relevant hypotheses and I be the number of irrelevant hypotheses (assuming, for simplicity, that they are all equally strong). Then define r as the proportion of relevant hypotheses;

$$r = \frac{R}{R + I} \tag{1}$$

In the above example, since there is only one relevant hypothesis, $R = 1$; but since there are four irrelevant hypotheses, $I = 4$. Therefore, $r = 1/(1 + 4) = 0.20$.

Mean Total Errors   As a general rule, the average or mean number of errors in a discrimination learning problem will be $(1 - r)/r$. Let T be the total errors and $\overline{T}$ be the mean total errors. Then,

$$\overline{T} = (1 - r)/r \tag{2}$$

This general rule arises from the assumptions of the hypothesis-sampling process, by mathematical argument. The argument is moderately difficult but will be given in detail so that the reader can follow step by step. Along the way, we shall encounter some predictions about how a discrimination-learning experiment should come out and can then compare the predictions with the data.

T is the total errors made by a given subject, but it is not the same for all subjects, since obviously one subject might accidentally sample the relevant hypothesis right away, and others might take many trials to hit it. To predict the average value of T, we must first consider how an average is calculated. If we had a large number N of subjects, we would find the total errors made by each, add up all these totals, and divide the total by N to get the average. We would get the same result if we first added together all the total errors made by subjects who made no errors, then all the total errors made by subjects who made one error, then all the totals of those who made two errors, and so forth, and finally divided by N. We would also get the same result if we added together all the errors of subjects who made no errors and at once divided by N, then combined all the errors made by subjects who made one error and divide by N, and so forth. This last step is the same as finding the proportion of subjects who made no errors and multiplying this by zero; then finding the proportion of subjects who made one error, multiplying by one, and adding this in; then finding the proportion of subjects who made two errors, multiplying by two, and adding this in; and so forth.

Let $p(0)$ be the probability of making exactly 0 errors, let $p(1)$ be the probability of making exactly 1 error, etc. Then, the theoretical value of mean errors is

$$\overline{T} = 0 \cdot p(0) + 1 \cdot p(1) + 2 \cdot p(2) + 3 \cdot p(3) + \ldots \tag{3}$$

and the sum goes out, in principle, to infinity.

Now every time the subject samples a hypothesis, it has probability r of getting the relevant hypothesis. If it gets the relevant hypothesis, it makes no more errors. The probability of making zero errors is simply the probability that the first hypothesis chosen is relevant, which is r:

$$p(0) = r$$

To make exactly one error, the subject must first choose an irrelevant hypothesis, on the basis of which it will make an error. Then it resamples, chooses a relevant hypothesis, and makes no more errors. The probability of choosing the irrelevant hypothesis first is $(1 - r)$, and the probability of then choosing the relevant hypothesis is r. The probability that those two samples are chosen in that order on the first two samplings is

$$p(1) = (1 - r)r$$

The probability of making some other number of errors, which we might designate by k, is the probability of choosing an irrelevant hypothesis on each of the first k samples and then hitting the relevant hypothesis. That is, in general,

$$p(k) = (1 - r)^k r \tag{4}$$

Now we can go back to equation 3 and replace the expressions $p(0)$, $p(1)$, and so forth, by their values as given by equation 4. We then get

$$\overline{T} = 0 \cdot r + 1 \cdot (1 - r)r + 2 \cdot (1 - r)^2 r + 3 \cdot (1 - r)^3 r + \ldots \qquad (5)$$

The first term is 0, and r can be factored out of all the remaining terms, yielding

$$\overline{T} = r[(1 - r) + 2(1 - r)^2 + 3(1 - r)^3 + \ldots]$$

To solve this equation we use a trick. First we multiply both sides by $(1 - r)$. Then we attempt to subtract corresponding terms. This is how it goes:

$$\overline{T} = r[(1 - r) + 2(1 - r)^2 + 3(1 - r)^3 + \ldots]$$
$$\overline{T}(1 - r) = r[(1 - r)^2 + 2(1 - r)^3 + \ldots]$$

Subtracting on both sides of the equals sign,

$$\overline{T} \cdot r = r[(1 - r) + (1 - r)^2 + (1 - r)^3 + \ldots] \qquad (6)$$

Notice that on the left side, $\overline{T} = \overline{T}(1 - r) = \overline{T} - \overline{T} + \overline{T}r$. On the right side subtract the first term of the bottom line from the second term of the top, the second term of the bottom line from the third term of the top, and so forth.

Equation 6 has the factor r in both sides, which can be factored out and canceled. Therefore, the expression reduces to

$$\overline{T} = (1 - r) + (1 - r)^2 + (1 - r)^3 + \ldots \qquad (7)$$

Now the same trick can be applied again. Multiply both sides of equation 7 by $(1 - r)$, and the result is

$$\overline{T}(1 - r) = (1 - r)^2 + (1 - r)^3 + \ldots$$

If this is subtracted from equation 7, the result is

$$\overline{T}r = 1 - r \qquad (8)$$

for all the rest of the terms on the right cancel out. Then,

$$\overline{T} = (1 - r)/r \tag{9}$$

which is the same as equation 2.

Distribution of Total Errors It was mentioned that this proof would not only verify that the mean errors is $1 - r/r$, but also make other predictions. Look back at equation 4. It gives the probability that a subject will make exactly k errors and therefore specifies the *distribution* of total errors. This is not a "bell-shaped" distribution such as one finds in elementary statistics but rather what is sometimes called a "J-shaped" distribution. More exactly, it is known as the "geometric distribution" because the probabilities form a geometric series like $\alpha, \alpha^2, \alpha^3, \alpha^4, \ldots$

An example of the distribution of total errors, as predicted from the theory, is shown in Figure 7.2. Two distributions, one for rapid learning ($r = 0.40$) and one for slow learning ($r = 0.10$), are shown. Notice that in both cases the most likely number of errors is zero, even when the mean errors is quite high. With $r = 0.10$, average errors will be $0.90/0.10 = 9.0$,

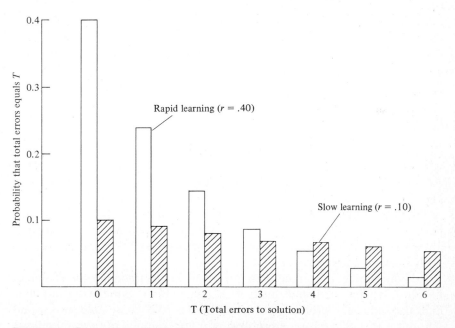

Figure 7.2 Theoretical distribution of total errors for rapid ($r=0.40$) and slow ($r=0.10$) learning. Note that in both distributions the most probable number of errors is zero.

and even though the mean errors is 9.0, the most likely value of total errors is 0. Because the distributions tail out farther than is shown in the graph, there will be some very large scores.

Does this mean that the subjects differ widely in ability? No assumption about differences in ability was made; and in fact it is assumed in the calculations that every subject has the same probability of sampling the relevant hypothesis after an error. Therefore, this wide spread of performances is predicted by the theory merely on the basis of the fact that random sampling—looking for the relevant hypothesis—is a risky business. Whenever this simple theory fits, individual learners will differ widely on the trial at which they master the discrimination, even if they are equal in potential.

This means that the average or mean error, though perfectly valid, is not particularly representative of the performance of a whole group of learners. Knowing the average trial of learning would not be useful for planning a school curriculum, for example. One could not plan to give just enough trials to obtain ten errors from each subject, knowing that the mean total errors would be ten. If the mean is ten errors, many subjects would make as many as twenty or even thirty errors. Good planning requires selecting an amount of training sufficient to get some fraction of the subjects, such as 0.90, to solution. However, for theoretical purposes, the mean total errors is the best single description of the difficulty of a problem and the speed with which it is solved.

METHODS OF MAKING A DISCRIMINATION
EASY TO LEARN

Consider a problem with two alternative possible correct answers, and with two redundant relevant cues. For example, one may be using cards on which figures are drawn in color. Suppose that the correct card is always a red triangle and the incorrect card always a blue circle. Then the problem could be learned as a discrimination between red and blue, or between a triangle and a circle, or both. It has two alternative correct answers, and this is because the two dimensions, color and shape, are both relevant and are redundant.

If the subject presented with this problem hits upon the cue of shape, he can solve the problem. Equally well, he might hit upon the cue of color, and also solve the problem—at least, he would become able to respond without errors. Therefore, a problem with two redundant relevant cues is easier than a problem in which only one of the cues is relevant, even though it might turn out that no subject knew there was more than one redundant cue. In fact, if there are, say, five dimensions in the stimulus, and if only one of them is redundant, we have $r = 1/5 = 0.2$; whereas if two of the dimensions are both relevant and redundant, $r = 2/5 = 0.4$. Mean total errors, also, would drop from 4.0 to 1.5, since $\overline{T} = (1 - r)/r$. Obviously, one way to make a discrimination easy to learn is to add a redundant relevant dimension.

A second way to make a discrimination easier to learn is to remove irrelevant cues. This is not at once apparent to a person trying to get a person or an animal to discriminate, say, a distinctive color. The experimenter naturally thinks about the color itself and tries to find a way to get the subject to pay attention to that color. However, his goals might be best attained by discovering what it is that the subjects do pay attention to—that is, what irrelevant cues are distracting them—and then removing these irrelevant cues.

According to equation 9, the average total errors is given by $(1 - r)r$. Now notice that $r = R/(R + I)$. A little algebra shows that

$$\overline{T} = (1 - r)/r$$
$$= [I/(R + I)]/[R/(R + I)]$$
$$= I/R$$

That is, the mean total errors is given by the ratio of irrelevant hypotheses to relevant ones. This means that if one can reduce the irrelevant hypotheses by half, one will reduce the mean errors by half. Reducing the irrelevant hypotheses by half has the same effect as doubling the number or weight of relevant hypotheses.

There are many examples, in everyday life, of ways that discriminations are taught by eliminating irrelevant dimensions. For example, the instructions on a complicated machine like an automobile engine often show a system of parts in an exploded or cutaway view. These drawings remove complications that would be present in a photograph of the whole engine; and the removal of parts that are irrelevant to the task at hand speeds up learning the necessary discriminations. It is relatively difficult to pick out the parts of the ignition system in a new automobile just by looking at the engine, but the task is much easier in a drawing which shows only the ignition system. Similarly, a person looking at a microscope slide might have great difficulty in finding and discriminating a bacillus, or rod-shaped bacteria, without considerable training. However, if the debris on the slide can somehow be removed from view, as by making a drawing of just the bacillus intended or making a photograph and then masking out everything except the bacillus, then learning of the necessary discriminations may be quite rapid.

A third method of making a discrimination problem easier is the use of an "emphasizer" stimulus (Trabasso, 1963.) This is an attention-getting stimulus that is used to direct the subject's attention to the locus of the relevant cue; it is particularly beneficial when the relevant cue is distinctive but is usually lost in a welter of irrelevant detail.

A discrimination may be difficult for either of two rather different reasons: either the relevant stimuli may be so small or so hidden that the subject cannot find them, or they may be perfectly visible but very similar. For example, a child may have trouble discriminating a small green spot from a small blue spot, even though the colors are distinctive, because it cannot find the little spots. It might also have difficulty discriminating a large green circle from a large blue circle, if the green is blueish, the blue is greenish, and in fact the two colors are very similar. If the difficulty has to do with finding the relevant cues, then emphasizers can be of great help. If the difficulty has to do with telling the difference between two obvious but highly similar cues, then emphasizers are of much less help.

When you try to teach a dog to open a door, you may make noises with your fingers, point his head toward the door, move the door, etc., all in an effort to get the dog to pay attention to the cue. Similarly, a lecturer may point to information on the blackboard, thereby attempting to direct the class's attention to it. A male ruffed grouse, seeking to engage a female in the mating dance, first makes booming sounds to attract her attention. The stickleback fish, inducing its egg-laden female into a nest, first swims directly in front of her to attract attention, then swims off toward the nest with a distinctive motion and rhythm.

EASY-TO-HARD TRANSFER OF TRAINING

The use of crutches, of simplification, and of emphasizers all can make a hard problem easy, but they have very different implications for the educational process.

The Effect of Adding a Redundant Relevant Dimension

The fact that you can make a hard problem into an easier one does not necessarily mean an important gain in the educational process. An example is the elementary reading book, in which pictures are added to the printed words. This gives the child two different ways to get the message. Furthermore, it is usually necessary to use the same passages over and over again. This means that the child might respond to (1) the words, which the teacher intends to be the relevant cues, (2) the pictures, which in some instances can substitute for the words, and (3) memory of what other children have been heard to say while reading. These three sets of relevant cues support three sets of relevant hypotheses, and the child can solve the immediate discrimination task using any of the three. This makes the problem much easier than it would be if the child had only the written words before him and no one else in the class had read them aloud. However, eventually the child must learn to read written words without pictures and without first hearing them read. Therefore, there is a hard "criterion" task that the child must master, and the fact that he can learn the easier training task is important only if he will, finally, really learn to read.

A similar situation exists in electronics, in which various circuits or types of wires are covered in red insulation, and others in green, blue, black, etc. A student can learn to discriminate the power from the ground, and various amplifying or logic circuits, by the color in which the wires are coded. If it were not for color coding, the student would have to make a much more difficult analysis of the wiring, identify components, and trace circuits to make the same discriminations.

If the student learns circuits by color coding, he will function perfectly well so long as the color coding he learned is used on the equipment he must analyze. However, if he must work with equipment that is wired all in one color, he is then faced with a new problem. If he had learned by the more difficult method of identifying components and tracing wires, he would be able to function without colors. Of course, if a change in technology makes all the components appear different, he is again stopped until he learns these new cues.

In both of these examples, the learner is given a second relevant cue with which to solve the problem. This second cue (for example, the pictures) is redundant in that it can give the same information as the primary cue (the printed words). Furthermore, the secondary cue is really "extraneous" in that, for example, if the child looks at the pictures, he is not encouraged to look at the words. Similarly, color coding in an electronic circuit is redundant with the actual functions (assuming that the color coding has been carried out intelligently) and extraneous in that looking at the color does not lead one to look at the actual components or to trace circuits.

To test the effectiveness of such methods of education, we employ what is called a "transfer-of-training" experiment. Such an experiment employs at least two groups from the same population. The control group learns only a certain test problem, which we may designate task B. The experimental group first learns a training task A, and then after completing task A is given task B exactly as it was given to the control group. Both groups are tested exactly alike on task B, so that their performances are comparable, and they should perform the same except for any effects of task A. If there is any effect transferred from the learning of A to the learning of B, transfer of training has taken place.

Consider the example in which a student learns an electronic circuit and can make the appropriate analysis by identifying components. Call the task of learning this analysis task B. A control group will be trained at once on task B. The experimental group, in contrast, will first be trained on task A, in which they learn the same analysis but with materials that are color-coded. Therefore, the experimental group might solve the problem by analyzing the task, by discriminating the colors, or both, and will solve it in relatively few trials. However, there is a question as to how well these subjects will do on task B, the analysis.

Essentially, the question boils down to how the subject learned the original problem. If the problem was learned by analysis of the circuit, even though color was available, then the plain problem without colors will also be solved with no further effort. However, if the original problem was learned by color, then when the colors are removed the subject will show no effect of the earlier problem and will have to learn the analysis during task B just as if he were starting from scratch.

Transfer will be all-or-none in such a problem. The learner will master the problem either by analyzing the circuit or by color. If he analyzes the circuit, he will perform perfectly well without color; if he uses the color in the first task, he will show no transfer and will perform exactly like a person who had never had pretraining.

Now suppose that we found that subjects made an average of twenty errors in learning the analysis, which is difficult, but made only an average of two errors in learning the problem with color. Would you expect many subjects to transfer to task B? Obviously, color makes the problem much easier; it seems, therefore, that many subjects must be using color. If so, then relatively few are learning the original problem by analysis, and therefore relatively few will show transfer to task B.

Remember that the mean errors is given by the equation

$$\overline{T} = I/R$$

For the analysis problem, mean errors was 20, so if the relevant analysis cues are R_a in number,

$$I/R_a = 20$$

With the color cues added, mean errors was only 2. Therefore, if R_c is the number of relevant color cues,

$$I/(R_a + R_c) = 2$$

These two equations can be combined to give an exact prediction of the proportion of subjects who will transfer. Dividing the first equation by the second, we get

$$\frac{I/R_a}{I/(R_a + R_c)} = \frac{20}{2}$$

so that, by some rearrangement,

$$\frac{R_a}{R_a + R_c} = 0.10$$

That is, of the total analysis with color cues given to the subjects in the pretraining task, the analysis cues make up only 0.10. Therefore, only one subject in ten (0.10 of the subjects) is expected to have used the analysis of the circuit in learning the problem, the other nine (0.90) having used the more salient color cue. The color-coded problem was learned rapidly, but this is not doing any good, since 90 percent of the subjects are not able to analyze the circuits but have merely learned the color coding.

In general, if the extra cue (like the color in the circuit or the pictures in a reading book) produces a great improvement in learning, then it will turn out that many people do not learn the real problem but instead rely heavily upon the crutch.

In fact, if we consider the total errors made both on the training and on the test problem, a remarkable constancy is deduced. In the problem requiring analysis but also giving color cues, a proportion of subjects, $R_a/(R_a + R_c)$, will solve the original problem with $I/(R_a + R_c)$ errors and will make no more errors. The remaining subjects, the proportion $R_a/(R_a + R_c)$, will make the same number of errors, $I/(R_a + R_c)$, on the first problem, will not transfer, and therefore on the second problem will make just as many errors as control subjects, an average of I/R_a. Combining all these parts,

$$\overline{T} = \frac{R_a}{R_a + R_c}\left(\frac{I}{R_a + R_c}\right) + \frac{R_c}{R_a + R_c}\left[\frac{I}{R_a + R_c} + \frac{I}{R_a}\right]$$

It takes a while to simplify this equation, but it comes out to

$$\overline{T} = I/R_a$$

which is exactly the number of errors expected if the subjects were trained immediately on the second test problem. The use of an extra cue, a crutch, does not help at all in reducing the number of errors subjects make, provided that everyone is eventually required to learn the primary cue. All that happens is that some time may be wasted, for subjects may spend a considerable time showing their mastery of the crutch, when they might as well be making errors and trying to learn the real problem— analysis of circuits, reading, or whatever.

The above calculations are not mere theory. A number of experiments done since about 1960 have confirmed these predictions. In particular, the work of Trabasso (1963), Trabasso and Bower (1968), and Levison (1972) is relevant to this question. Using laboratory tasks called "concept formation" which require specifically that subjects make a difficult discrimination in the presence of irrelevant cues, they have obtained quantitative results that agree almost exactly with the calculations given above.

The Effect of Removing Irrelevant Cues

The second way to make a problem easier is to remove irrelevant cues. When this has been done and the subject then solves the problem, that proves that the correct relevant cue is being used. In the electronics example, one might simplify the display so that only one very simple circuit is presented at a time, reducing the complexity often present in schematic diagrams. The subject then analyzes the circuit rapidly, because most of the irrelevant stimuli are removed. Similarly, in a reading class the experimenter might screen out the sounds and sights of the usual classroom situation, so that the child has nothing to look at but the book. This should have the effect of accelerating learning.

What happens when the usual irrelevant stimuli are put back into the situation and the subject is tested on the original task B? Experimental information is not complete; but in the experiments done, subjects transfer almost perfectly. Having found and mastered the relevant cue, subjects are not much disturbed by new, irrelevant cues. Having already solved the problem, they tend not to use the new dimensions coming into the situation and therefore are not disturbed by them.

This, of course, means that we can bring about almost perfect efficiency. By reducing irrelevant cues (if we can), we direct the subject to the relevant cue; and once he has found that, we can put the irrelevant cues back into the problem without confusing him. If the irrelevant cues could be reduced to zero, then the subject would make no total errors attributable to discrimination difficulties yet would transfer perfectly to the final task. In some experiments made around 1960, Trabasso (1963) showed that efficiencies of 10:1 were possible in the experimental laboratory. He used a final test problem in which subjects usually averaged twenty errors to learn but got his subjects to criterion in very few trials, averaging about two errors, by using this sort of simplification and removal of irrelevant cues.

This leads to a simple conclusion. Suppose that you want to teach some task B which requires a discrimination, and that the subjects make many errors learning task B directly. You might produce an easier task either by adding a crutch, or extra relevant cue, or by stripping away some of the irrelevant cues. Either method can reduce the number of errors made on this easier task to a low value. However, if you have added a crutch, you will eventually have to take it away, and then many of the subjects will be found not to know the solution to task B and will have to start learning over again. This procedure will give a net gain, in errors, of zero. But if you have removed irrelevant cues, you do indeed make the problem easy: when you put the irrelevant cues back in and return to task B, subjects will make very few if any errors.

For this reason, when you want to accelerate learning it is better by far to simplify the situation by removing irrelevant cues than by adding artificial relevant cues or crutches to the problem.

The Effect of Using an Emphasizer Stimulus

The third method of speeding up learning is to emphasize or otherwise point to the relevant cue. This method is useful mainly when the relevant cue is actually a small object or takes up only a small and secluded part of the stimulus field. Until the cue is located, the subject simply cannot learn the solution at all; after it is located, he should be able to retain the solution even if the emphasizer is removed. Therefore, this method should show perfect transfer, much like that obtained when we simplify the problem by removing irrelevant cues. The emphasizer should greatly reduce the search time and permit rapid performance that is never possible without the emphasizing stimulus.

Summary: Reducing Difficulties

There are three ways to make a difficult discrimination problem easier: (1) adding a crutch, or extra relevant cue, (2) clearing away irrelevant cues, and (3) using an emphasizer stimulus to point out the relevant cue. Of these, the first two can produce very fast learning and almost no errors, since average total errors T is given by I/R, the number of irrelevant cues divided by the number of relevant cues. Either increasing R or decreasing I sufficiently can make T very small. The value of the emphasizer depends on whether or not the difficulty in the problem arises because the relevant cue is inconspicuous, for the most an emphasizer can do is make the cue somewhat less conspicuous than the emphasizer itself.

If extra relevant cues are introduced to make the problem easier, then transfer is not very efficient when the extra cues are withdrawn. When irrelevant cues are removed to make the problem easier, performance usually remains steady when they are reintroduced, so that a tremendous gain in educational efficiency may be obtained. When an emphasizer is used, the evidence is that performance will remain steady after it is removed.

If you are a teacher, or in charge of a training program, or even just trying to make your own learning and performance more efficient, the first step must be to analyze the problem and determine the source of difficulty. If discrimination is a main difficulty, then you may be able to change the whole situation permanently and introduce a new cue. An example is the kind of standardized color coding used in some laboratories or by some electronic companies, which is perfectly consistent for all pieces of equipment. So long as you are working with equipment that follows your color code, you can take advantage of the rapid learning of new information based on the salient color hypothesis.

If you have to deal with a given situation, then there is little to be gained by adding relevant cues. You now must try to find out whether the difficulty is due to (1) a morass of irrelevant cues or (2) the smallness of the relevant cue. Usually, it is a combination of both of these factors. Then, a training program can be started that uses easier versions of the problem, made easier by removing irrelevant cues and emphasizing the relevant cue. This should speed up learning and yet permit good transfer to the original task that must eventually be mastered.

Obviously, if you are dealing with adult humans or with older children, it is possible simply to tell them what the cue is. Since this is the aid most commonly used, and since it is developed so powerfully as to handle almost any communication problem, the verbal message or instruction will often be a great help. It will fail when the subject simply has never before discriminated the cue required, or when the cue is something, like a complex shape, that is difficult to describe. A third possibility is that, like elegant phrasing of a musical passage, or like beauty in the human face, the cue you must learn is one that seems to elude anyone's descriptive powers. The other methods described above will work with any subject, human or animal, if the experimenter has the intelligence to apply them appropriately.

Finally, it should be restated that to teach or test a discrimination, it is not enough to have a clear instance of the cue—one must have both positive and negative instances, and sufficient irrelevant cues, so that the subject can really tell what is and what is not the correct answer. The test must be difficult enough really to require the discrimination. Otherwise, one can get into the trap of having a child appear to be progressing through school, and then discovering that in the fifth grade the child cannot read. How can this inability be "discovered" at that age? Because the tests of reading ability, as used day in and day out in the school, can be "faked" by a child who can answer well enough to satisfy the teacher without actually reading. Now, this does not mean that the child is dishonest—he is reading as best he knows how and may be successfully meeting the demands put on him by the teacher. However, the child is not doing what he must do in order to succeed in the world, for there is no way to "fake" reading in college or on the job.

Chapter 8

The Learning Set and More Complex Discriminative Skills

It seems a simple response to pick one of two objects as the correct one because it leads to food, and in a way this is a simple trick. The next question is how complex a problem animals can learn. The answer, of course, depends on the animal; our interest will center on primates since they are closely related to humans and share our kind of problem-solving ability. Particularly, we will be interested in the macacque monkey and the chimpanzee. The chimpanzee is a large, tailless, social ape of the Congo basin in Africa. The macacque is a genus of advanced monkey; the rhesus macacque, which comes mainly from India, where it is a prolific and citified inhabitant, is the most common in the laboratory. These animals, along with the relatively primitive cebus capuchin ("organ-grinder") monkey from South America, are the most capable in complex discriminative problems.

The apparatus used is interesting because it gives the reader a concrete picture of the situation facing the animal and also shows the important techniques necessary to test the advanced capabilities of animals. A schematic drawing of the apparatus is shown in Figure 8.1.

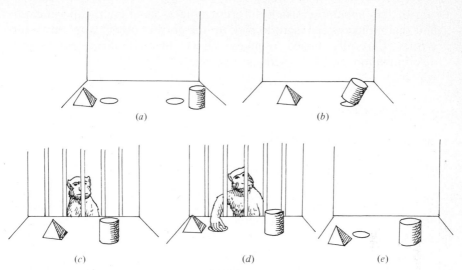

Figure 8.1   A single trial of discrimination learning in the Wisconsin General Test Apparatus. (*a*) Opaque screen is down so that the monkey cannot see anything. Two random objects are set near the food wells. (*b*) The cylinder, baited with a raisin, will be the correct object; the prism will be wrong. Objects are placed. (*c*) The opaque screen is raised so that the monkey can see, but cannot reach, the objects. (*d*) The tray slides forward, and the monkey chooses an object by sweeping it off the food well. This time, the monkey chose the wrong object. (*e*) The opaque screen is dropped, and the objects are withdrawn—the monkey cannot touch the cylinder until the next trial.

Between trials, the forward opaque screen is lowered to hide preparations from the monkey. The experimenter raises the screen nearest him, pulls back the sliding stimulus tray, baits one of the two food wells in it with a raisin or peanut, covers both wells with objects, and then lowers his one-way vision screen. At this time, the experimenter can see the objects but cannot be seen. The experimenter then raises the forward opaque screen so that the monkey can see and starts the stimulus tray forward with a slight jerk. This usually attracts the attention of the monkey, in which case the tray is slid forward so that the monkey can reach through the bars to choose an object. By dint of careful training, the monkey or ape is taught to push one of the objects aside and search the food well under it. The animal is not to grasp the object (which would lose it to the experimenter), or brush both objects aside, or otherwise disturb the smooth operation of the experiment. Taming and adaptation to the apparatus may take months, for rhesus monkeys, particularly, are wild and aggressive.

In this apparatus, using different objects as stimuli, experimenters find that monkeys can learn to pick up the correct object with only a few errors. Carefully tamed monkeys have learned their first object-discrimination problems with an average of $\overline{T}$ = 4.2 total errors, from which

$$I/R = 4.2$$

and the proportion of relevant cues is

$$R/(R + I) = 1/5.2 = 0.192$$

It is not surprising that monkeys can learn a problem in which a particular object is correct. What about a problem in which the food is not always under the same object? This would require a more complex behavior flow—not merely a discrimination between the objects (though this is necessary), but some other way of deciding which object is correct. The experimental task is to develop a problem in which the reward is not always under one object, but nevertheless can be predicted by some simple principle.

DISCRIMINATION-REVERSAL PROBLEMS

In a discrimination reversal, the discriminated objects remain the same but the rewards are reversed in the middle of a problem, so that the previously negative objects become positive, and previously positive objects become negative.

If the subject had merely learned responses to stimuli, then the reversal problem would completely disrupt him and should lead to negative transfer. That is, the subject on a reversal should be expected to perform worse than a control subject on the same task who had never had the original training.

In the first reversal, an animal subject does in fact show considerable difficulty, and its performance usually follows a distinctive pattern. First, for a few trials, the subject maintains the response habit or hypothesis that was working before. If, say, a black stimulus has been positive and white stimulus negative, and a rat has learned that, then when the black is made negative and white positive, the rat will make a few more responses consistently approaching the black stimulus. Close inspection usually shows that the rat slows down, hesitates, and generally shows conflict or uncertainty; and this uncertainty increases over the first few trials. Finally, the rat will make some response to the white stimulus for the first time, but this usually does not mean that it has solved the problem. It has merely broken the habit of responding to black, but it has not necessarily learned to respond to white. Instead, the animal is likely to regress to a position habit or some other irrelevant habit for a while before it finally adopts the new appropriate reversal problem (Lawrence, 1955). In its first reversal, the rat is likely to treat the reversed problem as a new problem; and after breaking the old habit it will to a considerable degree return to its original starting set of hypotheses.

However, suppose that the problem is reversed repeatedly. The animal first learns to go to black; when this is mastered, it learns to go to white; then when that is learned, it must go back to black; and so forth, for a series of reversals. Clearly, this experimental regimen, which requires the subject to master two opposite and conflicting habit systems, meets the requirements of our study of higher-level problems—the relationship between object and reward is not constant, yet the problem can be solved. To be exact, the problem can almost be solved—the subject may not be able to predict the particular trial on which the problem will next be reversed; but having once missed (and observed) the reversal, it can then respond correctly. In fact, one would expect some subjects to try to anticipate the reversal, since they might come to expect it.

In order to master a problem of this sort, the subject would have to develop a higher-order cognitive structure. That is, the two opposing behavior flows—in this case, one of approach to white and the other of approach to black—have to be integrated into a larger structure. A diagram of the needed structure is shown in Figure 8.2.

If this sort of higher-order cognitive structure can be developed, then the animal will be able to reverse rapidly from one habit to its opposite. Can animals really learn this ability? Dufort, Guttman, and Kimble (1954) showed that rats could learn to reverse a simple left-right position habit in a few problems; in fact, all their nine albino rats made one-trial reversals on problems 8, 9, and 10. The main results, in total errors per problem, are shown in Figure 8.3.

The rats were first trained against their position habit to go to one of two doors and were not permitted to correct if they failed to find the food. Notice that they made an average of 4.0 errors on the original problem, which therefore would probably have as an approximation

$$I/R = 4.0$$

In the first reversal, the rats made an average of 9.1 errors, an additional 5.1 over the initial learning. This is a clear example of negative transfer,

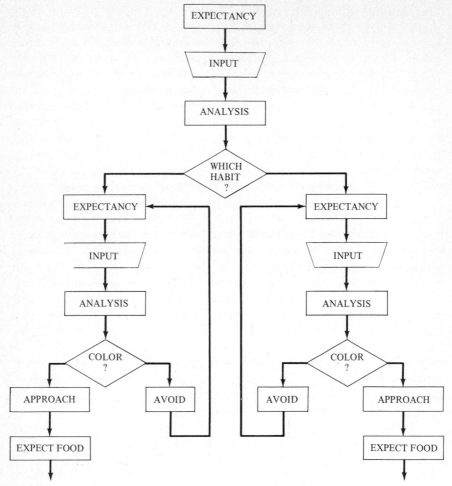

Figure 8.2 Second-order cognitive structure to control a discrimination-reversal-learning habit.

explained by the fact that the two behavior flows involved produce opposite, exclusive responses. Although we do not have detailed data, it is likely that most of the additional 5.1 errors were made during initial consecutive responses to the wrong side—that is, to the side that had previously been correct. After the first responses, the subject will go back to the kind of "random" responses made during original learning; and then after perhaps eight trials or so (4.0 errors), they will learn the new problem. After a few reversals, the "random" errors disappear, so that the animals make a few initial responses to the wrong side and then switch immediately to the correct response. By problem 6, the rats were making only about one unnecessary error in learning the reversal; by problem 7, almost all the rats switched immediately after once finding the food cup empty on a given side. As a control against the possibility that the rats might respond to the odor of food, the experimenters put food in the cups on both sides but locked the door to the wrong cup.

The results of the experiment clearly indicate that a structure like that shown in Figure 8.2 must be evolved but do not tell us what the input for the higher-level decision might be or what cue the animal discovers so as to choose the correct habit. Is it possible that the animal is holding some cue in short-term memory? Does the rat simply remember where the food was last, and try to go to that place? If the rat can remember the last place it found food, then it can perform perfectly. The higher-level input would be the memory of where food was, left or right, on the previous trial. If the food is remembered to have been on the left, then the left-going behavior flow would be called in. If the rat goes left and finds no food, this signals a switch to the right-going behavior flow.

One difficulty with this interpretation is that the experimenters ran

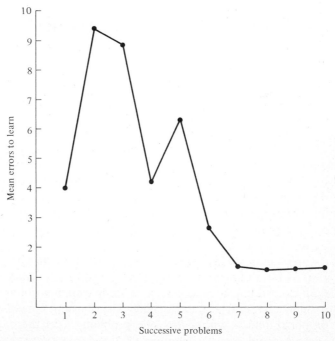

Figure 8.3 Performance of nine rats on successive reversals of a position discrimination. (*Dufort, Kimble, & Guttman, 1954.*)

only four trials a day; the rat, therefore, would often have to remember from one day to the next what response to make, and this is a long time for short-term memory. When House and Zeaman (1959) repeated much the same experiment with young imbeciles of low mental age (2 to 4 years), they found similar results, and they also often required the children to remember from one day to the next.

One interesting characteristic of repeated reversals, at least when the subject is a chimpanzee, is the side benefit the subject may obtain. Schusterman (1962) found that a chimpanzee, having learned to reverse back and forth with a given pair of objects, was almost immediately able to perform such reversals on a completely new pair of objects. What the chimpanzee had learned, apparently, was to choose the object that had just had food under it on the previous trial and switch from an object with no food—and this subject was able to transfer this concept to completely new objects.

The ability to transfer a learned behavior flow to new objects seems to have an important significance for the level of intelligence involved. The next section of this chapter deals with such transfer or generality of learning.

LEARNING SET AND REVERSAL-LEARNING SET

If a monkey or ape is given a series of discrimination problems, each problem using a new pair of objects, its performance will gradually improve. After 200 to 300 problems, the animal will be correct over 90 percent of the time on trial 2, the first trial on which there is any way for it to know the correct answer. This gradual, systematic improvement has been called the development of a "learning set" (Harlow, 1949). Figure 8.4 shows some typical learning curves, which were given in the first major report of this work by Harlow. What interpretation is to be put upon this result? The term "learning set" is curiously ambiguous. It indicates that the animal is developing the ability or tendency to learn; but it is an important question whether the change is in *ability* to learn—that is, in the parameter of the learning rate—or in some *tendency* or strategy adopted by the animal.

An analysis by Meyer (1951) indicates that improvement is *not* caused by a change in learning rate. Using data obtained from animals that were doing a series of reversal-learning problems, he plotted performance from trial 2 to learning. The learning curve—the improvement of performance within any one problem—was the same in all but the earliest problems. To summarize, the subjects' average learning curve moved 0.25 of the way toward perfect. If a group of subjects made 0.120

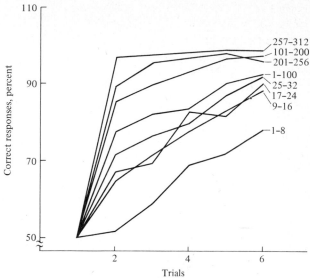

Figure 8.4 Learning curves for six-trial discrimination problems. Notice that learning is gradual on early problems but becomes very rapid by problem 200. (*Harlow, 1949.*)

errors on one trial, they would make only 0.090 errors on the next trial, for errors would drop by 0.25. According to this rule, errors would then drop to .0675, which is a 0.25 drop in errors from .090, and so forth.

What did change was the starting point of the curve. In a reversal-learning set the subject learns a new problem, and then the problem is unpredictably reversed. On the first trial of reversal, the subjects would always be wrong except for their efforts, sometimes successful, to anticipate the reversal. On the next trial, they could be perfectly successful if they did the reversal learning in a single trial. On early problems (1 to 36) on trial 2, the subjects make about 0.70 errors, showing considerable persistence in responding to the previously correct object; but then they learn quite rapidly on the next few trials. On problems 37 to 72 they show the same learning curve, but on trial 2 they are making only an average of 0.50 errors. By problems 73 to 108 their learning curve starts at an average of about 0.20 errors and again shows the same learning curve within the problem. Meyer's theoretical graphs are shown in Figure 8.5.

This looks very much as if the animals are not learning to *learn* but instead are solving these problems by some sort of "transfer of training," like the all-or-none transfer discussed in Chapter 7. Such data would arise

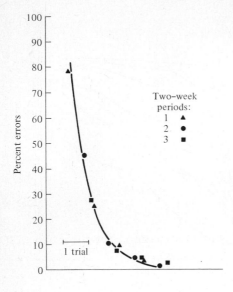

Figure 8.5 Meyer's graph showing that early, middle, and late learning curves in reversal learning set can be put on a single curve: later learning curves lie lower on the curve. (*Meyer, 1951.*)

if, on each problem, the subject either solved it without error or had to learn it by ordinary discrimination learning. In discrimination learning, the probability of solving the problem on a given trial is 0.25; the probability of solving it on a given error, then, is about 0.50. In such data, we find $c = 0.50$—which is to say, relevant and irrelevant cues are about equal, $R = I$.

The trouble with this interpretation is that the monkeys are continuously learning new problems with new stimuli and therefore cannot "already know" a problem after a single trial. The experimenters are careful to ensure that the problems are made up at random from a pool of objects, so that there is nothing common to all the correct objects. In other words, the monkeys appear to be learning a single, overall problem, but there are no relevant cues in the overall problem.

Still, there is one *abstract* characteristic common to all correct objects in a learning-set experiment. The subject can apply the general rule or strategy, "always pick the object that was rewarded last time, and always change object if the choice is not rewarded." More generally, this is a "win, stay—lose, shift" strategy, and it is defined with respect to the objects, not to their locations on the tray.

On trial 2, how will the animal tell which object to pick? He will have to remember which one he picked on the previous trial and then remember whether it had a raisin under it. If it did, he should pick it again; if not, he should reverse and pick the other object. The relevant property of an object is "having been reinforced on the previous trial."

The mechanism or information process by which this "cue" can be used would be something like this: Presented with a pair of objects, the monkey would search its recent memory. As soon as it retrieved one of the objects, it would try to remember whether it had a raisin underneath. If the object had not been picked by the subject, it would very possibly not even have been noticed (stored in long-term memory) and would not be available; the monkey would, then, have to look at the other object and try to produce a long-term memory of it. If this was successful, then the monkey would also have to retrieve information about the raisin, which would constitute an expectancy of food or no food under that object. In either case, this can lead the well-practiced monkey to an appropriate response.

Are these memories in short-term or in long-term memory? Leary (1958) showed that a monkey could develop a learning set while working on as many as nine problems concurrently—having one trial on each of nine problems, then returning for a second try at each problem, etc. This presumably requires long-term memory, for a human subject could hardly hold so much information in short-term memory. However, as might be expected, it is no simple matter to retrieve such information accurately when nine concurrent problems are being learned, and it has been shown that monkeys do better on one problem at a time than on several concurrent problems. (The same is true of human subjects, see Restle & Emmerich, 1966; Chumbley, 1967.)

Actually, monkeys can use short-term memory as well as long-term memory. Riopelle and Churukian (1958) showed that with a very short interval (10 seconds) between trials the animals did about 5 percent better than with a longer interval (60 seconds). With the very short interval between trials, the subject could remember which object was correct using short-term memory. When the animals were tested the next day, it turned out that they remembered problems learned with 60 seconds between trials better than problems learned with only 10 seconds between trials. The reason is not hard to see—when they could use short-term memory, they did; and as a result they sometimes did not put the information about the correct object into long-term memory at all. When tested the next day, they performed poorly because they did not have the information in long-term form.

There is more reason to believe that information about the correct objects is stored in long-term memory. Strong (1959) trained four rhesus monkeys on 72 pairs of objects, and tested them 30, 60, 90, and 210 days later. They were correct approximately 0.90 of the time, and this performance was almost as good as their performance on the day they finished training.

Finally, we can be quite sure of the fact that the raisin found under an object on trial 1 is serving as a cue, rather than having its effect through some sort of reinforcement. Riopelle, Francisco, and Ades (1954) showed that a marble under the correct object (on trial 1) was just as effective as a raisin, for it taught the animal where to expect food on later trials. In fact, the marble was *better* than a raisin, probably because when a monkey finds a raisin, it looks at the raisin and eats it; whereas when it finds a marble, it looks back at the object and tries to remember it.

There is one important difference between the ordinary discrimination-learning set and the reversal-learning set. In a discrimination-learning set, the animal should pick whichever of the two objects has had a raisin under it. In a reversal-learning set, the monkey must pick the object which had the food under it on the just-previous trial, so that it can shift when the experimenter reverses the problem. A reversal-learning set, therefore, requires finer discrimination and places the animal more directly under the control of the experimenter. It requires the animal to remember which object most recently had a raisin under it. In terms of a search of memory, it is no longer enough for the animal to search its memory for previous experience with the object—the monkey must search the most recent trials first, making a memory search that is selective in time. This means that memory for reversal problems over a period like 24 hours might be very difficult. No direct test of this hypothesis has been made as yet.

HIGHER-ORDER COGNITIVE STRUCTURES IN PRIMATES

Up to now in this chapter we have dealt with experiments in which the subject cannot attach his response permanently to any object or any property of an object, except the property that it has had a raisin under it before. In a reversal experiment, learning set, and reversal-learning set, the animal shows that it can respond consistently on the basis of somewhat abstract "cues" that cannot be seen in the animal's environment. However, the methods apparently used by the monkey leave us in doubt as to whether he is really using a higher-order cognitive structure. It would be more convincing if we could show a monkey shifting his response from one object to another consistently, and on the basis of some obvious principle that does not involve the use of rewards.

Oddities

In the experimental literature we can find a whole variety of such problems. One of the simplest to describe is the "oddities" problem. The animal is given three or more objects, all of which are alike except one, and the food is always to be found under the one odd object. This problem is well within the ken of the rhesus monkey and the chimpanzee.

The oddities problem does not require the animal to use his memory at all, except to retain and use the oddity principle. However, in one form of the oddities problem, the animal sees only three particular objects, two the same and the other different, and must choose the odd one. Such a problem, the *one-odd problem* (Levinson, 1958), can be mastered either as a discrimination of a quality in the object or as a true oddity problem. The actual mastery of oddity is relatively slow when the animals can respond to objects.

Levine and Harlow (1959) studied oddities with what they called "one-trial" and "twelve-trial" problems. In the one-trial experiment, the monkey saw a new set of three objects (two the same and one different) on every trial. In the twelve-trial problem, two objects were chosen and then the various oddity problems—AAB, ABB, BBA, and BAA—were made up using those two objects, for a period of twelve trials. At the end of twelve trials, a new pair of objects was selected and the experiment was repeated. Levine and Harlow used monkeys who had already had about 5,000 trials on discriminating objects. Their surprising finding was that monkeys did much *worse* on the twelve-trial problem than on one-trial problems. When the animals were taken off twelve-trial problems and put on one-trial problems, they immediately caught up with the animals that had always been given one-trial problems.

In a learning set, it seems to help the animal if a number of trials with the same pair of objects is given. The animal needs enough trials on a given pair of objects to form the discrimination between them, and then that problem can make a contribution toward forming a learning set. In the oddities problem, the opposite seems to be true. Why? Close analysis of the data reveals that in the twelve-trial oddity problem, the animals kept trying to do discrimination-reversal learning-set problems. That is, they would carefully note which object, A or B, had the raisin. If the display was AAB, and object B had the raisin, then on the next trial they would pick object B. Of course, the display might be ABB, in which case the raisin would not be under B. All right, the monkey would say, then the raisin is under A. It would continue to "track" the raisin for many trials. Unless a monkey happens to hit on the oddity principle, it can stay with this sort of tracking indefinitely. The monkey thinks it is still dealing with a reversal-learning experiment, though it might grumble that the experimenter now reverses the problem so often that it is very difficult to keep up. This tendency to track the object that has had the raisin on the past trial completely conflicts with learning the oddity problem.

Animals given one-trial oddity problems are faced with entirely new objects on each trial. They cannot go back into memory and find one of those objects associated with a raisin, because the objects are new. For this reason, the learning-set hypotheses are simply inapplicable and do not interfere with the monkey's attempt to learn the oddities principle and use it. As soon as the twelve-trial problems are stopped and a monkey is switched to one-trial problems, he finds nothing in memory and can no longer follow the object with the raisin—and this major interfering tendency is removed from consideration. Then the monkey can at once improve its performance.

All this confirms the belief that the discrimination-learning set is, actually, a tendency to use memory to identify which object previously had a raisin under it, and then choose that object. This is not a general improvement in ability to learn—it is just learning an appropriate tactic for solving such problems.

A problem involving the discrimination-learning set makes the subject very dependent upon the experimenter. The experimenter arbitrarily chooses which object will be correct for a given problem, and the subject must follow. In an oddities problem, on the contrary, the subject can always tell from the display which object will be correct. One way of seeing the difference is to imagine yourself a subject in the experiment. In the learning-set experiment, if the reward is not found under the object where you expected it, you must just learn that the problem has been reversed, and on the next trial you dutifully go to the other object. In an oddities problem, if the display is AAB and then there is no reward under object B, you would immediately report to the experimenter that something was wrong with the apparatus. You would be able to tell that an error

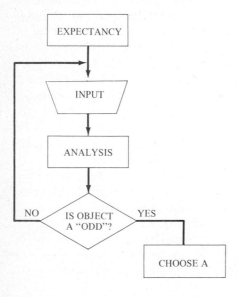

Figure 8.6 Flowchart for an oddities problem.

had been made because the general principle of oddities applies to every appropriate display.

Restle, Andrews, and Rokeach (1964), in an experiment using college students, showed that dogmatic subjects (those with relatively strong dependence on authority) did better than open-minded subjects on an experiment involving a reversal-learning set but that open-minded subjects did better at learning the oddities principle. This result is somewhat peripheral to the research discussed in this chapter, but it shows that the concept of learning sets and oddities as general cognitive processes can lead to predictions about human as well as animal behavior and integrates with the way the whole cognitive structure of the human personality is organized.

In oddities, the cognitive structure is relatively simple, and can be diagrammed as in Figure 8.6. The question in the flowchart as to whether object A is "odd" must be answered by a comparison with, say, the middle object, which in Levine and Harlow's experiment was never available to be chosen and was never odd.[1] If A is different from the object next to it, then it is odd. The subject must learn to respond to this property of being different from the middle object.

The importance of the middle object is shown by an experiment by Levinson (1958). She used the three-position oddity problem; but when a trial began, she used a transparent screen with a slot in the middle between the monkey and the objects. The monkey had to reach through and touch the middle object, and then the screen was raised so that it could reach the other objects and make its oddity choice. This meant that the monkey would definitely look at and pay some attention to the middle object. With this method, she had monkeys performing up to 0.95 correct in 500 trials, whereas Levine and Harlow, who did not use this method, had only about 0.70 correct after 3,000 trials.

It seems that the oddities problem, at least as generally used with monkeys, is well within the capacity of primate subjects but is difficult for incidental reasons. First, since the middle object is never correct, the monkey soon may come to ignore it; and if the animal does not look at the middle object, there is no way it can solve the oddities problem. Second, because oddities is a relatively complicated and advanced task from the point of view of most concepts of animal intelligence, it has been natural to use "sophisticated" animals for the study of oddities. This has actually meant using animals that had done hundreds of discrimination-reversal

---

[1]Levine and Harlow felt that their monkeys would show a "response bias" and would not choose the middle object as readily as the others. To avoid having this predilection complicate the data, they simply did not permit the monkeys to choose the middle object.

problems. These animals have developed the strategy of choosing at random when new objects appear, carefully noticing which of the objects is "correct," paying attention to that correct object, and then choosing it on the next trial. If an object that was correct is chosen and is not rewarded, the animal immediately studies the alternative object and switches to it. This technique conflicts with learning oddities in two ways. First, the animal does not look at the other objects so as to pick out which is odd and therefore really has no occasion to notice the oddities principle. Second, the animal has a behavior-flow system which tells it what to do after every trial, and as long as this behavior flow remains stable, the animal will not enter a search state and put information into memory.

Applications of the Oddities Principle   Why is the oddities problem so important? One reason is that it has been the behavioral basis for a remarkable series of studies of color vision in macacque monkeys by R. L. De Valois and his associates (DeValois, Morgan, Polson, Mead, & Hull, 1974). De Valois' problem was to determine the function of certain way-stations between the retina and the cerebral cortex—in particular, certain cell structures in the lateral geniculate nuclei of the thalamus. By measuring the function of cells at this level, he could determine what information arrives at the cerebral cortex. He was fortunate in finding that many cells in the lateral geniculate nucleus respond to one wavelength of light and not to others, which suggested strongly that they are involved in color vision (wavelength discrimination).

Because it is always possible to find brain functions that do not correspond to the true capacities of the animal, DeValois was not satisfied merely to observe nerve cells—he also wanted to know exactly what color vision these monkeys would display.

In principle, it should not be difficult to determine the color vision of an animal. If you want to know whether it can discriminate red from orange, you merely display the two colors side by side and always reinforce the choice of (say) red. If the colors are switched in position, the animal can solve the problem only by telling red from orange. True? Well, yes and no. To make the discrimination, the animal must be able to discriminate the red patch from the orange one in some way, but his success does not necessarily mean that he is making a color or wavelength discrimination. Perhaps the red patch is a bit darker than the orange one, and the animal is excellent at discriminating brightness. Well, then, you will say, the experimenter must just be careful to have the two colors produced by lights of equal brightness. But although the physical brightness can easily be equalized in the laboratory, lights of different wavelengths differ not only in hue but also in brightness even if produced by the same amount of energy. Yellows and greens appear much brighter than blues produced by the same energy. Therefore, in equalizing brightness, the experimenter will have to ensure that the two lights, red and orange, look equally bright to the animal. We can equalize the brightness for a human; but we must assume that the monkey's visual system may differ from ours, so that what is equal brightness for a human may leave a brightness differential for a monkey.

In experiments to measure the exact color discrimination of monkeys, one method has been to vary not only the positions of the red and orange lights but also their relative brightnesses. Sometimes the red light is brighter, sometimes the orange is brighter. If the monkey can still choose the red one consistently, he has shown a color discrimination that cannot be attributed to brightness. This method is dependable; but it is extremely tedious, and its worst difficulty is that it usually confuses the monkey, because the wide variations of brightness constitute a strong irrelevant cue. It is almost impossible to plot out the discrimination ability of a monkey by having it learn a sequence of discrimination problems—the labor in training and testing the animal on so many difficult problems is prohibitive, and the animal is put into so many difficult conflict situations that it is quite likely to show a neurotic breakdown before the experiment is completed.

DeValois and his students solved this problem by using a special form of the oddities problem. The monkey was put into a light-tight box with five small windows, each of which it could touch, closing a switch so that the response would be recorded. Correct responses were rewarded by a tube of grape juice.

On each trial, four of the five windows would be illuminated by patches of (say) orange hue, but of four different levels of brightness. The fifth window would be illuminated by a patch of red hue, of some fifth level of brightness. The animal was trained consistently to choose the odd hue, and the animals became so adept at this skill that their performance equaled, and even slightly exceeded, that of the human experimental assistants, who tried the same task by putting their heads inside the apparatus and attempted to select the odd hue.

This success means that the animals were performing at a very high level of precision on quite difficult discriminations. Moon and Harlow's monkeys were only about 70 percent correct on easy problems, whereas humans would be 100 percent correct; but DeValois' monkeys were just as good as humans. Why?

We have seen that the two difficulties with the usual three-object oddities problems are (1) that the monkeys did not look at the middle object and therefore could not pick up the oddities principle, and (2) that they continued to perform according to learning-set principles. DeValois, by using five windows instead of only three, made it more important for the animal to look at more than one window. Furthermore, because all five windows were correct equally often, the animals did not learn that the middle object is never correct as Moon and Harlow's animals did. Finally, DeValois' animals had never been trained on discrimination learning and discrimination-learning sets, and therefore they did not have this strong, conflicting behavior flow.

One major difficulty in testing the color discrimination of monkeys, as has been mentioned, is that a wide variation in brightnesses must be introduced, and these brightnesses constitute a strong irrelevant cue. DeValois got around this problem by using five different brightnesses. To an animal trained on the oddities principle, these five brightnesses do not lead to any response at all, since none of the five levels of brightness can be said to be the "odd one." Therefore, DeValois was able to introduce a wide variation in brightness without invoking a strong competing behavior flow.

A final point is that DeValois could test his monkeys on any hues he might want—with four oranges and a red, or with four greens and an aquamarine—and the animal did not have to learn anything new. Throughout the whole experiment the expert monkey merely had to determine which window was the odd color, and choose it, and it could get a slurp of grape juice on almost every trial. This avoided the conflicts, reversals of previous learning, and neurotic symptoms that accompany the usual methods of difficult discrimination learning.

The same general technique can be used for testing the perceptual powers of other animals or children in a variety of situations. Children presumably can learn the oddity principle relatively fast, and it can be used in many applications. Suppose that one is studying a child who cannot read, and it is possible that the difficulty is in mirror-image discrimination. As a simple test, if the child has learned oddities, one can ask him to pick the odd object from the following array:

```
q q q q q
q q q p q
q q q q q
```

or from the following array:

```
b b b b b
b b b b b
b d b b b
```

If the child simply cannot do it, then apparently he fails to discriminate between figures that are alike except for mirror images. If he makes the discrimination, then we know that he can see mirror images; and if he has trouble reading "bill" and "dill," the trouble does not lie in perceptual capabilities.

The usual way of teaching a child to see the difference between two things or pictures is to give them different names, and then teach the names until the child can consistently "tell the difference." This method usually uses the name in the natural language of the child; the result is that the child may have more difficulty in pronouncing and discriminating the names than in seeing the difference. If we merely want the child to see the difference, it is foolish to get all tangled up in a naming problem which is irrelevant to our purposes and may be beyond the capacities of the child. The oddities principle makes it possible to teach such a discrimination without using names at all; the child merely points to the one different object in an array. The difference by which the odd object is to be identified may be anything we want; and the child can quickly find it if he can make the discrimination. Presumably, if the differential cue is not an easy one to use, the child may be quite slow to make his response the first time but will soon learn to look for the differential cue. This last point is conjecture, however, since no experiment has been reported which shows that subjects, human or animal, if they have already mastered the oddities principle, will then improve on oddities problems in a way that can be attributed to "finding the cue," or discriminative learning.

Other Higher-Order Discriminations

Monkeys have been tested on a variety of tasks, variations of the ones described above, and have shown a high level of ability.

The opposite of oddities, in a way, is "matching from sample." In such an experiment the monkey is shown one object, the sample, in the middle, and is allowed to push it aside and get a raisin. Then the same object is shown with two others, one of which is like the sample. Monkeys were taught subtle color discrimination and were taught to ignore the position, size, brightness, and saturation of the objects while matching on hue (Weinstein, 1945). In matching-from-sample problems the animal must look from a sample to test objects, and a slight delay is involved. If the experimenter removes the sample before the matching test objects are shown, he gives what is called a "delayed-matching" test. Monkeys were able to handle a 5 second delay (Mishkin, Prockop, and Rosvold, 1962).

Oddities and matching from sample can be very similar problems. In one form of oddities, three objects are shown, but the middle one is never odd and is never correct. The animal must choose whichever of the two outside objects is unlike the middle one. Suppose that the same stimuli are displayed in the same way, and the middle object is never correct, but the animal must pick whichever of the outside objects is the same as the middle one. This would be a form of matching from sample.

Some of the skills and strategies required by these two tasks are the same. In both, the animal must first register the middle stimulus, then compare the other stimuli with the middle one, and finally choose according to whether the end stimulus is like or different from the middle one. Harlow (1942) required his monkeys to choose the odd one of three objects when the tray was one color, and the object that matched the middle one when the tray was another color. In other words, his monkeys were forced to learn both tasks, oddities and matching, and perform either one depending on the color of the tray. After 1,000 to 2,000 trials, the animals reached a high criterion on this very complex task.

Monkeys can learn to reverse discriminations whenever the color of the tray changes; and they can perform perfectly even with objects that have never been reversed before and with any change of the color of the tray. They can learn to pick the odd color when the tray is one color, and the odd shape when the tray is another color. In fact, given enough trials, monkeys seem to be able to adopt strategies that are quite complicated to explain to a human being. Since the animals succeed on such problems, we know that they have enough brain and intelligence for such tasks. It is true that some of the training regimes are long and hard, and the monkeys must be trained for thousands of trials; but we often do not know why the training takes so long. If you look back in this section, you will notice that some of the most complicated tricks were learned in the 1940s, when the techniques of animal training were not so advanced as they are today. Also, in many cases, techniques that seemed sensible or even necessary were later found to make the tasks difficult, mainly because the monkeys would not pay attention to the necessary stimulus.

Unfortunately, at the time this work was being done, there was little theoretical interest in the outcomes—learning theorists were concerned with rats and reinforcements. As a result, the field of animal intelligence is relatively stagnant at present. In recent years, however, many psychologists have begun to understand some of the strategies used by human and animal subjects in learning experiments. With some understanding of these strategies, and the ability to diagram their inner structure, we have now arrived at a point of determining the specific capacities of the higher primates, and perhaps extending these methods and concepts to the behavior of promising but less understood animals, such as dolphins, whales, elephants, and children in elementary school.

CONCLUSIONS

Learning sets, as Harlow himself has written, are a suitable model for the process of education. Within each problem the animal demonstrates learning and the mastery of a new situation; but during the whole long experiment the subject shows the gradual development of a generalized ability to solve new problems.

One of the first issues in learning theory was the question of specificity: whether an animal learned a specific habit, attaching a response to a stimulus, or whether it would develop a general faculty. The question comes from education—in learning Latin, is a child developing a precise and logical mind, or is he merely memorizing vocabulary and grammatical rules? Does mathematics develop a deductive capacity, or just mathematics? In general, the argument about general faculties was won by the specificists, who said that what an animal learns is the specific solution to the problem at hand.

However, ordinary experience shows us that this position cannot be right—a person does develop skills and abilities that transcend the specific situations in which they were learned. We learn to say sentences we have never heard, to play music we have never listened to, and to draw things we have not seen drawn. Necessarily, teachers teach simple things first before going on to the more complex problems that eventually must be solved. This is done on the assumption that learning one task can prepare the child to learn another, and therefore that what is learned is not perfectly specific.

Experimentalists have searched for this "nonspecific transfer," for ability that develops but is not just part of the task learned. Unfortunately, when you look for nonspecific transfer you first discard everything that is part of the original task, and then you have no idea what there is left to look for. Too often, "nonspecific transfer" has meant some improvement in performance that cannot be explained.

Recent studies of learning sets and higher cognitive processes in the monkey shed new light on this ancient question. Monkeys develop general strategies, like the "win-stay—lose-shift" strategy of a reversal-learning set, or the "match with other objects and choose the odd" that can be used in an oddities problem, almost irrespective of the particular objects presented. These strategies are general, not specific, in the sense that each strategy applies to a whole wide range of stimuli and responses, and is not by any means limited to the particular instances the learner has experienced. However, in another sense, these strategies are quite specific. The animal does not learn the oddities problem unless the stimulus properties are presented and seen, and there is no other way for the animal to solve the problem. The "win-stay—lose-shift" strategy is learned in simple discrimination-learning set but is not acquired merely by learning a single discrimination problem. Furthermore, learning to choose the object that was correct on the *previous* trial requires training with a reversal-learning set.

In other words, even within a rather narrow set of experimental procedures there are several different strategies, and the animal will acquire whatever strategy is demanded of it but will not learn strategies that are unnecessary or wrong. The monkey is not just becoming sophisticated; it is learning particular strategies that solve problems.

In education, therefore, we can expect students to learn those strategies that solve problems. We may intend to develop a large fund of readily accessible information and may use multiple-choice examinations to test our success. In such a situation, students may learn specific techniques for getting high scores on multiple-choice examinations, and these skills may transfer from one course to another, eventually giving rise to the chronic "A" student. It is always a shock to find such a student who, when given a topic for a term paper, is totally at a loss and turns in a dull and pedestrian paper that touches lightly on a hundred topics, as if the student were giving the answers to a series of multiple-choice questions he was never asked. Students in more progressive school systems may be rewarded mainly for having clever and original ideas; and such students may react to every new intellectual situation by trying to find some idea, however insubstantial, that no one else has expressed. Other students will outline, list, and memorize, and are perfectly prepared for routine examinations.

Each such student has reacted to a long period of training by developing a strategy, a system of rules that generate solutions to a wide variety of specific problems. Such skills are, of course, the natural product of education; the educator's main concern is that his students learn not just one but all the necessary and useful skills. At the same time, he wants the student to adopt a strategy of learning and understanding, not a strategy based merely upon techniques of taking tests. Methods of preparing microscopic notes, secreting them upon the body, and reading them unobtrusively will usually help a student get A's in courses with extremely factual examinations; but such skills have little application outside the classroom and therefore are not reasonable educational aims. On the other hand, methods of rapidly scanning a mass of technical material, selecting out the major points, and organizing and summarizing their content, will also help get good grades in college, but also will later be useful in many scientific, technical, and management positions.

How does a teacher ensure that his students learn useful strategies instead of useless tricks? Given a particular training regimen, what strategies will be adopted and what is it about the training history that shapes the strategy adopted? The experiments reported in this chapter give very clear answers to such questions for a few simple situations in the laboratory where monkeys are used. This is a narrow, flimsy, and misplaced platform from which to launch a whole education philosophy, but in many ways it is the best we have. Surely, these basic experiments must be extended to human learners, and many more complex strategies must be studied before we really know how to make the educational experience effective.

Chapter 9

Defensive
Behavior Systems

This chapter deals with the various mechanisms by which an organism protects itself from harm. The subject matter is divided into three parts: first, an account of how behavior can be shaped by the use of electric shock (punishments), mainly in such domestic animals as the rat, pigeon, dog, cat, and monkey; second, various real-life dangers to animals and the complex behavior flows available to deal with these threats; third, human beings and the fuller meaning of the concept of punishment.

BEHAVIOR CONTROL THROUGH ELECTRIC SHOCK

If there is one general symptom of mental disorder, or one orienting theme throughout the theory of clinical psychology, it is fear. A healthy person is motivated by love, desire for accomplishment, or ambition; but a sick person is motivated by fear. A person or animal controlled by fear is more directly under external control than one controlled by rewards. To understand how abnormal behavior works, psychologists have studied the effect of painful punishment on animal behavior. In order to control pain without damaging the animal, electric shock is used. The procedure is arranged so that it is analogous to various "real-life" situations.

Shocking a Specific Response (Punishment)

When a master tries to housebreak a dog, one method is to administer a noxious stimulus when the dog defecates or urinates in the wrong place; one method would be to slap the dog when it messes. In real life, such a punishment is likely to be administered when the offense is *discovered*— that is, long after it has been committed. The dog, consequently, has no obvious way of knowing the cause of the punishment. Most psychologists agree that such delayed and aimless punishment is useless in trying to remove a given response and have sought to describe more effective punishment.

Shock punishment has been administered to animals after three types of responses: (1) responses made spontaneously by the animal in the situation, (2) responses learned for food, and (3) responses learned to avoid shock. The results are different in the three cases.

First, consider a rat placed on a small platform that is raised a few inches above the floor of its enclosure. Placed there, the rat will soon step down. Now suppose that platform and floor are electrified, so that the animal gets an electric shock when it steps down. When the animal is next placed on the platform, it does not step down but remains on the platform for at least several minutes, usually until the experimenter gives up. The specific response of stepping down has been stopped by a single brief shock.

In this experiment, the animal has no particular reason to step down, though without shock it surely will in a short time. The expectancy of shock at the floor is quite sufficient to instigate a behavior flow that keeps the animal from exploring or leaving the platform, at least for a while.

The quickness of learning in this situation has been exploited for various studies of "consolidation" of memory traces. In the basic experiment, the animal is put on the platform, steps off, and receives a mild foot shock. Normally, the animal would surely appear to remember this experience and would stay on the platform in a test trial. However, the situation will change if the animal, after its foot shock, receives a strong electric current through the ears that produces a convulsion—what is called an "electroconvulsive shock" (abbreviated ECS). The ECS corresponds at least roughly to the "shock treatment" used on some mental patients. It knocks the animal temporarily unconscious and presumably scrambles current activity in the brain. If the ECS is given a few seconds after the foot shock, the animal when tested 24 hours later shows no memory of the foot shock and steps right off the platform. Control animals, that receive no foot shock, almost always stay on the platform for the required 10 seconds. If the ECS is delayed for even 2 minutes after the foot shock, its effect is sharply reduced, though some effects of the ECS appear even when it is delayed 2 or 3 hours. This research is discussed by McGaugh (1966). More recent research has shown that even if a memory trace has been disrupted by an ECS, the response can be reinstated by giving the animal a shock in another apparatus. This suggests that the effect of an ECS may be not to disrupt consolidation or destroy the memory trace, but to make it more difficult for the animal to retrieve its memory trace.

Suppose that an important response, like eating or sexual behavior, is shocked. What happens in such a case is that the basic instinctive response is severely inhibited; the animal becomes so nervous that it loses weight, and it may even starve to death rather than eat (Masserman, 1943 and later studies). As we have said in earlier chapters, eating is a complex behavior flow beginning with a specific expectancy of food. If the experimenter associates the appearance of food with painful shock, then a new expectancy is aroused which seems to take precedence over eating, and even though the food is there, the animal does not eat.

Suppose that a rat is trained to press a bar for food, and then receives an electric shock from the bar on a certain trial (Estes and Skinner, 1941). The result is that the response is not eliminated but rather is suppressed for 1/2 hour to 1 hour.

In a typical experiment, the rat is trained to press a bar for food and then on a certain day is put on extinction—i.e., the food is withdrawn. After a couple of hours, the rat will slow down and stop responding, after making about 500 responses. In a typical extinction experiment, the rat responds quite steadily for about 1/2 hour, then begins to slow down and even stop for short periods. By the end of 2 or 3 hours, the animal rarely presses the bar.

If, at the beginning of extinction, the rat receives an electric shock from the bar, it does not respond at all for a few minutes. It then begins to respond slowly and carefully, and at the end of 1/2 hour is far behind the control animals that received no shock. However, the punished animal increases its speed of responding as the effect of the shock wears off; and after about 2 hours it has made almost as many total responses as the control animals. Estes and Skinner concluded that the punishing shock did not "remove" the responses but merely suppressed them; and as the fear wore off, the animal came to emit all the responses it would have emitted without the shock. When this result is generalized to human behavior, it is sometimes interpreted to mean that punishment does not actually eliminate bad behavior but only suppresses and postpones it.

Bar pressing in the rat can be suppressed by a signal associated with shock, in what is called a conditioned-emotional-response (CER) procedure. First, a tone is paired with shock; that is, when the animal is standing around in a box, the tone comes on accompanied by an unpleasant foot shock. Then the shock is disconnected, and the animal is permitted to press a bar for food, which it has learned to do. Then, while the animal is working away, the tone is sounded; it is observed that the rat stops pressing the bar. The response is suppressed even though the shock was not paired with the response. This shows that punishment need not always be administered just as the unwanted response is made—a fear-inspiring stimulus can disrupt the response even if it is not paired with the response. However, notice that the bar press, in these experiments, has become the initiator of eating behavior; and electric shock is strongly incompatible with eating. Therefore, it appears that either shock or a signal for shock has the effect of bringing in a new behavior flow that is incompatible with eating and for that reason disrupts the bar pressing.

Hunt and Brady (1955) trained two groups of thirsty rats to press a bar for water. When the animals were working steadily, a clicking noise was sounded for 3 minutes. The "punishment group" were shocked whenever they pressed the bar during the clicking period. The "CER group" received a quick pair of shocks at the end of the clicking period. Both groups of animals stopped pressing the bar during the clicking noise; but the animals under the CER condition crouched and froze during the clicking noise, while the animals that were punished for bar pressing played with the bar, touching it lightly and then going to the empty water cup. In such "teasing," a rat would sometimes press the bar too far and give itself a shock. When this happened, the rat would show a mild startle response, withdraw from the bar, and in a few seconds return to play with the bar again.

These differences in behavior indicate the importance of apparently minor changes in procedure. The rats that are "punished" never receive a shock except when pressing the bar, and then only when they hear the clicking noise. Since the shock is highly predictable, it does not inhibit other behavior. The rats do not expect shock except when pressing the bar. If they are not pressing the bar, and are therefore safe from shock, they are likely to show the water-drinking behavior flow and initiate the bar-press response. Initiation of this response, however, brings up the expectancy of shock, and the response is stopped. These two behavior flows therefore may tend to alternate, so that the animal keeps "teasing" the bar. The rats under the CER condition, on the other hand, receive the shock no matter what they are doing and therefore are unable to make a specific prediction of a safe situation. These animals, therefore, show no active behavior flow in action during the clicking noise and remain immobile.

Usually, punishment of a response tends to suppress it, but there is one important exception. Suppose that an animal has learned a response, in the first place, to avoid shock, and then we try to abolish the response by punishing it—that is, by giving a shock whenever the response is made. In a general way this is similar to slapping a child for crying or chewing out a soldier for being timid. The animal does not suppress the response but instead usually gives more responses, thereby getting more punishments and then giving still more responses (Solomon, Kamin, & Wynne, 1953).

Establishing a Response (Avoidance)

It is possible to force an animal to make a specific response by giving electric shock if he doesn't. One way to do this is to use the animal's natural tendency to escape from shock. In a "shuttle box" the animal is placed in one compartment of a box, which is separated from a second compartment by a low hurdle. A conditioned stimulus is turned on—for example, a bright light. After 10 seconds, if the animal has not jumped the hurdle to the other side, shock is administered and left on until the animal jumps. Then the animal is put back into the first compartment, and another trial is given. The animal learns to escape the shock quickly, that is, to jump the hurdle the instant the shock starts. In many experiments, a rat or dog will learn to avoid the shock entirely by jumping the hurdle as soon as the light comes on.

In a true shuttle box, there are two compartments. When the animal has jumped from compartment A to compartment B, he waits until the CS light comes on and then must jump back from B to A. In this way, successive trials force the animal to shuttle between the two compartments. It is not at all easy to teach this to animals, and even cats and dogs may often take 200 trials to learn. Learning is much quicker in a one-way shuttle box, where the animal is always started in compartment A and sent to compartment B. In the one-way box, compartment B becomes a "safe" place, and the animal quickly learns to run to it, whereas in the two-way shuttle box there really is no safe place, and many animals merely freeze in place until the shock occurs. Denny (1971) developed a "jump-out" box to take advantage of the fact that when a rat's feet are shocked, it tends to jump up and down. In Denny's apparatus, the rat is placed by hand in a box about the size of a carton you would pack books in. All around the top of the box is a platform to which the rat can jump. On the first trial, the rat is placed in the bottom of the box, the door is closed, and in a few seconds a shock is turned on. Within a few moments, the rat jumps out of the box onto the safe platform above. On the next trial, the animal is placed again in the box and given a few seconds to jump out before the shock occurs. Most animals require only one shock to learn avoidance, and very few require as many as three shocks. Thus, learning avoidance in this apparatus is much faster than in the shuttle box. Denny's explanation is that his apparatus uses a natural response of the animal—jumping away from the shock—and gives the rat a distinctive safe place to go, where it can relax.

A number of experimenters have tried to teach a pigeon to peck a key to avoid shock. A typical procedure would be to illuminate the key for a few seconds. If the pigeon pecks the key in time, the light is turned out and no shock is given. If the pigeon does not peck in time, it receives a painful electric shock. Pigeons simply do not learn this task with direct training, and as of 1973 there was no published report of successful avoidance learning by pigeons involving a keypeck.[1] In the pigeon, pecking is not a defensive response: the pigeon's threatening behavior consists of flapping its wings and hopping about. In avoidance training, it is important to use a response that the animal applies to dangerous situations.

An interesting aspect of avoidance learning is the great difficulty of extinguishing a learned response. Remember that a typical response developed by food reinforcement would drop away when food is discontinued. When a response is learned to avoid shock, the experimenter can disconnect the shock and the animal will continue to avoid, perhaps for hundreds of trials (Solomon & Wynne, 1954; Denny, 1971). In fact, in the jump-out apparatus the animal may respond faster and faster on the average through a long series of "extinction" trials. Now during these trials the animal is not receiving any shocks; therefore, whatever drives the behavior should be getting weaker. An S-R theory should hold that since the stimulus is presented and the response is elicited, and nothing happens thereafter, the response should extinguish. An expectancy theory should hold that the animal again and again perceives the warning stimulus and gets no shock, and therefore should lose its expectancy that shock will follow the stimulus.

Four different explanations have been offered for the difficulty of extinguishing avoidance learning. First, since the animal is avoiding the shock anyway, it has no way of knowing that the shock has been

[1]Personal Communications, James Dinsmoor & Eliot Hearst, January 1974.

disconnected. This change, which the experimenter calls "extinction," is not known to the animal or available through any sensory channel; therefore it cannot change behavior. In ordinary extinction of a response motivated by the expectancy of food, the animal notices immediately that food has been omitted. A second explanation is that although the avoidance response may be motivated by fear or anxiety, the animal actually experiences very little anxiety because it makes the avoidance response so quickly. The only time the animal is in danger and should expect shock is for the brief period when the warning signal has sounded and the avoidance response has not yet been made. When the response is fast, this is a very brief interval, and therefore the animal actually experiences very little fear. The theory, of course, is that the animal will extinguish its fear only by being fearful and then avoiding shock. A third explanation is that the animal is actually going to a safe place, and its reward consists of arriving at that haven. Even during extinction the safe place remains safe, and therefore the response is always rewarded. A fourth hypothesis is that a traumatic event, like a severe shock, produces an irreversible change in the animal; and no amount of extinction training can reverse this change.

DEFENSIVE BEHAVIOR IN NATURAL SITUATIONS

There are two main theories of defensive response. First is the learning theory: that such defenses are, in the main, learned by direct experience. Pain, according to such a theory, is directly perceived and leads to a characteristic pattern of responses. This position was put in clear but rather unfavorable terms by R. C. Bolles:

> Once upon a time there was a little animal who ran around in the forest. One day while he was running around, our hero was suddenly attacked by a predator. He was hurt, and, of course, frightened, but he was lucky and managed to escape from the predator. He was able to get away and safely back to his home. The fable continues: Some time later our furry friend was again running around in the forest, which was his custom, when suddenly he perceived a conditioned stimulus. He heard or saw or smelled some stimulus which on the earlier occasion had preceded the attack by the predator. Now on this occasion our friend became frightened. He immediately took flight as he had on the previous occasion, and quickly got safely back home. So this time our hero had managed to avoid attack (and possibly worse) by responding appropriately to a cue which signaled danger; he did not have to weather another attack. And from that day hence the little animal who ran around in the forest continued to avoid the predator because the precarious-

ness of his situation prevented, somehow, his becoming careless or forgetful.

The moral of this tale, we are told, is that little animals survive in nature because they learn to avoid big dangerous animals. The ability to learn to avoid has such obviously great survival value, we are told, that we should surely expect the higher animals to have evolved this ability. We should also expect animals to be able to learn to avoid in the laboratory, and we should expand our theories of behavior to encompass such learning [1970, p. 32].

The second theory, put forward by Bolles, is that defensive reactions are generally innate and "species-specific" and belong to an animal's repertory of responses. According to this theory, the little mouse runs home when an owl appears "not . . . because it has learned to escape the painful claws of the enemy; it scampers away from anything happening in its environment, and it does so merely because it is a mouse" (1970, p. 33).

Defensive responses may be characteristic of species, but they are also elicited by specific situations. Each animal has several different defenses to use against different threats. Our understanding of defense behavior will be richer if we first investigate the various dangers animals must survive, and then study their resources and methods for survival. Three broad classes of dangers will be studied here: (1) illness, (2) predators, and (3) aggressive members of the same species.

Illness

If a wild rat eats poisoned bait and survives, it will thereafter avoid that bait (Richter, 1953). But how does the rat know that its serious illness was caused by the bait? The poisoner made every effort to make the bait taste good, and it is quite possible that many other things happened on the day the rat was poisoned; yet the rat seems to select out the bait.

Recent research has shown that this ability of the rat is no fluke and does not depend in any way on the nature of the poison. Revusky and Garcia (1970) developed the following technique in an important monograph. A rat is given only limited access to plain water each day for several days or weeks, so that it drinks only at a particular time. On a certain day, the water is flavored with harmless, sweet-tasting saccharin; and later the rat is made sick by some entirely independent means, for example by x-irradiation to produce radiation sickness or by injecting it with poison. Now there is no possible real connection between the sweetened water and animal's sickness, but still the animal shows an aversion for sweetened water and will soon learn to avoid it.

Is this ordinary avoidance learning? One new characteristic of this response to sickness is that the animal can be made sick 1, 2, or 3 hours after drinking the sweet water and will still learn to avoid it. This sort of delay between the CS (sweet water) and the punishment (becoming ill) is far longer than any that will work with ordinary shock avoidance.

Furthermore, the effect is specific to the *taste* of the water. In one experiment (Garcia & Koelling, 1966), the animal drank "noisy, bright water" that is, on a certain trial, when the animal drank its plain water a click sounded and light flashed. Then the animal was made ill. It later showed no aversion to drinking noisy, bright water. Another study showed that the animals had little tendency, when they became sick, to learn that water in a specific place was bad.

Two principles have come out of this research. The first is that animals pay attention to, and remember, unusual events. If a rat is used to getting plain water to drink and then is given saccharin-flavored water, this is a novel stimulus and apparently is well remembered. Then if the animal gets sick, it comes to avoid not the most recent situation it has been in but the most recent unusual or novel situation.

The importance of novelty is shown by a study in which a rat tasted saccharin-flavored water and was not poisoned. Later, the usual procedure of tasting saccharin-flavored water and being poisoned was followed, but the solution was "then quite resistant to association with poisoning" (Rozin & Kalat, 1971).

The second principle is that certain stimuli are relevant to certain later events—the taste of food or water is relevant to sickness, and the animal will single out not just any novel event, but particularly a novel *taste*, to avoid.

These principles are not limited to eating and drinking. In study by Garcia and Koelling (1966), poisoning was not the only kind of punishment used. Half the rats were shocked when they drank, during a punishment session; the other half were poisoned. It was found that when the animal was poisoned after drinking saccharin-flavored water, it thereafter avoided sweet water; but when it was shocked for drinking saccharin-flavored water, it showed no avoidance of sweet water at all. On the other hand, remember that often when a rat had been poisoned, it did not show an aversion for "bright, noisy" water—that is, for drinking water with these external stimuli attached. However, when the rats were shocked in the presence of bright, noisy water, they showed a strong aversion to it, just about the same as the rats poisoned after drinking saccharine-flavored water. In other words, taste is perceived as the "cause" of poisoning; noise and sound are perceived as the "cause" of shock.

These studies show that the rat, at least, has a well developed system for avoiding poisoning. First, it tends to eat the same thing it has always eaten; if it samples a new food, it seems to pay very close attention. If it then gets sick, it develops an aversion for the unusual food.

Defense against Predators

A second danger, at least for wild animals, is the predator. To avoid predators, the prey animal must be able to recognize them in time and then must take some appropriate action that at least reduces its chances of being killed for food.

The problem of recognizing a predator depends, of course, on the particular sense organs of the prey, the stimuli given off by the predator, and the range or distance at which the predator must be detected if the prey is to be provided with protection. For example, if the prey can run faster than the predator, then it need only detect the predator outside striking range; whereas if the prey is relatively slow, it may require a much longer lead to escape.

Are there stimuli that identify predators and are innately known to prey animals? Probably not, for a simple reason. Suppose that built into rabbits was an instinctive response to fear the particular odor of a fox. In the next generation, any genetic variant of foxes with a different odor would have an advantage in catching rabbits, would thrive, and presumably would have more cubs than other foxes. Within relatively few generations, the surviving foxes would be those that did not smell like foxes, and the rabbits who had an instinctive fear of the smell of a fox would have no advantage over rabbits that did not. Predators are selectively bred not to have any identifiable characteristic that prey animals could possibly use to avoid them.

How, then, does a prey animal detect predators? It must watch out for unexpected attacks by camouflaged and undistinguished-looking predators that walk very quietly and stay downwind. The smallest stimulus, then, may be the only cue to imminent danger. But if the prey animal freezes or flees at every turn of a leaf, it will exhaust itself and starve to death. Fortunately, fear responses habituate quite rapidly. If the animal senses some stimulus and initiates its defense system, it may begin by turning all senses in the direction of the new sound to investigate it further. This initiates a behavior flow with an expectancy of more signs of an approaching predator. If there actually is no predator, the behavior flow will simply loop for a while and then be interrupted by some other behavior, like eating. When this happens, that particular stimulus no longer initiates an expectancy of danger, and the animal's defense response becomes habituated to it.

This means that all "familiar" stimuli, which might originally have been feared, are soon ignored by the animal. The animal receives stimulus information but does not initiate an expectancy of danger and therefore can carry out its daily business of living. However, if any unusual stimulus occurs, to which the animal is not already adapted, the fear response will appear at once. Thus, the system of defense against

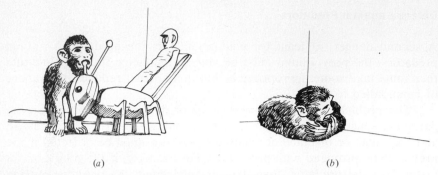

(a)   *(b)*

Figure 9.1   (a) Infant monkey exploring and manipulating a toy. (b)
Infant frozen in terror without the mother surrogate. (*Harlow,
McGaugh, & Thompson, 1971.*)

predation is primarily initiated not by specific stimuli but instead by any
unfamiliar stimulus.

A number of predator-type stimuli do elicit strong fear responses,
however. For example, a looming stimulus produces rapid escape behavior and many young birds fear a bird shaped like a hawk (Tinbergen, 1951).
In addition, animals are often terrified by being put into strange surroundings. A rat placed in a fairly large enclosure will defecate and urinate, will
often panic, and will either rush around looking for a safe place or become
immobilized. When Harlow studied the importance of mother love, his
test of an infant monkey's emotional stability was to put it into a strange
room with strange objects about. In this situation, the infant monkey
would freeze in terror unless its mother or mother-surrogate was present.
If the (familiar) mother was there, the infant monkey would at first cling
to her and then begin making small exploratory excursions, reducing the
surrounding field to familiarity. After a reasonable time, the fear responses would be gone and the baby monkey would play and explore (Harlow,
McGaugh, & Thompson, 1971). Contrasting infant postures are shown in
Figure 9.1.

Defense against predators consists of one of three mutually exclusive
response systems: freezing, fleeing, or fighting. Freezing is a typical
response of animals that hide to avoid predators, and especially of the
young of deer, monkeys, rabbits, and rodents. Predators who hunt by eye
are usually very sensitive to movement in the environment. An animal
that is perfectly still is difficult to see and of course makes no noise; only
its scent can give it away. When an animal is fearful but perceives no
definite immediate threat, it is likely to freeze.

Fleeing involves locating the predator and then heading in the
opposite direction, or at least in a course that will avoid the predator. If

the prey animal is not faster than the predator, it will use various evasive actions, changing direction erratically to avoid capture. However, in most cases the prey is not so much fleeing away from the predator as fleeing toward a safe place—a nest, sanctuary, or refuge. A squirrel fleeing a dog runs to the nearest tree; if it is being chased up a tree by a cat, it will try to find a small entry or a very weak branch. Groundhogs and chipmunks will dive into their burrows; birds take to the air; and fish swim into inaccessible tangles of weeds.

The differences between freezing and fleeing indicate some reasons for the behavior of rats in laboratory situations. Rats can quickly learn avoidance responses if fleeing is involved; but since a very important part of flight is the sanctuary, the experimenter must provide a safe place in order to get rapid and stable learning of an avoidance response. Since shock administered by an experimenter is not accompanied by any way of locating the predator, it is not surprising that rats freeze in the presence of shock, particularly in an apparatus without any safe place.

As a graduate student, I tried to study rat learning in a shuttle box. The danger signal was a light above the rat; when the light came on, the rat was to traverse the hurdle. Instead, all the rats froze. The problem is explained by Hediger (1968): hares, and presumably rats, flee from land predators, but their defense against birds of prey is immobility. The overhead warning light evidently elicited the defense against birds, and the rats froze.

The third defense against a predator is fighting. One might think, at first, that this a rare defense, because an animal would not be prey if it were a formidable fighter. However, not only predators are fierce, and a vegetarian diet does not necessarily result in a peaceful nature, as is illustrated by the rhinocerous and the African buffalo.

Fighting presumably is a last resort for an animal that has been discovered and caught. An example of a battle between two lions and a small buffalo cow, filmed in Africa, was traced by P. Leyhausen (Lorenz & Leyhausen, 1973) and is shown as Figure 9.2.

Defense against Aggression

Many animals maintain home territories, gather and protect mates or herds, or establish hierarchies of leadership. In most anmals, these functions are accomplished by driving away intruders or rivals and by dominating subordinates, and aggressive displays are employed.

There is usually very little difficulty in identifying the stimulus in an aggressive display. Unlike the predator, who would like to be mistaken for a harmless passer-by, the aggressor is trying to dominate his opponent and wants to be believed. Although there is no absolutely fixed pattern of

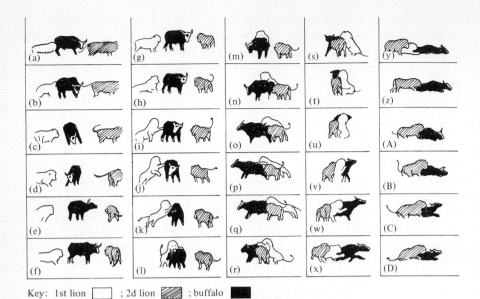

Key: 1st lion ☐ ; 2d lion ▨ ; buffalo ■

Figure 9.2 The two lions have got the buffalo between them and each *in turn* makes an advance toward the buffalo, thus forcing it to keep continually turning round in order to show its next oppressor its horns each time. The last of these maneuvers is shown in (a-g). In (h-j) the first lion jumps at the buffalo from behind and throws its two forepaws over the buffalo's croup (k). The buffalo tries to turn toward it, but the lion holds fast and likewise springs around with its hind-legs (l-o) or is passively swung around by the buffalo, thereby losing contact with the ground with its hind-feet for an instant (p). Having landed again, it fastens its teeth into the buffalo's rump in addition, pulls it backward (q) and at the same time farther around in a circle in the old direction, pressing (r-v) and finally pulling it down (w-x) in the process. The second lion has moved around with them in a narrow circle, but so far without interfering. Only when the first lion has brought the buffalo down at the rear does it approach (y-z), grasps the buffalo in the shoulder with its teeth as it struggles to get up again (A), then, straining backward, pulls it down onto its side (B-D). The second lion lets go of the buffalo's shoulder and takes a bite somewhere behind the head, adjusting its grip twice. It is impossible to discern the exact details, however, partly because of the tall grass and partly because at the vital moment a hyena runs past between the head of the buffalo and the camera. (*Lorantz & Leyhausen, 1973.*)

aggressive behavior, it usually involves a certain complex of postures and gestures. The aggressive animal stares balefully with open eyes, looking fixedly at its opponent. It moves stiffly in a slow, steady advance. It usually makes itself as large as possible, as by puffing out its feathers or standing its hair on end (piloerection). It shows teeth if it has them or displays other weapons prominently. It may make harsh, sudden sounds, such as the growling of a dog or the hissing of a cat. These more steady behaviors may be interrupted by sudden rushes toward the opponent. Many horned animals actually come into contact, butting and driving one another back. The deadlier species may attack, but the attack in many cases is limited, carried only to the point where the other animal either retreats or counterattacks. Postures of cats, showing mixtures of attack and defense, are shown in Figure 9.3.

Obviously, in this kind of aggression between members of the same species, the two animals involved are fairly well matched. For that

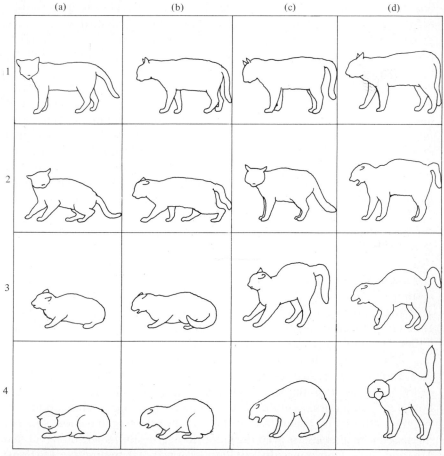

Figure 9.3 Expression of readiness for defense or attack in the cat. 1 (a-d) horizontal: from "neutral" to maximally aggressive; (a) 1-4 vertical: from "neutral" to maximally defensive. The other squares show corresponding superimpositions. No posture has been interpolated, all are drawn from photographs or film. Under suitable conditions every stage may be experimentally elicited in the same animal. (*Lorantz & Leyhausen, 1973.*)

reason, aggression is a common *response* to aggression, and the aggressive behavior of an animal has strong elements of fear and submission.

The two main responses to aggression are (1) cringing and (2) counter-aggression. The cringing response is found in dogs and wolves, and in a well-regulated canine community such a response will terminate the aggression. In many animal communities, such aggression-submission dyads become well established, so that the leaders of the society do not have to threaten other animals but are immediately treated with deference: the submissive animal makes its submissive response before aggression can even begin. Counteraggression often begins with *retreat*, in which the animal backs away from the aggressor. This is quite unlike flight, for the retreating animal does not turn its back, does not take evasive action, and does not primarily seek a safe place. Instead, it faces the enemy, follows its movements, and keeps its attention on the aggressor.

Retreat and fighting are controlled, in many animals, by territory or personal space. When one animal enters the personal space or territory of another, the occupant begins an aggressive display; and in most cases the intruder will at once retreat from the territory. This is a mechanism that keeps members of a species from bunching too closely and thereby running the danger of exhausting their food supply or being easy prey.

The responses of retreating, fighting, or submission may be made by a rat when shocked, particularly if there is some particular object in the environment that can be identified as the source of shock. An example is the bar in a Skinner box, which can be bitten by the rat or pressed in an aggressive display, which in the rat sometimes involves standing erect and using the front paws.

Notice that punishment works very well in removing instinctive responses and will suppress eating and various responses, like bar pressing, that have been connected with the eating behavior flow. Evidently, electric shock instigates defenses of the kind used against either predators or aggressors and thereby takes the animal completely out of its eating behavior system. The particular defense elicited is not easy to predict, because electric shock is not typical of either the threat represented by a predator or that represented by an aggressor: it is a completely unnatural stimulus. Furthermore, the domesticated laboratory rat may, after many generations of laboratory breeding, have lost some of its specific responses to predators and to aggression, since survival and breeding in a laboratory do not depend on intact instinctive systems. Although very precise research has been done, with exact control of the rat's history and environment, and with precise measurement of the electric shock administered, it is possible that these studies are difficult to interpret because the situation is not one of those to which rodents have a regular response, and the animal chosen has a rather amorphous repertoire of responses.

SOCIAL CONTROL

In most human societies, social control is attained mainly by coercion and punishment. Malefactors are forcibly overpowered and arrested by law officers; may be handcuffed and later jailed, losing their freedom of movement and control of their personal property; are treated without respect; and are criticized, scolded, and generally dominated by society. The degree of physical brutality used varies considerably from society to society; particularly, the use of brief, painful punishment may be contrasted with long but physically painless incarceration.

Many psychologists and social scientists decry this use of punishment. They argue, following Skinner and Estes, that punishment merely suppresses a response which will reappear as soon as punishment is terminated. This is a prediction based on sound experimental foundations and supported by the high rate of criminal recidivism—that is, by the fact that most prison inmates, once released, again commit crimes that return them to prison. It is also argued, with some force, that incarceration is a highly unsatisfactory form of punishment, since it is costly and, rather than reforming the prisoner, often constitutes an advanced course in criminal methods. According to the usual psychological theory, criminal behavior must have some cause, and the "cure" of crime must be directed to these underlying causes rather than to the superficial behavior of the criminal.

To a great extent, these criticisms are justified, and the data sketched in this chapter tend to support them. However, we also need some justification for the fact that almost all societies use punishment as a main way of controlling behavior. A reason for this can be found in the discussion of aggression and submission in animals. A criminal is a person who threatens people, who in one sense or another intrudes on their personal space of possessions or welfare. The response to such intrusion is aggressive—that is, a rough and fierce display intended to drive the intruder back and force him to submit. Society, through the strong arm of the policemen, makes a fierce response to the criminal, and by means of display and social attack tries to make the criminal submit. A criminal who submits and is truly "penitent" can be accepted, in a submissive role, within society. That is what the law tries to accomplish; but one major problem of our society is that the law is not successful in enough cases.

Remember that aggression and submission are different from the predator-prey relationship in that aggression and submission occur between members of the same social group or species. The aggressive display and the submissive act both contain an element of the theater, even though the consequences are serious and real. The aggressor acts fierce in order to dominate, and the other may act submissive in order to pacify the aggressor—the behavior of each is aimed at producing an effect in the other, and in that sense both are somewhat like actors on a stage.

The aggressive and dominating force of the law is an effort to gain the upper hand over the criminal. But suppose that the criminal does not feel himself to be a member of the same social group as the policeman; suppose that to the criminal the threat is actually an incursion or attack by an outsider. Then submissive behavior is not natural, and instead the criminal may flee or hide like a prey animal, or he may fight. In other words, such a criminal does not show the submissive behavior required of him for successful social interaction. The law cannot function correctly, because the criminal does not accept the authority of the law. Frustrated, the legal system may either escalate its aggressive behavior or give up the whole effort to obtain submission and merely put the criminal away where he cannot be seen.

It seems certain that a better method of social control, based upon what is known about punishment and reward, will eventually arise. However, although the human is not a typical animal, it is well to realize that individuals and human societies face some of the same problems faced by animals and have some response systems similar to, if more elaborate than, those found in animal societies.

Skinner (1948, 1971) has said that human societies can be based on the principle of positive reinforcement, of rewarding good behavior and extinguishing or punishing bad behavior, and that this method is more efficient and effective than our traditional arrangements. However, Skinner gives no reasonable account of why we have the old ways, except that human society is irrational and that its leaders will not listen to Skinner. These old ways grow out of standard animal responses to intrusion and are predicated on the assumption that both aggressor and victim recognize themselves as parts of the same society and have appropriate responses. In other words, the policeman must believe that he is protecting society and asserting its valid demands; and the criminal must feel himself part of that society and must be willing to accept responsibility as a part of it so that he can be reformed and allowed back into its good graces. That traditional system fails not because it is intrinsically unsound but because society includes subgroups that do not recognize one another, contrasting patterns of social behavior, and a collapsing system of legitimate authority. The first step in reforming criminal law may be to bring criminals back into society to reestablish the social ties between criminals and law-abiding citizens, and thereby to establish some system of accepted and effective authority.

Chapter 10

Recognition

When a stimulus is perceived, it must be recognized and identified before it can be a sure guide to action. Before kicking a dog, one must be sure that it is in fact a dog, not a lion. A man should recognize his wife before kissing her.

Recognition is not a difficult task, in general. People are often amazed, when they think about it, that they can recognize a friend a block away walking in the opposite direction. They might be equally amazed at their ability to recognize letters and words in a book; and if they were Chinese and could recognize 20,000 or more complex characters, they would be even more amazed. In fact, the human mind is a remarkable device for recognizing all sorts of people and things.

In recent years, the psychological study of this process has been given high priority, because computers do not recognize any wide variety of things. To feed information into a computer, the information must be digested by human workers and then reduced to a very specific and artificial form. It may be given to the computer in the form of punched cards, punched paper tape, magnetic tape (usually prepared by a computer in the first place), or certain combinations or patterns of rapid electrical pulses (usually composed by a computer). The practical difficulty is that human subjects use written or spoken words and numbers, whereas the computer cannot use such stimuli at all. Conversely, the form of information used by computers is unintelligible to the human. As a result, humans spend long hours at keypunch machines preparing data for computers, and the output of a computer is often limited by the cost and delay involved in getting needed information into the computer.

This situation presents an obvious problem to the computer engineer: to program the computer to read the same kind of information that people read. For practical business purposes, the most important tasks would be, first, to read handwriting, or at least hand-printed data; and, second, to understand spoken instructions and data.

When an engineer sets out to make a computer do what every normal human can do, he naturally takes at least a long look at the behavior of the human. If his task is merely to produce a "reading machine"—that is to say, to have the computer accomplish the intelligent act of reading by any convenient means—then he is working on what is called "artificial intelligence." If he attempts to have the computer perform this intelligent act in the same way humans do, then he is "simulating" the process—that is, making a computer process that is similar to the human process as well as having the same end product.

It is interesting that computers, despite their great speed and power, have great difficulty reading. This engineering difficulty has raised interest in how humans do the job. Since computers cannot even read single handwritten letters very well, the first problem is pattern recognition.

The reader of this book identifies letters so rapidly and with such precision that he probably cannot, at once, see what the problem could possibly be. But if we think about various computer programs that might do the job, we can see certain theoretical issues that would not otherwise be apparent. This is one of the ways that computer-oriented research has often stimulated cognitive psychology in the past few years—by showing that certain tasks, easy and familiar to the ordinary person, are very difficult to simulate on a computer and therefore are not so obvious and easy as they seem.

There have been three general approaches to pattern analysis in the computer: the "perceptron," the template-matching device, and the feature analyzer.

PERCEPTRONS

A "perceptron" (Rosenblatt, 1958) is basically an S-R device. It has a matrix of sensing cells (roughly corresponding to a bit of the retina) on

Figure 10.1   As the image of the letter A falls on the sensory matrix, a certain pattern of stimulus points are activated. This is the basic form of input to the perceptron.

which an image of a pattern is put. An example would be Figure 10.1, which shows the letter "A" imposed on a sensory matrix, and the resulting pattern of stimulus points. Each of the sense receptors (there are eighty-four in the device shown in Figure 10.1) can be connected or not connected to the response "A." The receptors not stimulated would not be connected with response "A." More generally, the perceptron program is likely to strengthen and weaken connections between points and possible responses.

This is an "adaptive" process in that it begins without any knowledge of what patterns might have what names, or even of what patterns are possible. Repeated trials would build up selective connections between certain points in the matrix and the responses with which they most often are connected.

An obvious objection is that many points in the matrix would be stimulated with many different letters. When such a point is stimulated, the perceptron would have many different possible responses and would not know which to make. This is true; but when a whole pattern (e.g., the letter "Q") is presented, a great many sensors are stimulated, some of which will lead both to "Q" and "R," others to both "Q" and to "C," and the largest number to "Q." Thus if the perceptron can take in the degree to which the given pattern resembles (overlaps with) each of the possible letters and can somehow compute the "strongest" response, it might do quite well.

Perceptrons have been tried; but they are very disappointing. They learn very slowly, and typically have improved only slightly after hundreds of trials through the alphabet. Even when they do finally learn, perceptrons are quite inaccurate, misclassifying a sizeable fraction of the letters of the alphabet (Uhr, 1966). If a perceptron learns while it works, reading clear text, it will gradually develop rather strong biases. For example, "E" and "F" have many elements in common. In addition, since "E" is much more common in English than "F," the perceptron will more often be reinforced for saying "E" than for saying "F" when in doubt, and will therefore eventually develop a pattern of always saying "E" to both "E" and "F." Such a device can hardly be said to read.

The reader should notice that the perceptron is a simple embodiment of S-R theory. The stimulation of its elementary receptors is a stimulus, and the identification of the letter is a response. When the teacher tells the perceptron that what it has just seen is, say, an "F," this acts like a reinforcement, increasing the connection or association between the given stimulus pattern and the response. Thus the general failure of perceptrons can be taken as a point against a simple S-R theory of identification or recognition of letters.

Not only is the perceptron slow to learn and inaccurate; it is also inflexible. When it has learned the alphabet as well as it can, and is then presented with exactly the same alphabet but drawn only half as large, it must begin all over. If the letters are slanted somewhat to the right, or are drawn in thinner or thicker strokes, or otherwise modified, the perceptron sees a new pattern with which it does not know how to deal and must therefore begin anew. A human being can recognize letters through many distortions, and can usually read unusual handwriting or printing fairly well, but the perceptron shows no such abilities. Furthermore, when the figure and ground are reversed, so that a white letter is printed on a black background—a situation with which the human has little difficulty—the perceptron goes completely wrong. In fact, if one printed two copies of the alphabet, one black on white and the other white on black, mixed them up, and offered them to a simple perceptron, it could not improve at all; the two examples of, for example, "A" would be completely opposite and the perceptron could not learn a single response to both of them.

TEMPLATE OR PATTERN THEORIES

Templates (Neisser, 1967) are expectancies or images corresponding to the form the subject is trying to recognize. If the stimulus agrees closely enough with the template, then the identification is made; if there is any serious discrepancy, the identification is rejected and the system tries a new template.

This approach does not tell how the subject may acquire the templates or learn the response to each. The perceptron learns connections between points and the names of letters by simple association. The template theory does not attempt to account for the process of learning.

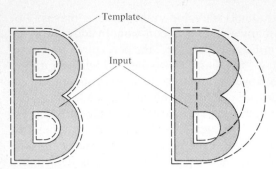

Figure 10.2 The template of "B" fits an input "B" perfectly and does not fit input "D."

The perceptron is unable to identify letters well because there are so many common parts to letters. The block letters B, D, E, F, H, K, L, M, N, P, and R all have a straight vertical bar on the left. The stimulus elements from this bar cannot be consistently associated with any one of the responses. The template theory, on the other hand, deals with complete *patterns,* or *Gestalts,* and therefore need not be bothered by common elements. Figure 10.2 shows how a given pattern of input would be compared with the templates for "B" and "D," and how the common elements do not interfere at all with identification. In the right-hand panel of Figure 10.2, there are discrepancies between the input (B) and the template (D), and these discrepancies would be enough to eliminate identification of the input as "D." The fact that the input fits template D at some points is immaterial, since it does not fit the template everywhere.

Template theory differs from perceptrons in two ways. First, it is not based on a simple, elementary S-R learning model; second, a match requires that the template and input agree in all respects, whereas a perceptron adds up partial matches.

Estes (1969) discusses a pattern-learning theory as the solution to what he called the "overlap problem," namely, the theoretical complications placed on an S-R theory by the fact that people can distinguish precisely between two patterns whose stimulus elements may overlap considerably. It is obvious that college students can learn one response to the nonsense syllable VEK and another response to MEK, even though the two overlap considerably. Similarly, one can identify "B" and "R" differentially despite the overlap of much of the two stimulus figures. Estes' approach was to say that responses are attached not to component elements but to the patterns (templates) themselves. Then, if a new stimulus matches the pattern, it is identified accordingly. Various patterns may be quite different, even though if analyzed they would have many components in common.

A template or pattern theory can help solve some difficulties of a simple associationist theory, but it does have serious difficulties, which stem from its way of handling patterns. Figure 10.3 shows what will happen if the letter "B" is printed with a slant and then compared with a template that is upright. Notice that the input will not fit the template, and identification will not be made. Similarly, the other inputs shown in Figure 10.3 will also be rejected, even though a human reader would recognize them all as examples of the letter "B." The advantage of the template or pattern theory is that it can ignore common elements and require a match of the pattern. However, this means that the template must match not just at some points but at all points. Any irrelevant change of the input from its usual form, then, will lead to a rejection: the input will not agree with the template, and the figure will not be identified.

The reading performance of a human being is quite different from this, for he can recognize a letter through many deviations; through changes in size, shape, and color; and through other distortions. The pattern or template theory is at a loss unless it sees an exact pattern to which it has a response.

The subject might in fact use the pattern or template principle if the pattern shown was identical with some stored template. If shown a new stimulus that did not fit any stored pattern, the subject would be forced to generalize. In this case, he would analyze the pattern into its components and respond to these components like a perceptron, element by element. This model worked reasonably well with certain random dot patterns (Schoeffler, 1954) as templates, but it does not explain the human's ability to make precise identifications of certain distortions of the stimulus pattern.

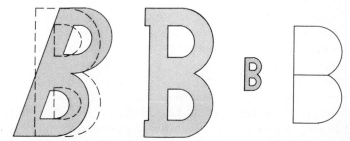

Figure 10.3   The template of "B" does not fit slanted, fat, small, or skinny forms of "B."

CRITICAL FEATURES

A third theory of identification is that an incoming stimulus is first analyzed, not into simple elements, but according to certain properties it may have. An example is "phonemes" in speech. A phoneme is a speech sound that may show some physical variability but has a particular significance in the spoken language—for example, /t/, which signifies both the sound made at the beginning of the word "tin" and that made at the end of the word "bat," even though the two sounds are quite dissimilar (the /t/ in "bat" being essentially silent in normal pronunciation). It is possible to analyze a spoken language into phonemes, which are the various component sounds or sound categories used, but this does not tell us all there is to know about phonemes. For example, consider the phonemes /t/ and /d/; they are alike except that /d/ is voiced and /t/ is not. The same difference exists between /f/ and /v/. In English, being or not being voiced is an important property of phonemes.

A thorough analysis of the important properties of English phonemes has been developed but will not be given here, mainly because of the difficulties of presenting such information in written form. However, E. J. Gibson (1969) has developed a system of distinctive features for what she calls "graphemes," the elements of written language. The graphemes, in this experimental case, are the twenty-six letters of the alphabet printed in capital block letters.

The features were generated mainly from the intuition of the investigator, but with several constraints. (1) The features had to be *critical*, present in some members of the set but not in others, so as to present a contrast. (2) They were defined as *relational* so as to be invariant under changes in brightness, size, and perspective. (3) They should yield a unique pattern for each grapheme. (4) The list should be reasonably economical; at worst, there should certainly be fewer properties than letters. Such a set of distinctive features is shown in Table 10.1. To understand this table, notice that a plus sign (+) is entered in the table if the grapheme has the property in question, and a minus sign (−) otherwise. Consider the letter "A." Is there a straight line? Yes. If so, is there a horizontal line? Yes. Is there a curve? No. Is there an intersection? Yes. And so on.

Notice that the pattern of features is unique for each letter, so that twenty-six letters can all be separately identified on the basis of only twelve features. The features are relational in the sense of being unchanged by changes in brightness and size; but there is some question about perspective transformations, at least in the case of symmetry. The economy is not bad, since only twelve features are used to discriminate

Table 10.1

Features	A	E	F	H	I	L	T	K	M	N	V	W	X	Y	Z	B	C	D	G	J	O	P	R	Q	S	U
Letters of the alphabet (block)																										
Straight																										
Horizontal	+	+	+	+	−	+	+	−	−	−	−	−	−	−	−	+	−	−	−	+	−	−	−	−	−	−
Vertical	−	+	+	+	+	+	+	+	+	+	−	−	−	+	−	+	−	+	−	−	−	+	+	−	−	−
Diagonal /	+	−	−	−	−	−	−	+	+	−	+	+	+	+	+	−	−	−	−	−	−	−	−	−	−	−
Diagonal \	+	−	−	−	−	−	−	+	+	+	+	+	+	+	+	−	−	−	−	−	−	+	+	−	−	−
Curve																										
Closed	−	−	−	−	−	−	−	−	−	−	−	−	−	−	−	+	−	+	−	−	+	+	+	+	−	−
Open vertical	−	−	−	−	−	−	−	−	−	−	−	−	−	−	−	−	−	−	−	+	−	−	−	−	−	+
Open horizontal	−	−	−	−	−	−	−	−	−	−	−	−	−	−	−	−	−	+	−	+	+	−	−	−	+	−
Intersection	+	+	+	+	−	−	+	+	−	−	−	−	+	−	−	+	−	−	−	−	−	+	+	+	−	−
Redundancy																										
Cyclic change	−	+	−	−	−	−	−	+	−	−	+	−	−	−	+	−	−	−	−	−	−	−	−	−	+	−
Symmetry	+	+	−	+	+	−	+	+	+	−	+	+	+	+	+	−	+	+	+	λ	−	+	−	−	−	−	+
Discontinuity																										
Vertical	+	−	+	+	+	−	+	+	+	+	−	−	−	+	−	−	−	−	−	−	−	−	+	+	−	−
Horizontal	−	+	+	−	−	+	+	−	−	−	−	−	−	−	+	−	−	−	−	−	−	−	−	−	−	−

Source: From E. J. Gibson, 1969, p. 88.

among twenty-six letters. However, an information-theory approach would hold that with a perfect system of classification, one could actually discriminate among $2^{12} = 4,096$ different things with twelve distinctive features, and yet only twenty-six are discriminated by this system. No more than six features would be needed by an "optimal" system—that is, a system optimal as regards the quantities used by information engineers. Of course, the block capital letters were not designed by engineers and therefore may not be even nearly optimal.

However, as Gibson herself points out, efficiency is not the most important criterion of a system of distinctive features. Hypothetical features should make some psychological or physiological sense. In defending her system, Gibson points to neurophysiological research with frogs showing the significance of straight-line images on the retina; to work on cats suggesting that the orientation of a line in a receptor field (e.g., horizontal, vertical, or diagonal) is responded to differentially by specific cortical fibers; to research on form discrimination by humans showing that the distinction between "closed" and "open" can be discriminated by even very young children; and to Piaget's statement that intersection is also distinguished at an early age.

One of the most serious problems with this system is that although the features discriminate among letters, they become ineffective when

Table 10.2

	Letters of the alphabet (block) and nonsense figures								
	∀	∃	Ŧ	Ꮒ	⅂	ǂ	Ӿ	Ɯ	ᗡ
Features	**A**	**E**	**F**	**H**	**L**	**T**	**K**	**M**	**D**
Straight									
Horizontal	+	+	+	+	+	+	−	−	−
Vertical	−	+	+	+	+	+	+	+	+
Diagonal ╱	+	−	−	−	−	−	+	+	−
Diagonal ╲	+	−	−	−	−	−	+	+	−
Curve									
Closed	−	−	−	−	−	−	−	−	+
Open vertical	−	−	−	−	−	−	−	−	−
Open horizontal	−	−	−	−	−	−	−	−	−
Intersection	+	+	+	+	−	+	+	−	−
Redundancy									
Cyclic change	−	+	−	−	−	−	−	+	−
Symmetry	+	+	−	+	−	+	+	+	+
Discontinuity									
Vertical	+	−	+	+	+	+	+	+	−
Horizontal	−	+	+	−	+	+	+	−	−

presented with patterns other than letters. Table 10.2 shows a number of stimulus patterns that meet all the conditions of certain graphemes yet are obviously not letters. For example, the upside-down "A" has the same features as "A," the rotated "E" has the same features as "E," and the distorted figure has the same features as "F."

It may be argued with some justice that this system is designed not to handle all possible arrangements of lines but only to discriminate among letters, given that a pattern is known to be a letter. Still, such a system should be sensitive to those properties of a letter by which it is recognized—and it certainly is not difficult to read the somewhat irreverent expression shown in Figure 10.4 in distorted letters.

To remove this limitation of the system of distinctive features, the theory should not only list the features but also say how they are arranged. It is not enough to inventory a letter and say that it has horizontal and vertical lines, intersections, horizontal discontinuities, and a cyclic change, and is symmetrical; the particular arrangement of these parts must also be known in order to tell "E" from "Ǝ".

This criticism is not easy to overcome, although it certainly cannot be construed as a criticism of Gibson's work. In fact, the criticism itself stems from earlier work by Gibson and others on the discrimination of letter-like forms (Gibson, Gibson, Pick, & Osser, 1962).

Precise measurements of the frequency of errors of confusion have been made by Townsend (1971a, b) and provide the material for a test of Gibson's model of distinctive features. Geyer and DeWald (1973) used these data to test the adequacy of Gibson's theory, and a variation of it that they had developed, along with a related set of features given by Laughery (1971). Of these, Geyer's most recent set improves on the earlier sets mainly in that it permits *amounts* of certain features to be taken into account; for example, convex or curved segments are in units of a quarter-circle, so that "J" has only one such segment, "D" has two, "C" has three, and "O" and "Q" have four. Geyer's system also distinguishes between vertical symmetry (A, M, T) and horizontal symmetry (B, D, K). His refinement reduces errors in prediction of the actual data by about 40 percent and therefore is a significant, though still small, improvement.

Lists of features give some account of the properties by which we recognize letters but do not describe the process by which the letter is analyzed. One theory is that the perceptual process goes through the various features in some order, making a series of decisions until it can definitely identify the letter. An example is a computer program by Feigenbaum and Simon called the "elementary perceiving and memorizing machine" (abbreviated EPAM). EPAM is a *serial* processer and uses what is called a discrimination net, a process common in computer thinking but completely compatible with behavior-flow theory.

Part of a possible discrimination net for using Gibson's set of distinctive features is shown in Figure 10.5. In this diagram the system is arbitrarily arranged to test the features in the order in which they appear in Table 10.1. Notice that in this discrimination net, the system first asks if the figure has a straight horizontal line. If the answer is "yes," it takes one branch; if "no," it takes the other. This individual process is itself an elementary behavior flow, in that it involves an expectancy (for a horizontal line somewhere); an input (from the stimulus field); an analysis of the figure to select out any horizontal line irrespective of color, thickness, length, etc.; and a decision process depending on whether or not the analysis matches the expectancy.

If the stimulus does have a horizontal line, then the answer at the first step of the discrimination net is "yes," and the next question asked is whether or not the stimulus has a vertical line. Suppose that the answer is "no." Table 10.1 shows that only three letters have a horizontal but not a vertical line: "A," "G," and "Z." An efficient net might test for a

Figure 10.4 These figures would all be identified as specific letters by Gibson's feature system. Can you read the word?

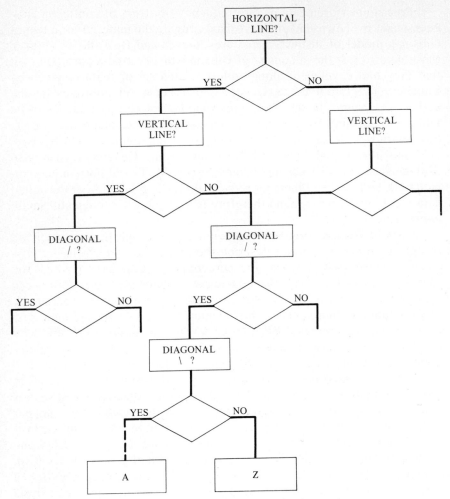

Figure 10.5 Part of a discrimination net to recognize letters by features.

horizontal opening (open H), pick off "G," and then look for an intersection, which would separate "A" (which has one) from "Z" (which does not). It is not known, at this time, whether the system is efficient in that sense or merely goes through all the possible distinctive features in a rigid way for each letter.

This kind of discrimination net, no matter how it is organized in detail, has the characteristic that it can reliably identify or recognize each letter; and since it does so on the basis of a set of features, it can recognize letters that differ in size, thickness of strokes, tilt, etc. Furthermore, because each recognition theoretically requires a whole series of small discriminations using simple information flows, such a theory can predict that some errors will be more probable than others. For example, notice from Table 10.1 that "K," "M," and "H" have many features in common, whereas O and D have quite different features. In one of Townsend's main experiments (1971a) he found that "D" was mistaken for "O" with probability 0.12, one of the highest frequency errors in the whole matrix; "O" was mistaken for "D" with probability 0.05. In contrast, "D" and "O" were mistaken for "K," "M," and "H" only about .01 of the time. The probability that "K," "M," and "H" will be confused with each other varies from 0.01 to 0.10. It appears that under the conditions of the experiment (in which there is a very brief presentation of the letter, as a flash) the subject would more often miss a feature than mistakenly think he had seen what was not there. If the viewer misses the corners in "D," he will mistake the figure for "O." As was mentioned above, "D" was called "O" more often than the converse. "M" was called "H" with probability 0.10 but "H" was called "M" with only probability 0.03, which suggests again that the viewing conditions often kept the subject from seeing fine detail. The interesting fact is that these missing details lead the subject to misidentifications, as if he had made one wrong turn in the sorting tree and then proceeded to "recognize" the wrong letter. The details of such experiments are the basis for modern theories of letter recognition.

The feature-analytic approach to letter recognition has been discussed in detail by Neisser (1967), on the basis of a computer simulation developed by Selfridge and Neisser, called "Pandemonium." According to this model, which envisions a considerable cast of characters in the head, letter recognition is a three-stage process.

First, the incoming information is analyzed into features. These features are then sent ahead to a set of "demons," each representing a particular letter of the alphabet. Each demon waits for any feature that would indicate that its letter has been seen. For example, the demon for "A" is waiting for a set of features including horizontal and diagonal lines, intersection, symmetry, and a vertical discontinuity. This can be determined by looking back at Table 10-1, finding "A" at top, and then reading down the column for plus signs. The set of plus signs tells what features demon "A" is waiting for. Whenever a demon receives a feature matching its list, it begins calling out. (In more neural terms, such an agreement may be said to increase the recognition strength of that letter.) If the demon then receives a second feature, it raises its voice. From Table 10.1 it can be seen that every feature is positive for at least two letters. The vertical curve, positive only for "J" and "U," is the least common feature; symmetry, positive for sixteen of the twenty-six letters, is the most common feature. When a letter is shown—for example, "K,"—then a set of features are sent forward corresponding to the six positive features (plus signs in the table) of the letter "K." Now begins a complex process. The first feature in the list (reading down) is a vertical straight line; when this feature is sent forward, it arouses demons for the letters E, F, H, I, L, T, K, M, N, Y, B, D, P, and R. Each of these demons begins calling out. Suppose that the next feature is the first diagonal straight line. It arouses demons A, K, M, V, W, X, Y, and Z. Those already aroused raise their voices; others begin to call out. As we go down the list of features, more and more demons are aroused, and some begin to call out louder and louder. By the time we get to the bottom of the list of features, it is conceivable that all twenty-six demons are sounding off. Of these, however, the demon for the correct letter, "K," will be loudest. The reasoning is simple enough: *every* feature raises its voice, whereas no other demon will have its voice raised by *every* feature, since no other letter has all the features of "K." Therefore, "K" will have the highest recognition strengths of all the letters, and the system can recognize that the correct letter is "K." The last stage of Pandemonium consists of a single demon, perhaps Beelzebub himself, who listens to the cries of the demons before him and decides who is loudest.

This analysis shows that a general approach using a system of appropriate critical features and complicated measurements and comparisons of recognition strengths can in principle arrive at correct identifications of letters. The Pandemonium model selects a response from among many competing responses on the basis of a small difference in total strength and therefore must be sensitive to random fluctuations of stimulus energy, pressures of rapid information processing, any failure of demons to stop sounding off when one letter is removed and a new letter is considered, and any other disturbance. The human process of identifying letters, especially during rapid reading, is simply not that sensitive.

INFORMATION FLOW—TEMPLATES AND LISTS OF PROPERTIES

Template theory has trouble picking out the important characteristics in a stimulus and tends to respond too much to global, average, or unimportant parts; a property-list theory, on the other hand, selects what is important but has difficulty organizing and integrating the various properties it uses. Therefore, deciding between the two theories is uncomfortable and unsatisfying.

The concept of an information flow provides a solution to this problem of information processing. The expectancy that occupies the first box of a flow is the template; therefore, an information-flow theory will include templates. The expectancies will not be fixed, stored "pictures" of the object, but instead will be subject to modifications based on particular situations. If a printed line is in a certain type, then expectancies will be adjusted to expect letters of that form. If a situation is one that arouses anger, then the expectancy will take account of the angry expression on a face. In this way, the expectancy theory shows a degree of flexibility like that intended, but never actually attained, by early perceptrons.

The information flow also involves an analysis of the input, and this analysis is often highly selective. If we expect a letter "Q," then the input stimulus is subjected to a piecemeal analysis seeking the small tail at the lower right; if we expect a "C," attention will be directed toward a gap. The process of analysis picks out abstract information about the stimulus and matches the result of this analysis against the expectancy. This is the essential part of the "distinctive-feature" analysis intended by Gibson in her analysis of graphemes. A rigid system of properties, able to analyze all possible letters, is less efficient than having a special analysis for each letter, tuned to make particular needed distinctions. A feature model with no overall expectancy or template against which the analyzed stimulus can be matched is rather easily fooled by a figure that shuffles the arrangement of feature-bearing elements. The human eye is not so gullible.

A person reading fluently is in a rapid process of generating the message. As his mind moves along the message, it will come to points of choice and will then have to extract information from the printed page to make the necessary decisions. If the person expects a given word and does not see anything to contradict his expectancy, he will probably pass on. That is, in fluent reading, the individual unitary behavior flow is as shown in Figure 10.6.

As the individual reads, he generates a sequence of expectancies. As long as the input information as analyzed matches the expectancies, the process of generation of expectancies simply continues smoothly along. If at some point the subject sees something that does not agree with his expectancy, he must stop and determine where he went wrong. Notice that this is not exactly the process to be expected if a person merely views one letter, presented for 1/1,000 second, and then tries to tell what it is. In that artificial laboratory situation the individual might make errors, confusing one letter with another, when no such confusions would take place in fluent reading.

If reading of letters is an information flow, then the theoretical problem is not to decide between template-matching and feature-list

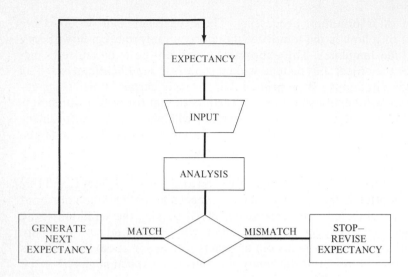

Figure 10.6 Flowchart of continuous reading, that progresses rapidly from letter to letter and word to word unless stopped by a mismatch.

theories. The template corresponds to the expectancy that always initiates a flow, and the feature list corresponds to the output of the stimulus analysis—and we have argued that stimuli are always analyzed. The information-flow theory requires that we recognize both the template-matching and the feature-list properties of the process of reading and recognizing letters. Also, we must realize that the templates are expectancies and therefore will be generated by the subject at the time he is reading, on the basis of what he has read, his "line of thought," contingencies in the English language, and so forth. A template theory must take account of this strong organization of the available templates or expectancies and the very complicated system upon which they are based. Furthermore, there can be no single, fixed feature list, since the features are the output of a stimulus analysis. As we saw when studying the response of a herring gull to its eggs, the mode of analysis depends upon the behavior flow that is in control. Therefore, as expectancies are generated during the process of reading, there will be a concomitant change in how the stimulus input is analyzed. In simpler language, the subject will look for different properties of the input, depending on what letter he expects. A single fixed list of features, such as that taken from Gibson and shown in Table 10-1, is at best an approximation or overall average of the systems of analysis actually used by the subject in recognizing letters.

Chapter 11

Structure of Memory

When we speak of the use of memory, we ordinarily mean a specific kind of memory—namely, memory for information that is fairly old, not something that happened one second ago, for example. We also tend to mean the process of actually retrieving and reperceiving an experience, rather than merely using information that may have come from past experience. We may contrast memory with perception in that memory is of past, not present, events; with imagination, in that memory is of events that actually did happen; and with knowledge and skills, which use past information directly without retrieving the events on which the knowledge is based.

However, in our more abstract definition of memory, the above distinctions can easily be blurred. Perception of an event involves memory of things that have happened for at least a very short time, so that they can be integrated with what is happening just at the present. As a person listens to a sentence, he must remember the first words in order to combine them with later words and make sense of the whole. A person playing tennis must not only see the present location of the ball but must remember where it has been in order to calculate its trajectory and move to strike it properly. In the experimental laboratory, stimuli are often presented so briefly that the subject cannot respond until the stimulus is actually gone. This means that he responds to a memory—that is, to past information rather than a concurrent perception.

In modern memory theory, this sort of very-short-term retention, which is actually part of the perceptual process, is thought of as a variety of memory. Such memories have specific content and organization, decay at specific rates, and are utilized in specific ways. This sensory memory is sometimes referred to as a "sensory buffer," which is analogous to the input buffer of a computer.

Another kind of memory different from what we usually call "memory" is the means by which, for example, a person retains a telephone number from the time he looks it up in the telephone directory until he has completed dialing it. There are many examples of such *short-term memory:* remembering digits while adding a column of numbers or performing long division, storing a group of words before typing them, and remembering the cards just played in a hand of bridge. Such information is often retained for only a few seconds or minutes, in contrast with regular memory. Sometimes short-term retention is attained not by what we would call "memory," but by the simple process of rehearsal—repeating the information to oneself until the task is completed. However, since performance is certainly controlled by past information, we should call this a variety of memory.

What we usually mean by memory is a longer retention of words, sentences, actual events, pictures, etc. It often requires some conscious effort to memorize such information; and every student is aware that retrieval at a later time may be difficult and uncertain. This process is what is now called "long-term memory."

Finally, some information is not so much something that is memorized or remembered as something that constitutes the very structure and substratum of our minds. If I ask you whether a canary is a bird, you will answer "yes." You might very well say that you do not *remember* that a canary is a bird; you *know* it. Merely knowing the definition of the word "canary" is enough to establish that it is a type of bird, and you do not need to remember a specific canary you have seen, or the occasion on which you learned the word, to answer the question. Clearly, your answer to the question depends upon some past experience, however, and in this general sense therefore depends upon memory. Such memory is sometimes called "semantic memory," since it relates mainly to the meanings (semantics) of words rather than to the words themselves—but it seems both more natural and more accurate to refer to this kind of general memory as "knowledge." Readers with philosophic interests may realize that this is a psychological meaning of "knowledge" (the information is deeply embedded in the mental structure of the person), not a philosophical meaning (in the sense that it is surely true, or believed without question). What is knowledge in the psychological sense can certainly be false in the philosophical sense—not only false, but ill-founded. If a person's mental structure is unrealistic, then some of his fundamental structures may be absurd.

In summary, then, the modern abstract theory of memory distinguishes four levels: sensory, short-term, and long-term memory, and knowledge.

The process of remembering and using past information is divided into three phases. First, the information must be entered into the appropriate level of memory. It has become clear that a person does not necessarily remember an exact perception that he had; instead, he modifies the information, extracts from the perception certain information that will be retrieved, and perhaps places this information in a new form for the purposes of memory. This process—preparing information for memory—is called "coding."

Once the information has been coded, it is placed in memory and must then be retained, undisturbed, until needed. This process is called "storage."

Finally, when a question is asked or when action is required, the stored information must gain control of the active mind. It must become conscious, or at least change from the relatively passive or potential state of being stored into a more active state. This process is called "retrieval."

With these concepts, it is possible to construct a table showing the distinctions between the different levels and processes of memory. Table 11.1 shows the four kinds of memory and the three processes and briefly describes each process at each level of memory.

A regular progression can be observed in Table 11.1. As the level of memory becomes deeper (going from the top of the table to the bottom), the information is more completely processed in coding, its storage becomes more permanent and protected from interference, and the process of retrieval becomes more and more complex.

An interpretation of this theory is that as information is taken in by the subject, it is progressively processed (Craik & Lockhart, 1972). If the processing is interrupted at any point, and the subject is asked to remember, then all he can remember is what he has already processed. If the information is only slightly processed, memory is pictorial and brief; if the information is more completely processed, memory becomes more abstract, deals with more and more meaningful aspects of the stimulus,

Table 11.1 Levels and processes of memory

Level	Processes		
	Coding	Storage	Retrieval
Sensory buffer	Sensory; critical features, contours, colors, sizes, pitches and timbre.	Rapid spontaneous decay; often less than 1 second. Subject to interference.	Immediate so long as information exists.
Short-term storage	Material is identified and named; often coded in words; but full meaning is not stored. Literal memory for words.	Retained well with no interference; rapidly forgotten with memory load (10-30 seconds). May be held by rehearsal.	Rapid serial search; one digit retrieved every 35 milliseconds.
Long-term storage	Meaning of word is extracted; specific word or grammar may be lost. Images, mnemonic systems.	With no interference, information is retained indefinitely, for days or weeks. Retrieval becomes difficult.	Systematic retrieval systems help; search of "search sets," using mnemonic systems.
Knowledge	Fitted into general cognitive structure; understood.	Permanent unless cognitive structure changes.	Aroused in normal functioning of thought process.

and is more nearly permanent, and its arousal is more integrated into general cognitive functioning.

SENSORY BUFFER

The original theory of the sensory buffer was that the sense organ itself could store sensory information for a short while, as in an afterimage in the eye, or else that there was some deeper structure in the brain (perhaps in what are called the "sensory-projection areas" of the cortex) in which raw sensory information was stored while being integrated. After enough information was collected in the buffer, it would be organized and sent forward to the short-term memory.

More recent thinking suggests that even the information collected by the senses is coded and analyzed immediately. In vision, there are several levels of such analysis. First, the figure may be segregated from the background. Second, the figure itself may be analyzed into a contour versus an interior. Third, contours or lines may be analyzed as having curves, bends, or gaps; when such information is missing or lost, the eye tends to perceive a straight line. Fourth, the interior of the figure can be analyzed as to color (hue and brightness, often analyzed in relation to the illumination) and such surface properties as texture and contour.

This sort of information, processed at only a very superficial level, cannot be retained for any length of time unless it is processed further. Rapid decay or instability is understandable; for if the information does not become part of some more important structure, it should be replaced by other incoming information that may be more important.

If we think of information flows as a tree structure, sensory information is at the very tip of the branches. The letter "I" is a part of English lexicography, is a capital letter, and is printed black on white: these properties represent three higher levels of the cognitive tree. The letter is tall and thin with small protuberances at top and bottom and with no bends or curves: these properties may be distinctive features for the particular letter of the alphabet. The position of the stimulus, its color, and the properties having to do with figure versus ground are of even lower order, and more sensory. Sensory coding represents a low level of processing. If a quick view of the letter cannot be processed high enough in the tree to become connected with language, then it can be retained only very briefly.

Retrieval

In experiments, it appears that there is no retrieval process from this "sensory buffer." The reason is obvious: the information exists only at the very surface of the cognitive system and either is used immediately to form a larger structure or disappears.

SHORT-TERM STORAGE

When a letter is flashed on a screen, a subject takes a short while to integrate the various properties he has observed and to identify the letter, using the rules described in Chapter 10. At that point, the information no longer is merely visual, in the form of contours and areas, but is integrated into a more comprehensive language system. Similarly, when a word is spoken, the listener analyzes the course of intensities and frequency and interprets it as a phoneme, or speech sound. At that point the sound is part of his language system and is no longer merely auditory.

The process of identifying involves taking various sensory information, already coded into edges and forms, and analyzing it to see if it conforms to linguistic or other more significant cognitive systems. Most of the research on short-term storage uses verbal stimuli, and therefore the process of coding the information is often close to what we would call "naming." However, information can be coded into short-term storage in other forms, depending upon the content of the storage. If movement in nearby grass corresponds to the possible approach of a weasel, this information will be integrated and fitted into a highly significant behavior flow that will send a fieldmouse into defensive behavior. Similarly, a glance at a picture may permit a person to recognize the face of his representative in Congress without enabling him to be sure who the person is or having any idea of his name—still, the interpretation is enough to put the information into short-term memory.

In experimental work, information in short-term storage does not last for a long time. The reason presumably is that the information is integrated into the language system but not into anything more central or permanent. When a person has seen the letter "J," identified it, and perhaps pronounced "jay" to himself, he has not attached the information to any ongoing behavior flow that will continue for a length of time. If the person is an experimental subject and knows that he will be expected to remember what he has seen, then he can keep the linguistic element "jay" active for quite a while, by the simple process of rehearsing it—that is, by saying it over and over to himself. He need not give the letter any deeper meaning (such as by attaching it to a name, thinking of it as a fishhook, etc.) if he is undisturbed and can simply keep the same structure active until questioned. This is about what a person does when he looks up a telephone number in the directory and repeats it to himself over and over until it is dialed.

This process of simple rehearsal—retaining the information flow by exercising it over and over—soon collapses if the information to be retained is increased beyond a small amount. It is generally agreed that the average subject can retain only somewhere between three and nine unrelated items. The difficulty in ascertaining the exact number results from problems in defining "unrelated" items. The three digits in the group 6 4 9 are probably all independent; but the digits in 3 4 5 may make up only one item; and the digits in 5 5 8 may make up two items. The three consonant letters X K M are probably three elements for most subjects, and this is true for many three-consonant (abbreviated CCC) letter groups. But the usual consonant-vowel-consonant nonsense syllable (abbreviated CVC) may be only one item, as in VEL; possibly two, as in YAH; and even three, as in XAJ. These differences might depend upon how pronounceable the syllable is; the first (VEL) is completely pronounceable; in the second, "YA" can be pronounced, but "H" must be introduced some other way; and the third (XAJ) has no dependable pronunciation (either of "XA" or of "AJ") in English. Similarly, common words are probably functional elements (CAT, THE, SEE) and groups of words may become one element (THANK YOU).

When a person is trying to retain information for a short term by rehearsal, he may be thought to construct a special information flow that carries just the information needed. When more information is to be rehearsed, this information flow must be expanded to include the new information. The person might rehearse one element, for example, "A," in the behavior sequence A-A-A-A . . . ; but when a second element, "B," is to be introduced, he must become able to produce the behavior sequence A-B-A-B-A-B- . . . As more and more information is loaded onto it, the rehearsal process becomes larger and larger, with more and more decision points; and as a result the possibility of error increases. In verbal rehearsal, the output of the system is the source of input; if, therefore, the person makes a mistake in rehearsal memory, he disrupts the input and may therefore lose more of his short-term memory.

The fairly rapid decay of information from short-term storage results from the fact that the information is not integrated with any larger meaningful system but is supported by a special information flow that merely rehearses the information. As more and more information is put into this system, or as the rehearsal process is otherwise disrupted, the special information flow may collapse. The person is then unable to regenerate the information, and the item is lost.

Retrieval

When the information is still retained in this relatively superficial form, how is it retrieved? Retrieval consists of regenerating the information from the small information flow within which it is embedded, without any complicated process of search. However, the information is not immediately available, as in the sensory buffer, especially if there is any volume of information in short-term storage.

Remarkable studies by Saul Sternberg, which will be discussed in detail later in this book, indicate that when information is firmly held in short-term storage, it can be retrieved at a very rapid rate. If you count as fast as you can, either aloud or silently, you can probably count to 10 in about 1.0 seconds, a rate of approximately 100 milliseconds per digit. However, when attempting to retrieve digits rapidly from memory, subjects seem to be able to retrieve one digit in about 35 milliseconds— three times as fast as verbal rehearsal. According to Sternberg's results, digits held in memory can be retrieved only one at a time, in serial order. Of course, if the information is integrated into a more complex structure, then other methods of search are possible.

LONG-TERM STORAGE

If a person must remember information for a long time, rehearsal methods are inefficient, because, first, only a very small amount of information can be held in rehearsal at a time, and second, rehearsal interferes with and is disturbed by other mental activities. Therefore, whenever a person must either hold more than a few items of information or hold information for longer than a matter of minutes, the information must be processed more deeply and integrated into more stable information structures.

Instead of simply naming letters, for example, or at most pronouncing a syllable, a person attempting long-term memory will extract the meaning of a word. In fact, if a nonsense syllable is to be learned, people often go to some lengths to find some associated meaning. Uninterpreted sounds are difficult to remember for any length of time; but once a meaning is found, there are many different ways to organize it into a deeper behavior flow. One early study of this sort of memory is by Bartlett (1932), who showed that English college students, when learning American Indian folktales, would paraphrase the story and even supply a plot, since the stories did not follow any familiar Western European plot line. This is an example of how information is assimilated to an existing cognitive structure. In order to get new information into existing information-flow systems, the learner usually begins by interpreting individual items or words according to their usual meaning.

However, some situations in life and many experiments require a person to retain large amounts of information that have no obvious structure. An example would be trying to remember the names of a number of people one has just met. This problem is particularly important for salesmen and politicians. In a settled rural community, family names may have great significance and given names may also follow detectable and meaningful patterns; but in a mobile mass society these patterns are disrupted, and very little organization can be detected in people's names. How, then, is one to remember everyone's name? If there is no real structure to what is to be learned, the learner may use an artificial "mnemonic system." He might, for example, attempt to identify some noticeable characteristic of each person that can be associated, through a flight of fancy, a pun, or a sound association, or in some other way, with his name. If a man named Terry Vincent has a rough, weather-beaten complexion, the first name might be associated with terry cloth, which also has a rough surface, and the family name may be associated with "invinceable." The learner might then construct for this face the image of a Roman warrior. By this system, the name and face are connected with a meaningful structure. Many mnemonic systems advise people to use images; and indeed it has been found experimentally that imagery is an important aid to long-term memory (Bower, 1970a ; Paivio, 1969).

When information is tied into a meaningful system of images and special associations, it becomes part of a larger structure that may be relatively active throughout much of the learner's life. A politician may use his system for remembering names every day; and though he will not use all its detailed devices, he will at least keep the higher-level information flows active. So long as the structure is active, it is usually possible to

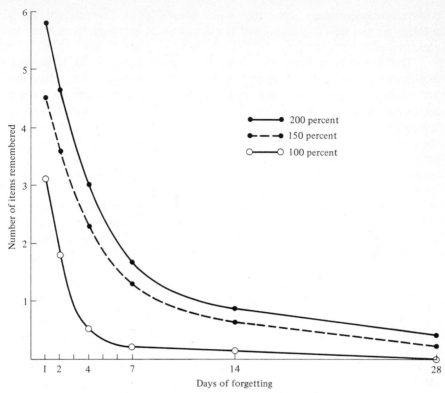

Figure 11.1 Forgetting curves as a function of "overlearning." (*Krueger, 1929.*)

generate a particular name, which can be derived from the general system.

In the laboratory, psychologists have traditionally used nonsense-syllables instead of names, or have made arbitrary connections between words (paired associates) and had college students try to memorize lists of such pairs. If a given list is just barely learned, then something like half of it will be forgotten after 24 hours, and there may be considerable forgetting within 4 hours. If there are a few trials of "overlearning"—that is, a few trials with the list after the subject can first get through it without error—memory is much more stabilized (Krueger, 1929). Suppose that a subject takes eight trials to learn a list well enough to recite it once without error. If he is then given eight more trials to overlearn, this is called "200 percent learning." The results of Krueger's experiment are summarized in Figure 11.1, which shows that many more items are remembered after 200 percent learning than after 100 percent learning. In fact, after 2 days the subjects in the 100-percent-learning condition remembered about 1.8 items; the subjects in the 200-percent-learning condition remembered about that much after 7 days. Overall, the extra training on the first day increased the duration of memory from three to eight times.

The rapid forgetting of meaningless word lists, as in Krueger's experiment, results from several factors: the words do not have any importance to the subjects and therefore are not tied into any very deep cognitive structures; moreover, the whole selection and arrangement of materials, and the method of training, are designed to produce an appropriate rate of forgetting. However, it is interesting to note that forgetting occurs steadily for a period of weeks, indicating that this sort of material is integrated into cognitive structures some of which survive for quite a long time.

Once the subject has first mastered a list and is then given a few more trials on it, his performance continues to improve: that is, he responds more quickly, more confidently, and more precisely. During this period, subjects no doubt edit and improve the cognitive structures holding the material and integrate low-order structures into higher-order patterns. Even if the experiment does not put any such patterns into the stimulus materials, subjects will find subtle patterns or will even invent connections between parts of a task. This process of editing can result in a more stable structure, which remains active and available for a longer time than the simple minimum structures used at the first correct recitation. However, it appears from Figure 11.1 that these more stable products of overlearning rarely survive a month and would no doubt disappear completely after a few years.

Retrieval

It is not a simple matter to retrieve information from long-term storage, at least in laboratory tasks. One reason is that in most experiments the material learned consists of disconnected lists of words or nonsense syllables that do not easily form an overall organization.

If the task involves recall, and the person must dredge up and produce a name, word, or piece of information, then there are several stages in arriving at the response. One is to analyze whatever cues are present to direct the search process—for example, you may see a person's face and try to remember his name. All the cues of the face are available, though if, say, it is a man and he has recently grown a beard, some of these cues may misdirect memory. This process of using external cues is exactly like discrimination learning (Chapter 5) except that the response is not merely a choice but the initiation of a search of memory.

Once the search is started, some relatively high level of the cognitive tree is activated, and the process begins generating lower-order branches (switching to lower-order information flows) to generate a particular name. When a name is generated, this in turn sets up a strong expectancy of a "fit" between the name and all it conjures up, a process of recognition. When such a fit occurs, then the name is firmly remembered. Sometimes no name at all is generated from the part of the tree entered; and sometimes various possibilities are generated but rejected as arousing wrong expectancies—such names are thought of but not recognized.

The speed and certainty of recall, therefore, depend on several factors. The various possible stimuli, to which different names must be given, must be distinctive (Restle, 1964b; Polson, Restle, and Polson, 1965). If two such cues are very similar, errors will result: one name will be given to different stimuli. The size of the search set is important. If the subject has a large number of stimuli to recall, then the search process is slower (Shiffrin, 1970). If the information to be recalled is itself well organized, then it is possible for the generating process to go directly to the information sought. On the other hand, if the information has little internal organization, the process of generating it is more nearly random and is quite slow and uncertain.

SEMANTIC MEMORY AND KNOWLEDGE

The normal human mind is furnished with vast amounts of information. One major kind of information is the language one speaks, both its grammar and what is called "semantic memory"—the ability to remember the meanings of words.

Memory for words is usually tested in the laboratory, but rarely initiated there—experiments on semantic memory use words already known to the subject and merely try to find out the nature of the meaning known to the subject. Therefore, it is not easy to determine how the meaning was coded in the first place; but it is perfectly possible to study the results of that coding.

One well-known experiment uses the "tip of the tongue" phenomenon, which was described by the famous early American psychologist William James:

> Suppose we try to recall a forgotten name. The state of our consciousness is peculiar. There is a gap therein; but no mere gap. It is a gap that is intensely active. A sort of wraith of the name is in it, beckoning us in a given direction, making us at moments tingle with the sense of our closeness and then letting us sink back without the longed-for term. If wrong names are proposed to us, this singularly definite gap acts immediately so as to negate them. They do not fit into its mould. And the gap of one word does not feel like the gap of another, all empty of content as both might seem necessarily to be when described as gaps [1893, p. 51].

The "gap" described by James corresponds to the expectancy in an information flow. The expectancy is perfectly specific as to the input that will match it, but in this case the expectancy itself cannot generate the required response to fit itself. Recall that in an information flow, along with the expectancy there is an analysis of the input information. When a person searches for a word, he may make partial matches between the word recalled and the expectancy of the word desired when a word is generated that partly matches the gap. If we want to know something about the information flows that correspond to rare words in the lexicon, we may study words that almost fit expectancies and see in what ways these words may fit. The result should tell us something about both the gap and the analysis of words that decides whether they fit the gap.

Brown and McNeill (1966) gave college students definitions of rare words (for example, "apse," "nepotism," "cloaca," "ambergris," and "sampan") and asked them to give the words. Some subjects either knew the word or clearly did not know it. But with fifty-six students and forty-nine words, there were 360 instances of the "tip of the tongue" phenomenon: the subject did not know the word at the moment but was searching for it. When this occurred, the subject would be asked to give the number of syllables and the initial letter in the target word, and to list words of similar sound and words of similar meaning.

This study showed that the subjects in the "tip of the tongue" situation would often have the first letter correct (56 percent of the time; which is very good, considering the number of letters in the English alphabet). It was also found that the subjects were quite accurate in guessing how many syllables there were in the target word; see Table 11.2, which shows that 132 of 242 guesses were correct, and even wrong guesses were often close. The subjects also apparently had some information about which syllable of the test word was stressed; and they tended to match letters at the beginning and end of the word more than in the middle. In a number of cases, subjects had the correct suffix when they did not have the word itself.

There may be other features of a word that is on the tip of the tongue—an experiment of this type will yield the information the experimenter looks for. However, we can conclude that when semantic information is coded, the word itself is coded not merely in its specific all-or-none form, but also in terms of more generic features such as length, stress, initial and final letters, and suffixes.

But what is the form of the meaning attached to the word? This also seems to be not only specific but also organized into general and more specific information. When college students are asked to sort various common words (with brief definitions) into piles according to how similar

Table 11.2 The "tip of the tongue" experiment
Frequency with which subjects guessed that words had various numbers of syllables, and the actual number of syllables in target words

Actual number	Guessed number				
	1	2	3	4	5
1	9	7	1	0	0
2	2	55	22	2	1
3	3	19	61	10	1
4	0	2	12	6	2
5	0	0	3	0	1

their meanings are, they spontaneously form hierarchical, taxonomic organizations: for example, two animate things are more likely to be judged similar than an animate and an inanimate thing; two human beings will be judged similar more than a human and an animal; two men will be judged similar more than a woman and a boy (Miller, 1969). When the subject must decide whether or not a word is a member of a given category, the smaller the category, the faster he decides. If he is directed immediately to a small subcategory (e.g., asked to name cities in England) he is faster than if he is given a broader category (e.g., asked to name cities in the world). Furthermore, the various meanings of words are clearly connected in various ways. One concept may be similar or opposite to another, may be a subset of another, or may be related to another in a variety of ways—as the experiencer, owner, object, etc.

Such information in semantic memory is retained for a very long time, apparently on the basis of general linguistic activity. Since a word and its meaning have many properties, it is not necessary to refresh every particular low-frequency word to keep it available: the various properties and higher-level linguistic structures can be maintained, provided that the person reads, converses, and thinks. For this reason, retention of high-level semantic information is very good, despite the fact that many of the words are rarely encountered and never spontaneously used.

Retrieval

Retrieval from semantic memory is a fairly systematic process of search. Given a category, subjects can enter their memory right at the level of that category, for search time does not depend on whether we search a high- or low-level category (Freedman & Loftus, 1971). Once the category is entered, items in the category are generated and compared with the expectancy until the correct one is found. If a category is exhausted and the desired word is not found, then the process must move up to a higher level and generate new categories.

SUMMARY

Modern memory theory distinguishes the three processes of coding, storage, and retrieval of information. There are various levels of memory, including sensory memory, short-term storage, long-term storage, and more meaningful semantic memory and knowledge. This chapter has pointed out the relationships between these types of memories and memory processes and shown that they are all related to one another. The chapters that follow will go into these questions in more detail, giving a more complete picture of what is known about memory and related cognitive processes.

Chapter 12

Sensory and Short-Term Memory

As was noted in Chapter 11, information is processed continuously from the time it first reaches the receptor until it is integrated into the individual's personality or discarded. We may want to study the sensory buffer, but in actuality information goes into it and out of it continuously. When an experimenter tries to study the buffer, he asks the subject certain questions; but the subject's answers may be based on information in short-term memory or even in long-term memory. Since the mind works as an integrated unit, attempts to tease out separate processes are necessarily indirect. Much of the story of recent research on short-term memory has to do with experimental methods employed to get new facts about the mind.

Some brief comments about scientific discoveries may be in order here, so that the student will be prepared to evaluate discussions of new methods. These new methods almost always yield scientific information that was not previously available. A really interesting innovation will be doubted, repeated in other laboratories, and subjected to intensive study and criticism—but all this follows merely because it does seem to yield genuinely new information. A layman may ask why a scientist who brings forth a valued discovery is subjected to such intensive critical scrutiny. Actually, such criticism is itself a form of praise—it is an expression of true interest.

If a new method is intensely and successfully criticized, does this mean that it has been shown not to be valuable? Very rarely. When a new phenomenon has been discovered, the very nature of the situation is that we do not know what it is. Consequently, there is room for disagreement about the nature of the phenomenon and exactly what the research findings signify, and such disagreement will continue until finally one view prevails. Many scientists will put forward alternative ideas and interpretations, each of which must be considered and either accepted, refined, or finally rejected.

In most human pursuits, we tend to say that if we have a good idea which fits our findings, it is good enough; there is no need for troublemakers who invent opposing ideas for no particular reason. In science, however, we are sure of the correctness of a view only to the degree that we can eliminate all alternatives. Ideas can be eliminated only if they are considered. New suggestions serve to test the prevailing ideas; and even if a new suggestion proves to be wrong, it can serve to strengthen the more correct theory.

SENSORY MEMORY

When an image falls on the eye briefly, shown by a tachistoscope[1], the light may actually strike the eye for only 50 milliseconds; but the sensory information persists longer than that in a form available to the brain. Similarly, when a listener hears a melody or a sentence, he can hold parts of the auditory information while he attempts to analyze the whole. Presumably, touch stimulation and the feedback from movements also persist in a similar brief form.

"Sensory memory" refers to information that is not recoded from its original form into a name but remains sensory in nature. Visual sensory memory is called "iconic" storage; auditory sensory memory is called "echoic." An iconic image is not exactly like a visual perception; for example, in the perception of a moving object one must be able to distinguish its present from its past location and therefore must be able to separate a current image from a sensory memory. The point is that

---

[1]A tachistoscope is a laboratory device for presenting a visual field very briefly, usually for only a few milliseconds (thousandths of a second).

information in iconic or echoic memory has not yet been processed into a new, nonsensory form.

Most of the research on iconic memory has dealt with human subjects reading individual letters in a tachistoscope. When a letter is presented, an image in the shape of the letter immediately falls upon the retina of the eye. The light energy so distributed gives rise to the firing of cones in the eye, which in turn may stimulate bipolar and ganglion cells, eventually leading to the transmission of impulses back through the lateral geniculate nuclei of the thalamus to the occipital lobe of the cerebral cortex. This chain takes some time; and it is not mere transmission, for at various stages of the stream of neural impulses various items of information are extracted. At the first stage, the brain is not aware of the letter itself and does not know its name—it merely has information about size, shapes, angles, intersections, etc. This preverbal information, which is not yet sufficient to identify the letter or has not yet been used to identify it, is in iconic storage.

How can one study such short-term sensory memory? Suppose we present a stimulus very briefly to the subject—for, say, 1 millisecond—and then ask him what letter he saw. If the illumination was set high enough, he will tell us correctly. Does this mean that the letter can be identified in 1 millisecond? Not necessarily. Suppose that in the 1 millisecond the information was merely placed in iconic storage; and that then, some fraction of a second later, the information was retrieved and the visual system at its (relative) leisure extracted the distinctive features and identified the letter. Then the subject could take some more time, think of the name of the letter, and initiate the verbal response. We really do not know how long any of these activities would take.

The experimental problem is to measure sensory storage in the face of the fact that information will almost always not merely be processed as sensory memory but also identified and then stored in another form of memory.

Sperling (1960) devised an ingenious approach to this problem. He knew from earlier studies that subjects could not accurately remember as many as nine letters from a single tachistoscopic exposure. His hypothesis was that the nine letters were all registered in the sensory memory but that they could not all be recognized and reported rapidly enough; therefore, they faded from the sensory memory before their names had been determined. He realized that if he presented a rectangular array of letters, as in Figure 12.1, for a brief time—say, 50 milliseconds—he could ask the subject just to report just one row. And a person *can* report three letters with perfect accuracy. But this does not give us a clear

T   D   R

S   R   N

F   Z   R   **Figure 12.1** Typical letter array for
Sperling's experiment.

idea about the sensory memory, because if the subject knows in advance which row he will have to report, he may read just that row and not store the others at all. Sperling hit upon the idea of showing the stimulus and *then* signaling to the subject which row—top, middle, or bottom—he should report. To prevent any interference, he used a tone as his signal. A high-pitched tone indicated that the top row should be reported, a middle tone indicated the middle row, and a low tone indicated the bottom row. If the tone occurred immediately after the visual display, subjects reported the critical row with almost 100 percent accuracy. But if the tone was delayed for even a fraction of a second, the subject would have to hold the whole array of nine letters in sensory memory until the tone told him which row to report, or else he would have to start processing information from the whole array. In Sperling's experiment, if the subject were given no warning signal, he would be able to name only about 4.5 of the 9 letters, which is to say that any given letter had a probability of only 0.50 of being reported. If given the tone right at the end of the 50-millisecond display, subjects were able to give an average of 2.8 of the 3 items required, which is a probability of 0.92 correct. If the tone were delayed 150 milliseconds, only 2.5 of 3 items could be remembered, a proportion of 0.82 correct. With a delay of 500 milliseconds, only 2.1 of 3, or 0.70, of the items could be reported correctly. With a delay of 1,000 milliseconds (1 second) only 1.8 of 3 items, or a proportion of 0.60, could be reported correctly. This last figure is fairly close to the proportion correct when no warning signal is used (0.50), and the experimental results are often interpreted to mean that the sensory storage is lost in about 1 second (see Figure 12.2).

Sperling's original interpretation of this experiment is that the information is stored in purely visual form, almost as an afterimage, and that this purely sensory storage decays rapidly and is nearly gone after about 1 second. If the subject is told which items to report while the image still persists he can read off the image and give the correct responses. If there is too long a delay, the image has faded and the subject cannot read it off.

An interpretation more in accord with the depth-of-processing theory is that the information extracted from the brief visual flash is processed further, finally being named, and that the name is slipped into a rehearsal routine so that the letter can be reported. When all the nine letters are shown, the subject can get only about four or five items into his rehearsal buffer and hold them. If the subject is told which line to report, he can process the letters in that row all the way to the rehearsal buffer and not process the other two rows. Now suppose that the experimenter waits 500 milliseconds before giving the tone that tells the subject which row to report. After 500 milliseconds the subject will have carried processing of several of the letters to completion, and they will be entering the rehearsal buffer. The signal is too late to prevent the process from going through; the subject, therefore, cannot concentrate his processing capacity, and especially his rehearsal list, on just the row signaled. The instructions clearly tell the subject to report only items in the indicated list; if he has processed the wrong items, that is just too bad. Any letter that does not get into the rehearsal list will be lost, since the subject has no other way of remembering it in this sort of structure.

   Massaro (1970) has been able to demonstrate a kind of auditory or "echoic" memory. In his experiment, he first showed that his subjects could accurately discriminate between very short (20-millisecond) presentations of a high tone (870 hertz) and a low tone (770 hertz). These notes correspond roughly to the A above middle C and the G a whole tone below A. Such a discrimination is not very difficult for practiced subjects,

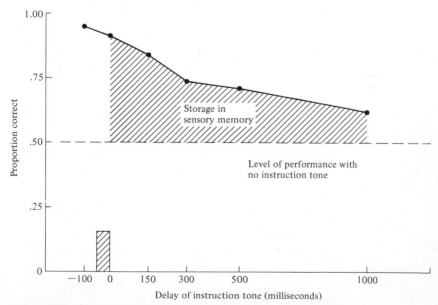

Figure 12.2 Result of Sperling (1960) experiment. A 3×3 letter matrix is displayed, followed by the instruction tone telling *S* which row to report. During delay the information is held in sensory memory.

even when pure tones of very short duration are used. Next, Massaro used these two test tones as "grace notes," playing them for 20 milliseconds and following them with an intermediate tone of 820 hertz. The intermediate tone lasted for 500 milliseconds and was used as a "masking" tone. Now, if the 20-millisecond grace note was immediately followed by the masking tone, subjects were barely able to make any discrimination; they were correct in discriminating between the two grace notes on only 0.60 of the trials. However, if Massaro delayed the masking tone a fraction of a second—for example, for 250 milliseconds—the subjects performed much better, correctly discriminating the grace notes with a probability of 0.90 correct. The average data are shown in Figure 12.3.

This effect can be demonstrated simply on a piano. Play the notes A sharp and A flat, say, on the piano, very staccato, and you find that they can easily be discriminated. Now play each as a grace note to A natural, holding A natural for a longer time than the staccato A sharp and A flat, and you find that the two sounds are very much alike and would be difficult to discriminate. You will feel that the grace note, though it can be heard, is "swallowed up" by the much longer and more impressive main note, or "masking tone."

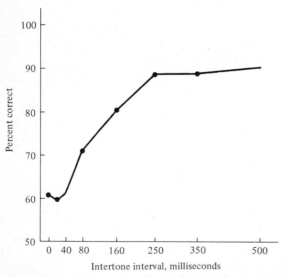

Figure 12.3 Ability to identify the first tone improves as the second tone is delayed. Apparently the second tone disrupts processing of the first.

Does this mean that the effect arises merely because the masking tone, being held longer, dominates the auditory tract and is, in effect, a much stronger stimulus? Massaro (1971) tested this hypothesis by varying the duration of the masking stimulus, sounding it for 50, 100, 200, and 400 milliseconds. A 50-millisecond masking tone is not much longer than the grace note; but the result was that the duration of the masking tone makes no difference. This is not what would be expected if the masking tone had its effect simply because it was a stronger auditory stimulus.

Another possible explanation is that the masking tone, because it is very similar in frequency to the grace notes, takes over the auditory channel. However, Massaro found that if the masking tone was quite different from the test tone, up to almost an octave away, the same effect was still obtained: a steady improvement in discrimination with longer delays of the masking stimulus, most of the advantage accumulating by 250 milliseconds.

Finally, one might adopt an idea found in some visual work, and say that what the person hears is merely the "sum" of the two tones. However, Massaro has handled this possibility nicely in another experiment in which the "masking" tone was played first, followed by the test tone: that is, the main note before the grace note. If the process were one of summation, this procedure would have nearly the same results as the original experiment, so that a delay between the two tones would improve discrimination. In fact, however, when the masking tone came before the test tone it had no effect at all; the subjects could discriminate the test tones about as well as they did without any masking tone at all.

These results, taken all in all, make it difficult to escape Massaro's conclusion that the masking tone interferes with the processing of the test tone and that it takes something of the order of 250 milliseconds to process a brief tone well enough to discriminate between two notes a whole tone apart. If the masking tone enters the system within this 250 milliseconds, it interrupts the processing of the test tone and prevents discrimination.

Recently, Turvey (1973) has studied backward masking in vision and separated out two processes which had confused the literature. The basic experiment is to show a target such as the letter "T" and follow it closely in time with a masking stimulus—under a variety of conditions, this masking stimulus makes the target disappear. Since the mask occurs after the target, the procedure is called "backward masking."

One kind of backward masking is a simple result of the slowness of the eye: the eye "integrates" energy from both the target and the mask and tries to analyze the resulting blurred signal. This kind of masking is more or less the same forward or backward, appears to occur right at the retina (for one thing, if the target is shown to one eye and the mask to the other, there is little masking), depends on the two stimuli occurring closely in time, and is very much affected by the amount of energy in the target and the mask.

The second kind of backward masking is best seen by using, as a mask, a pattern of stimulation that contains many characteristics of the target letter. For example, the mask can consist of a collection of short bars about the width and length of those found in block letters. Such a mask stimulus is analyzed by the visual system much as a letter would be and sends forward a collection of distinctive features of the type used to identify letters. It does not depend much on the energy in the two stimuli and is as effective when the target is shown to one eye and the mask to the other as when target and mask fall on the same retinal surface. The amount of masking depends upon the time from the onset of the target to onset of the mask. When target and mask are about equally bright, the mask wipes out the target if it begins within about 130 milliseconds after the target has begun. Actually, different subjects in Turvey's experiment produced quite different values of this figure—from about 65 to 200 milliseconds. This suggests to Turvey that the results reflect masking and interference quite high in the information process, at a point where individual skill, strategy, and experience can have a large effect on how well the subject can respond.

SHORT-TERM MEMORY

A typical example of short-term storage is remembering a telephone number from the time you read it in the telephone directory until you have finished dialing it. To maintain such a memory, a person often rehearses or repeats the message over and over to himself. He may learn it so well that he can remember it later (putting it in what is called long-term storage), but he may also just hold the information briefly, for a few seconds or minutes.

One of the first measurements of short-term memory was by Peterson and Peterson (1959). They would show the subject a nonsense syllable and then give him a three-digit number; the subject would have to count backward from the number by threes—274, 271, 268, 265, 262, etc.—at a rate of one count per second, and then try to remember the syllable. The mental arithmetic is not at all easy at a pace of one count per second, and therefore the subjects were unable to rehearse the nonsense syllable. They also quickly forgot it; the nonsense syllables showed a rapid forgetting curve, as Figure 12.4 indicates. Notice that the forgetting curve is slower than that in sensory memory; forgetting is more or less

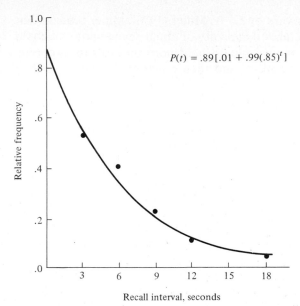

$$P(t) = .89[.01 + .99(.85)^t]$$

Figure 12.4 Proportion of correct recall as a function of recall interval. (*Peterson & Peterson, 1959*.)

complete by 15 to 18 seconds, and the half-life is somewhat over 4 seconds.[2]

At first it appeared that the prevention of rehearsal drove items out of short-term memory. However, in a dramatic demonstration, J. Reitman (1971) showed subjects a single nonsense syllable and then had them spend a period of time listening intensely for a weak tone in noise: although the subjects reported that they did not rehearse the syllable during the listening period, they did not forget the syllable. This result has been repeated (Shiffrin, 1973).

At this writing, we do not know exactly what activity causes rapid loss from short-term memory. It seems that counting backwards by threes puts a heavy load on short-term memory, since the subject must remember one number, perform a subtraction (which may involve "borrowing"), and then reconstitute the result. Reitman's listening task, on the other hand, though it prevents rehearsal, does not engage the subject's memory. Such an interpretation suggests that a person has a certain fixed ration of memory to use, and if he uses it for one purpose it will be unavailable for other purposes.

---

[2]A "half-life" is the time it takes the curve to drop halfway to zero, or to whatever its asymptotic value may be. It is a good characteristic way of describing a simple forgetting curve like that shown in Figure 12.4.

This idea was put forward by G. A. Miller (1956). Miller thought that short-term memory had a limited capacity of about seven units and could accommodate no more; if people actually hold more, they do so by grouping stimuli into meaningful "chunks," and then remembering no more than seven chunks.

As information enters the mind, it often is not integrated, and it must be retained during the process of analysis. Miller's idea is that some small fixed number, about seven, can be held before being organized. If this idea is correct, then information is lost from short-term memory when it is pushed out. Short-term storage has a limited and fixed capacity. New items can be remembered perfectly until the capacity is filled; but after that, when the next item is brought into short-term storage, something has to go. According to a mathematical and experimental analysis by Atkinson and Shiffrin (1968), when the storage is full and a new item is introduced, any item in the storage may be forgotten. One might suppose that the oldest item in short-term storage would always be the first to be lost, or at least that older items would be more likely to be lost than newer ones. The data indicate, however, that any item in storage can be lost and that the victim is chosen essentially at random.

How does the information in short-term memory differ from information in the sensory buffer? Items in short-term storage are coded as the names of letters, or words as pronounced. One piece of evidence is given by Conrad (1964), who showed that when a subject is trying to remember letters shown on a screen in short-term memory, he makes confusions that reflect not similarity of appearance but similarity of the sound. That is, "E" and "F" look alike but are not confused in memory; "S" and "F," which sound alike, are more frequently confused. This clearly suggests that the picture of the letter has been translated into its name, and that errors arise when subjects confuse such names—even though the subject does not read any of the letters aloud.

The distinction between memory of visual features and memory of names is nicely shown by the experiments of Posner, Boies, Eichelman, and Taylor (1969). In these, the subject is shown two letters and must say whether they are the same or different. The instructions make it clear that "A" and "a" would be considered the same. Now, in a series of trials in which various pairs of letters are shown, some the same and some different, some capital and some lowercase, consider only pairs of the form "A a" and "a A." For the subject to see that the letters in each of these pairs are the same, he must identify the letter in each case and compare his identifications. To see that the letters in the pair "a a" or the pair "A A" are the same, the subject can use the visual appearance of the stimuli without identifying them. Matching on "physical identity" is much faster than matching that requires a process of naming; the difference in reaction time is approximately 90 milliseconds.

What happens if one letter is shown briefly, then there is a pause, and then the other letter is shown? If one letter follows the other immediately, then the "A A" match is 80 milliseconds faster than the "A a" match. At 0.5 seconds between stimuli, the difference in reaction time is only about 55 milliseconds. Somewhere between 1.5 and 2.0 seconds, the advantage of using physical identity is gone. This suggests that the shape of the letter can be retained for approximately 1.5 or 2.0 seconds.

Posner and his associates were able to go further than this and show that a subject not only could hold a visual image for a couple of seconds but could in fact generate an image of a letter after just hearing its name; and that image is just as useful a template for matching as the memory of a visual presentation of the same letter would be.

The way they showed this was simple but telling. The subject would first receive one letter, which might be either shown visually ("a" or "A") or spoken. Then another letter would be shown, and the subject had to say whether the second letter was the same as or different from the first. We already know that if the first letter is physically the same as the second letter capital, matching will be about 90 milliseconds slower. Now suppose that during a whole session the subject knows that the second letter will always be a capital, though he does not know what letter it will be. If the experimenter *says* the letter, the subject is able to imagine capital "A," and when capital A is shown as the second letter, the response comes quickly—just as quickly as if he had been *shown* capital "A."

These results show that there exists a visual short-term memory extending somewhat beyond the very short, fraction-of-a-second sensory memory. This sort of memory can be retrieved from long-term memory and used even without a visual stimulus. Still, its features are not verbal but maintain some of the *visual* characteristics of a capital or lowercase letter, for example.

In most of the experiments discussed so far, the subject has been shown a letter and asked questions that can most easily be answered from the name of the letter. It certainly is easier to maintain the verbal *name* of a letter by repeating it over and over to yourself than to maintain an image of the distinctive features of the *picture* of the letter. Therefore, in most short-term memory experiments the subjects have gone from the visual image to its name and retained the name in short-term memory. But Posner, Boies, Eichelman, and Taylor (1969) seem to have shown that the information pathway does not necessarily proceed from visual to verbal. In conclusion, it must be said that we do not know that information in short-term memory is coded differently from information in sensory memory; the idea that information is recoded from visual to verbal in order to enter short-term storage, though often true, is not always true—there seems to be such a thing as visual short-term memory.

Perhaps the difference between sensory memory and short-term memory is that information in short-term memory can be generated and regenerated by the subject; it is in a form that can be rehearsed. Ordinarily, we think of rehearsal as "saying it over to yourself," implying that the information is verbal. However, it is apparently possible to rehearse visual images, nonverbal sounds, tactile sensations, and motions. When information is coded in a form that can be regenerated, then it is in short-term memory. Neisser (1967), using earlier data, called this short-term memory "active verbal memory," and said that "it is characteristic of active verbal memory that information is recoded rather than simply echoed" (page 223). The nature of the recoding is not perfectly known, but apparently the subject finds some cognitive structure from which he can generate the items.

One way to regenerate material is to repeat it over and over, but this is not the only way. The subject may detect more general patterns in the incoming information and may use these patterns to regenerate the sequence. If a subject must remember the digits 1 4 9 1 6 2 5, he might simply repeat the string over and over to himself; but if he notices that it can be grouped into 1   4   9   16   25, and that these are the squares of the first five integers, he then has a new recoding, a new system by which the numbers can be generated. Given such a system, the subject does not need to rehearse continuously. To make a subject forget information remembered by such a system, it not sufficient to interrupt his process of rehearsal; it is also necessary to confuse or disrupt his system. This is often accomplished by loading on a number of new items of the same type but generated randomly by the experimenter. Such a string will give the subject difficulties. Since the items are of the type he has been using, he will probably apply his generating system to the new items; but since they are generated at random, it is probable that the subject's system will eventually fail. This produces forgetting by "interference."

If information in short-term memory is there because it can be generated by a system, then the information is forgotten whenever that system is prevented from functioning. The steps necessary to produce forgetting from short-term memory cannot be laid out in advance by a general theory until we know just what generating scheme the subject is using to remember.

Retrieval from short-term memory is really misnamed; the subject has the information by virtue of being able to generate it, and "retrieval" is simply a matter of carrying out the process of generation. For this

reason, it often appears that such retrieval is very simple and unconscious. But does it take time? The outstanding set of studies on this
question are by Sternberg (1970). In a typical experiment, Sternberg's
subject has memorized a list of digits, say, 2, 5, 6, 8. He is given a signal,
then is shown a digit, and as rapidly as possible must say "yes" (it is in the
memorized set), or "no" (it is not). Since the subject is completely ready,
because he has received the signal, there is no problem about having the
memorized set activated in short-term memory. He does not actually have
to "retrieve" in the full sense of recalling items in the set; he merely
performs a matching operation of some type, like recognition.

   Sternberg first asked: Does the subject test the whole memory set at
once, comparing the test stimulus with all items simultaneously, or are
items retrieved from short-term memory one at a time and compared
individually with the test digit? If the items are tested simultaneously,
then it should make almost no difference how many there are; whereas if
they are retrieved serially, reaction time should increase linearly with the
number of items in the memory set. Reaction time may depend on many
factors—time to read the test item, time to search short-term memory,
time to make the comparison or match, and time to respond. Most of
these components will be the same regardless of how many items are in
memory. However, if short-term memory is searched one item at a time,
serially, then the time to search short-term memory will be proportional to
the number of items in that memory. Total mean reaction time *(RT)* will
then consist of a part, *K*, that does *not* depend on the size of the set, plus a
part that is proportional to the size of the set, *s*. Let *h* be the average time
it takes to search a given item, and

$$RT = K + h \cdot s$$

This is a linear equation, and if the mean reaction time *RT* is plotted as a
function of set size *s*, the data should fit a straight line with slope *h* (time
to retrieve a single item) and intercept *K*, where *K* includes many factors.
The data from two of Sternberg's experiments are shown in Figure 12.5;
in each case the best-fitting straight line has been drawn. In these
experiments, the reaction time does increase linearly with the size of the
set, as would be expected if the retrieval were serial; and *h* is about 38
milliseconds—that is, it takes about 38 milliseconds to retrieve each digit
from short-term memory.

   If retrieval is serial, one possibility is that the search of memory is
self-terminating, stopping when the wanted item is found. The subject is
thinking of one of the digits in his set, and the test digit is shown. He
compares his retrieved memory with the test digit and decides if they are
alike. If they are, he says "yes"; otherwise, he retrieves the next digit in

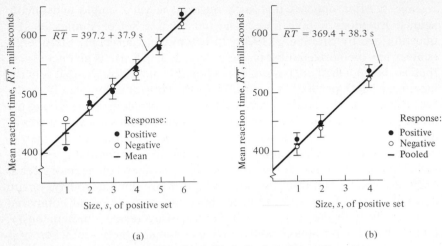

Figure 12.5 Mean time to decide if a digit is in the "positive set" as a function of the size of the positive set. (*Sternberg, 1970.*)

his memory and makes the same test. This process of retrieving a digit and testing it is repeated until the subject either finds the matching digit in memory and matches it with the test digit or discovers that he has exhausted his memory bank and has not found the test digit—in which case he says "no." This appears to be a plausible procedure for serial search of short-term memory, but Sternberg has shown that it is wrong.

Suppose that a subject has four items in memory and searches until he either finds a match or exhausts the set. If the test item is in his set, then he may find it first, second, third, or fourth; and each of these possibilities takes a different number of retrieve-and-test operations. The average number of operations is 2.5. If the test item is not in the search set, it takes four operations to determine this. This would suggest that "no" answers would be slower than "yes" answers; but the overall time is not a good fact on which to base the conclusion, because the process of deciding to say "no" may be different from the process of deciding to say "yes." However, consider what would happen if the memory contained only two items. If there is a match, this can be found with one or two searches, an average of 1.5; whereas if there is no match, it takes two searches to discover this. As the size of the memory set is increased by one, the number of searches increases by 1.0 in the case of "no" responses but by an average of only 0.5 in the case of "yes" responses. Not only will reaction time increase linearly with the number of items in the search set, but the slope of that straight line will be twice as steep for "no" responses as for "yes" responses.

The results of Sternberg's experiments as shown in Figure 12.5 are clear: the two functions, reaction time as a function of number of items in memory for "yes" responses and for "no" responses, are parallel. When an extra digit is added to the search set, it will increase the time to make a "yes" response by about 38 milliseconds, and it will also increase the time to make a "no" response by 38 milliseconds. How can this be? The fact that $\overline{RT}$ increases linearly with the number of digits in the search set seemed to require a serial search, but the fact that an added digit has the same effect on "yes" and "no" responses seems to disprove this.

Sternberg notes that the reaction time increases by only about 35 milliseconds per item, which corresponds to a retrieval rate of about thirty digits per second. If you try to count as fast as you can (either aloud or silently), you will find that you cannot generate digits, even in this simple way, faster than about ten per second, or 100 milliseconds per digit. How, then, can short-term search be so fast?

The subject may generate all the items in the search set and compare each with the test digit, but he does not at that time decide or notice whether he has a match or a mismatch—he just hurries on to the next item in the search set. When a match is made, though the subject does not stop to notice it, his mind "flags" the match. Then, when he has reached the end of the search set, the subject goes back and checks for a flag to see if he found a match or not, and responds accordingly. The length of the search set merely affects how long it takes to get through the set, and in this process (called "exhaustive serial search" of memory), a "yes" trial takes just as long as a "no" trial.

This may seem rather peculiar, but Sternberg has a plausible argument. He holds that the process of deciding whether a match has been made may be slower than bringing information out of short-term memory and comparing it with a test digit. Therefore, the subject would be foolish to make this decision with every digit—it is faster to search through a few extra digits, taking only a few extra milliseconds, and reduce the number of difficult and time-consuming decisions. Even if deciding itself is not very time-consuming, Sternberg goes on, we may consider that this experiment requires two different processes: first, retrieving the memory and comparing it with the test digit; second, deciding whether a match has been obtained. If the subject went through the list comparing and deciding about each item, he would have to alternate between the two processes. Alternating or switching between processes may itself be quite time-consuming and effortful. If so, it will help the subject to segregate his two kinds of tasks, doing one and then the other. This itself would be enough reason for the subject to make all the comparisons first and then return and make his decision.

This theory of an exhaustive serial search explains the figure of only 38 milliseconds per item in memory, because the process of comparing is here separated from the process of deciding, which is relatively time-consuming. Second, this theory explains why the increase in reaction time per item in memory is the same for "yes" responses as for "no" responses: The subject goes through the entire list in memory in either case, continuing to the end of the list even if he makes a match early in the list, and then finally making his decision.

This process of searching short-term memory is justified by Sternberg on the basis that it is very efficient and saves several milliseconds. The subjects working in Sternberg's experiments were highly practiced and motivated to answer the simple questions as fast as possible. Therefore, it is quite possible that they gradually adopted a special strategy or technique for searching short-term memory; and we may either take Sternberg's findings as an analysis of how information is retrieved from short-term memory in general, or think of them as the result of a special task and situation.

Recent work has shown that a change in the task may bring about a very different search process. DeRosa and Morin (1970) used a procedure formally like Sternberg's; but instead of always giving the subject a "random" and scattered set of digits to recognize, they also gave sets that are adjacent, like (2,3,4,5). This subset was searched faster by about 25 milliseconds than a set scattered out like Sternberg's; what is more to the point, the numbers 3 and 4 were found more rapidly than the numbers 2 and 5. Furthermore, the negative response given to the number 6 was relatively slow, whereas response to the number 7 was faster, and the number 9 was very quickly said not to be in the set. Evidently, when it will help them, the subjects can search these small sets of numbers using the meaning (magnitude) of the digits. The serial search found by Sternberg is, perhaps, a response to the task of identifying one of a scattered and "random" set of digits in memory.

Another set of experiments, by Theios (1973), has shown that if some digits are tested for more often than others in a long series of trials, the subjects become faster at identifying the digits that are asked for more frequently. It appears at first glance that this is totally at odds with Sternberg's search process; and Theios suggests an entirely different, parallel search. Recent work by Shiffrin and Schneider (1973) suggests that in such a situation the subject may expect a single one of the digits and wait for it. If that digit is tested, he says "yes" very rapidly; if not, he then goes through a serial search approximately as Sternberg said.

These results indicate that college students can find and adopt an efficient strategy for almost any task they may be given. The exact workings of the resulting cognitive process are difficult to determine and may be of considerable interest. However, when dealing with cognitive processes, one should never forget their flexibility and ability to adapt to the situation before them. Every process, however "basic" it may appear, is always under the control of more general cognitive systems. By the time a subject becomes highly practiced and expert at a given experiment, he may have adopted a strategy of cognition, interesting in itself but shared by no other living being.

Chapter 13

Long-Term Memory and Memorizing

A memory stores information for a substantial time so it can be used later. Although we are interested in human memory, it can be helpful to think briefly about simple computer memories. One kind of information which a computer must store in memory is called "data." The basic idea of storing data is to lay out a series of locations within the computer. Each of these locations has an "address" which always remains the same. When working, the computer will put data into these locations. Therefore, if a piece of information is stored in memory, there must be some way of knowing its address; when the information is needed later on, the address must be obtained, and the information at that address can then be fetched.

This structure is minimal for any working memory: the information must be stored, and it must be stored at some definite address; When the information is to be used, the address must be available, and then the information must be retrieved from that address. This seems obvious enough, but many naïve theories of memory, especially those based on physiological or chemical theories of memory, fail to take account of these requirements. For example, it is sometimes argued that information can be stored in the brain by modifying large chemical molecules—DNA, RNA, or something else of that sort. Such molecules have thousands of tiny units strung together, and the theorist sees this as a miniature computer card: by modifying this or that point in such a molecule, one could store vast amounts of information. What such theories often forget is that the information not only must be stored but must later be retrieved. Any system that stores a large amount of information will necessarily have a retrieval problem. The information must be stored at distinct addresses; and at the time of retrieval the brain must have some way of knowing the address of the information wanted.

Is information about a particular situation stored in a particular spot in the brain?

When K. S. Lashley (1929) finished his heroic attempts to localize memory "engrams" (an old word for actual stored memories, which would correspond to words stored in a computer's memory), he concluded that they were not localized anywhere. He was never able to cut out a certain part of a rat's brain and then show that the rat had forgotten certain learned habits but retained others. When an experimental psychologist attempts to test human memory, he does so by asking the subject questions; when the subjects answer the questions, it is not at all clear that they are using only a faculty of "memory"—they seem to use all their faculties, capacities, strategies, general knowledge, and skills.

Therefore, to a psychologist the first difference between computer memory and human memory is that computer memory clearly exists as a separate entity, whereas there is good reason to question whether human memory has a similar independent existence.

A second, more definite, difference between computer memory and human memory is that a computer will remember anything it is told; human beings, in contrast, quickly assimilate and clearly remember material that is *meaningful* but rapidly confuse and forget material that is *meaningless.* A list of ten nonsense syllables, like XAJ and KUH, is difficult to memorize and will usually be forgotten within a day or two. A fragment of poetry such as "Tyger! Tyger! burning bright/In the forests of the night" is learned on one exposure and remembered indefinitely. In fact, there are different levels and kinds of meaningfulness; and so far as memory is concerned, almost every possible interpretation of a concept is correct. Even among nonsense syllables, some are very unmeaningful (like XUH) and others much more meaningful (like TID), and we can more rapidly learn the more meaningful ones. (Subjects can successfully say which words are more meaningful, can give more associations to them, and can pronounce them more rapidly and surely. Also, close examination shows that meaningful nonsense syllables use letters that are more frequent in the subjects' language and in other ways conform more closely to its rules of spelling and pronunciation.) Most words are easier to remember than nonsense syllables. Infrequent words are harder to learn than common ones. Words that have a concrete meaning are easier to remember than words with more abstract, and often more indefinite, meanings. Words grouped into meaningful categories are remembered better than words given in meaningless order. Sentences are remembered better than ungrammatical strings of words; and sensible, meaningful sentences are remembered better than nonsense sentences. Finally, well-organized paragraphs are easier to remember than disorganized ones. Therefore, at all levels and in every sense of the word "meaningfulness," meaningfulness affects memory.

In order to imitate the properties of human memory, recent computer systems have complicated the form of computer memory. Instead of merely having an address with some data in it, they add a "link." That is, along with the data that belongs at that address, they add another address. The program is then written so that when given an address, it not only can extract the data but also is led to another address. When information is put into such a data structure, the proper approach is to link together pieces of information that are related and belong together.

This sort of data structure finds some things easy to retrieve and others very inaccessible. A certain address—say, the one that refers to the learner himself—may be linked from many other parts of the memory system. That is, the word "hat" may be stored with a link to the self, yielding something like "my hat"; the word "mother" may link to the self, yielding "my mother"; and so forth. If for any reason the learner should need to think of himself, he would soon get there by thinking of almost anything else and following the links—before long they would lead to this very central concept. A more peripheral concept, like "aardvark," on the other hand, can be reached by almost no links—perhaps by one from "ant" and another from "proboscis," but not by very many.

Such a system defines the meaningfulness of an item of information as representing the number of other addresses that point to its address. This is a computer model of an associational theory of memory structure. There are several interesting elaborations of this system. Instead of direct links between addresses, there may be certain conceptual way-stations; or the various kinds of links can themselves be labeled "relations"; or the whole system can be given a more organized structure, somewhat like the books in a library, so that data is "content-addressable"—that is, the address of an item of data depends upon what the item means, much as the location of a book in the library depends on what the book contains.

ACQUISITION OF NEW MEMORIES

The process of acquiring new memories can be studied in many contexts. Two basic experimental procedures will be described to give a sample of what is known.

Free Recall

In a free-recall experiment, the experimenter reads a list of about ten to fifty words, one after another, at a rate of about one word every 2 seconds. When the experimenter has finished, the subject writes down all the words he can remember, in any order. Most subjects first write down the last few words and then any others they can remember; and they do not do very well on this task.

According to memory theory, each word heard by the subject is put into short-term memory, where it is rehearsed and processed. While it is in short-term memory it may at any time be copied over into long-term memory. Only a limited number of items can be held in short-term memory; when it is full, something is bumped out. Two facts agree very well with this hypothesis. The last few words in a serial list are usually given first by the subject and are relatively likely to be remembered. According to the theory, this is because those words are in short-term memory and can be spilled out without ever going into long-term memory. It has been shown that if the subject has to do arithmetic for a few minutes after hearing the list, he has lost all the advantage of short-term memory: the last few words are no easier to remember than words in the middle of the list. This is presumably because the arithmetic has occupied short-term memory and driven out all the words from the list.

The first three to five words of the list are remembered better than words in the middle of the list, though not from short-term memory. The theory is that when the first word comes in the short-term memory is empty, and the subject therefore can put his full attention to the first word. It stays there while the second and third words are given, because short-term memory has a capacity for several words. When the subject gets to the sixth or seventh word, his short-term memory buffer is full, so that subsequent words are lost quite quickly. The first few words have the advantage of more time in short-term memory and therefore an increased probability of being copied into long-term memory.

This theory has recently been supplemented by studies of the particular processes subjects go through when they are learning a free-recall list. One fact which has emerged is that subjects tend to rearrange the words in the list, trying to form clusters of related words, to put the words in a sentence, etc. This is discovered when the subject tries to give back the list and is found to have rearranged it. Some subjects try to fit the words into sentences and perhaps into a kind of connected story. Others form images, and some will try to develop an imaginary scene in which all the words of the list are represented.

The subject's problem, in free recall, is one of generating the list of words. To do this he needs some system for generation, which might consist of a higher-order information-flow structure. If a person can construct a complex scene and then divide it into parts, and the parts into parts, in such a way as to generate a large number of expectancies, he is likely to be able to recall a relatively large number of words. Furthermore, he will remember words that do fit his theme and forget words that he cannot fit in, and he will tend to give related words together in his output. A subject working in such an experiment may analyze a word in many ways, trying to find a memorable characteristic or connect it in some way into his system; and there is reason to think that the ability to remember a word depends upon the depth of processing to which it has been subjected (Craik and Lockhart, 1972).

Paired Associates

In paired-associates learning the subject is shown a list consisting of pairs of words. One word is designated the "stimulus"; the other is the "response."At the time of testing, the subject is shown the stimulus member of each pair and is required to produce the response member. A typical list might include pairs such as these:

> CURDLE—house
> RAPID—bogus
> TURTLE—outline

There might be perhaps twelve pairs altogether. The subject is shown the list of pairs, and then is shown the stimulus items (CURDLE, RAPID, etc.) and tested to see how many response items he can supply. Then he will be given another trial with the twelve pairs, presented in a new order, at random.

This task is different from free recall in that the subject does not have to generate the whole list but must merely give one response when cued with the stimulus. However, he must find one particular response and is usually given only a couple of seconds to do so; and since the words are given in random order, the subject cannot know in advance which response word he will need next. Therefore, he needs rapid, pinpoint retrieval based on the cues given in the stimulus words, but he does not necessarily need an overall scheme.

When presented a word pair, the subject analyzes the pair, seeking some association that will take him from stimulus to response. Both the stimulus and the response words have many characteristics or aspects toward which he might turn his attention. His task, in learning, is to generate information flows until he hits on one that (1) analyzes the stimulus term to yield a unique cue, so that he will not be confused with other stimulus terms later, and (2) provides some way to generate the response term.

A subject who studies an item in this way, may be said to be finding a "code." A subject may hit upon many possibilities when studying a pair, and many will not work. (There are lists of many different degrees of difficulty; but if the pairs are made of common words or if the stimulus is a word and the response is a numeral, approximately half of the items can be learned on a given exposure.) When the subject studies an item and arrives at a given code, he has no way of being sure whether that code will or will not succeed in yielding the response term later. Of course, when tested the subject may find that he has forgotten the code he wanted to use or that he remembers it but it fails to generate the response. In that case, he will not continue to use the same code but will try another on the next training trial.

What is the probability that the subject will "learn" an item on the first trial? Although we do not know just what this will be, we may call it c, the porbability of hitting upon a satisfactory code; then $1 - c$ is the probability that the subject does *not* have a satisfactory code. What is the probability that a subject will learn an item after having once failed to learn it? All he can do is to code the item, and the probability that he will hit a satisfactory code is again c. Now the probability of learning with exactly one failure is $(1 - c)c$, which is the probability of failing once but then succeeding the next time. What is the probability that a subject will fail exactly twice and then learn the item? This probability is $(1 - c)^2 c$, since each of the two failures have probability $(1 - c)$, so that the joint probability of two failures is $(1 - c)^2$, and we then combine this with the probability c of success after the two failures. In general, the probability of making exactly N failures and then learning is given by

$$\text{Probability (exactly } N \text{ failures, then success)} = (1 - c)^2 c.$$

This is called the "geometric distribution," because the successive probabilities of 0, 1, 2, 3, etc., errors form a geometric series, which generally would be of the form $1, a, a^2, a^3$, etc. In our case, we use $(1 - c)$ for a.

This distribution of errors has been found to a close approximation

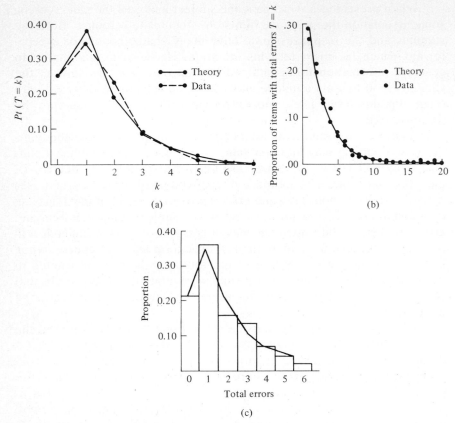

Figure 13.1 (a) Distribution of *T*, the total number of errors per item (*after Bower, 1961*). (b) *After Polson, Restle, & Polson, 1965.* (c) *After Restle & Greeno, 1970.*

by a number of experimenters. A few examples are shown in Figure 13.1.

There is an important implication to this finding. Suppose a teacher is trying to teach a list of information to children in school, and they do not all learn the information at the same time. One theory, which is implicit in the minds of many of us, is that some of the children are just too stupid to learn or that some of the items are just too hard for the children. Patience would not be rewarded, according to this theory, but just would be waste of the teacher's and the students' time. With such a system of instruction, the teacher continues working with the children until about half or three-quarters of the material is learned by most children, and then goes on to something else. The findings in Figure 13.1 show, however, that a child may have failed to learn an item three or four or even ten times and still have as good a chance of learning it as at the very beginning. According to the all-or-none coding theory, the subject initially has a probability c of learning the item; and after he has failed N times he still has the same conditional probability of learning, c. This means that teachers should not give up just because a few children do not have all the material—this is to be expected. Working on the basis of this theory, a teacher should come to expect that as teaching progresses, a certain fraction of the material will be mastered during each session. If one-half is learned the first hour, then half of what is left will be learned the next hour, and half of what is left beyond that will be learned in the third hour, etc.

Of course, this all-or-none theory does not have to be accepted as axiomatic. Any teacher working with several students or with a large amount of material of approximately equal difficulty can experiment with the theory simply by continuing to teach for an extended time and measuring the probability of mastery of an item of information over time. This approach has implications for teaching a whole class, for determining optimal class size, and for working with a course like mathematics in which each section of the course depends upon mastering all previous parts. Some of the consequences are found in Restle (1964a), where it is pointed out that it is almost impossible to teach a long course in which each item depends on mastery of the last one unless individual students receive individual attention and the pace of the course is adjusted to individual accomplishment. Almost no one will otherwise get through a course with twelve topics, each depending upon the preceding one, and it does not matter whether the teacher is too fast or too slow. Teaching must be adjusted to the individual learner.

The all-or-none theory was not easily accepted, and many experimental tests have been made. In fact, there are many experimental situations, including some kinds of paired-associates learning, in which learning is not strictly all-or-none. (For a review of such experiments, see Restle, 1965, p. 320.)

It is not possible to track down all the possible reasons why an experimenter might not find all-or-none learning, but a few situations are clearly understood. When experimenters used consonant-vowel-consonant (CVC) nonsense syllables, such as MEK or ZOV, one CVC being the stimulus and the other the response, the result was often some degree of gradual learning. One reason is that the subject may misspell a CVC even if basically he has learned the association—in technical terms, the response requires "integration" (Rock & Heimer, 1959). Therefore, in many experiments using nonsense syllables, the subject must not only learn the association but also learn to integrate the response syllable. This entails at least two processes. Even if each process is all-or-none, the two processes would not yield all-or-none learning. Another cause of multi-stage learning is that various pairs of stimulus items in a paired-associates list may be similar enough to be somewhat confusing. If so, the subject may have to learn not only the association but also a discrimination between similar stimuli. This has been shown to result in two stages of all-or-none learning (Polson, Restle, & Polson, 1965).

A natural conclusion would be that simple learning of an individual item proceeds all-or-none if it involves no difficulties of stimulus dis-crimination, response integration, etc. However, many experimental tasks require multistage learning; and when the experimenter finally separates the stages, he will understand the structure of the learning task he has set for his subjects.

There are various ways a subject might encode paired associates, and some are highly efficient. One method is to rehearse the pair of words over and over as quickly as possible, trying to pound them into one's memory; but this is the most inefficient and wasteful method of memoriz-ing that has been tried experimentally. Another method is to try to generate a sensible sentence linking the two items (Bobrow & Bower, 1969). The results of two paired-associates experiments are shown in Figure 13.2. Notice that subjects do worst when trying to associate two

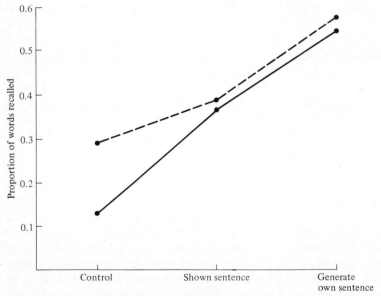

Figure 13.2 Memory for words is improved when they are embed-ded in a sentence, and still more when the subject generates his own sentence. (*Bobrow and Bower, 1969.*)

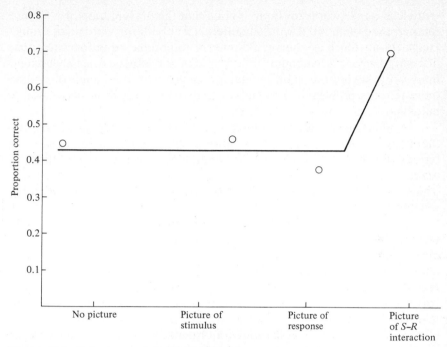

Figure 13.3 Paired associates are learned faster when a picture showing S-R interaction is provided. The result is not attributable merely to pictures of stimulus and response separately. (*Wollen and Lowrie, 1971.*)

words (e.g., "cow—ball"), better when given a sentence as context ("The *cow* chased the rubber *ball),* and still better when they must generate some sentence combining the two words. Other experiments indicate that when the subject is given a sentence he may merely mouth it and not really process it into his semantic system; but when he generates a sentence, he works harder and processes the two words more deeply.

Another way of remembering paired associates is by visualizing or imagining a scene. The most effective way to do this is to develop a scene in which the images connected to the two words interact in some strong way (e.g., for the pair "cow—ball," imagining a cow balancing on a large ball). It is not nearly so useful merely to picture the stimulus, as it should be if images helped the subject discriminate the stimulus item. Nor is it very helpful to picture the response term, as it should if the image helped the subject form a conceptual peg for retrieval (Paivio, 1969). Another possibility is that an image of the response term would help make the response word more available, but pictures of the response term do not help at all. Figure 13.3 shows the results of an experiment (Wollen & Lowrie, 1971) in which subjects were shown pictures related to stimulus words, response words, or both. Notice that the presentation of a picture relating the S with the R word is quite helpful both for words that arouse images easily (such as "horse," "flower," "umbrella") and for words that do not ("impact," "vacuum," "link"). Similar effects can be obtained merely by having the subject imagine such pictures, though of course there is some problem in knowing exactly what images the subjects may be using.

In addition, subjects can search out intermediary associates between the stimulus and response words, note graphemic or phonological similarities (the "clang" association, as in combining "burgle" with "turtle"), or classify the concepts signified by the two words (as when "horse—train" is remembered because both terms can serve as means of transportation).

Such methods are meant to work item by item, but subjects usually try to remember the whole list of pairs given (there are usually between eight and twelve pairs per list) by finding a general rule. For example, one can make up a list of nonsense syllables in which the response is simply the stimulus spelled backwards: pairs like RIJ—JIR, XAH—HAX, and so forth. Such items are not learned separately; instead, the whole list is learned singly as soon as the rule is educed. As has been shown by Polson (1967), subjects may start learning an organized list item by item; but as soon as they catch on to the general rule, they rapidly learn all items. For more detail on this topic, see Bower (1970).

THE NATURE OF CODES FOR NONSENSE MATERIAL

The idea that a learner detects a pattern or codes new material is correct, but it raises the further question: What sort of a pattern might exist in a random list of nonsense syllables? To answer this, we must see what subjects actually do in memorizing experiments. In one early study, Adams and Montague (1967) reported four general classes of such "codes," which they called "natural-language mediators."[1]

First, in learning to associate pairs of common words, subjects most often used sentence associations. These consisted of placing the two words in a sentence, or relating them to a scene in which they would be connected. An example is the pair "inshore—victor," for which a subject reported that he "thought of troops landing on a shore." This kind of association was used in 50 percent of the pairs in a second list, when subjects were getting used to a fairly difficult task. Second, subjects

---

[1]In their associationistic language, the term "mediator" signifies that the subjects were not simply associating a stimulus word to its response but doing something else. The phrase "natural language" distinguishes their observations from mediators taught by the experimenter.

related the two words to a more general concept or idea. For example, when learning the pair "retail—wealthy" a subject would give the association "money." This type of association was observed 13 percent of the time. Third, subjects made the "clang" association, in which two words are connected because their sounds are somewhat alike; for example, learning "retail—fatal," a subject said that "the two words sound alike." Notice that they do not have to be homonyms (sound exactly alike) or rhyme, or have any other strict relationship; in this case, the words would rhyme except that the vowel sounds are different. Fourth, subjects learned some word pairs by abstracting letters, usually initial letters, and making the relationship between them. An example: When learning "portly—unearned," a subject succinctly stated, "P—U." These last two types of association occurred 4 percent and 3 percent of the time, respectively. The subjects said that they learned the remaining 30 percent of the items "by rote," without any known or conscious form of association.

A recent study of how Stanford students remember nonsense syllables (Prytulak, 1971) has revealed that such syllables are transformed into more meaningful and memorable entities, usually words. Prytulak discovered a "transformation stack," or sequence in which such transformations are tried. A major problem a subject has in a memory experiment is to reconstruct the original nonsense syllable from the code he remembers, and the best or top transformations in the stack are those that are most likely to lead to a correct reconstruction. The best transformations are identity (PIN—"pin"), adding a suffix (LOV—"love") and adding a vowel inside (WOD—"wood"). These all resulted in successful reconstruction about 0.88 of the time. Another transformation added an internal consonant plus a suffix (FEX—"flexible") or added a vowel internally plus a suffix (PYM—"payment"). These transformations result in reconstruction about 0.75 of the time. A substitution of the consonant that leaves the pronunciation unchanged—(KUT—"cut") produced nearly 0.50 retrieval. Relatively unsuccessful transformations (reconstructed with probability about 0.20) are those that substitute for the vowel, and then also make inserts of consonants, such as ZYT—"zest" and JYZ—"jazz."

Whereas Adams and Montague emphasized the *linguistic* relation when a subject associated "inshore" with "victor" by thinking of troops landing on a shore, more recent research has emphasized the use of an *image.* In one line of research, Paivio (1971) has collected voluminous evidence that a word is easy to remember when it easily arouses an image. Concrete nouns like "woman" are easier to remember than more abstract nouns like "theory," and this is irrespective of whether the words arouse few or many verbal associations. Paivio's interpretation is that people remember by the use of images wherever possible.

Bower (1970a) has discussed the use of imagery in memorizing and shown that when subjects are instructed to use vivid and peculiar images, they can learn lists of words with remarkable speed and certainty. Given the pair "fish—table," for example, the subject might be instructed to repeat and rehearse the words over and over during the 4-second study interval. The result is very poor performance. Alternatively, the subject can be instructed to imagine "interactive scenes," for example, a fish with a bib on, sitting at a dinner table. (Notice that the image is not of a fish on a table, for that would not be unique; one might remember the fish on a dish, or get the table right but remember a ham steak.) When subjects learn to imagine interactive scenes, memory capacity can be increased at least tenfold.

The psychological literature contains a classic description (Luria, 1968) of a man called S. who was remarkably talented and had trained his memory so that he could make a living as a performer, using his unusual ability to form and retain images: "When S. read through a long series of words, each word would elicit a graphic image. And since the series was fairly long, he had to find some way of distributing these images of his in a mental row or sequence. Most often (and this habit persisted throughout his life), he would 'distribute' them along some roadway or street he visualized in his mind" (Luria, 1968, pp. 31–32).

In fact, the errors S. made when he was still inexperienced were not so much errors of memory as errors of *perception.* For example, in a list he forgot the words "pencil" and "egg." His explanation, quoted by Luria, was this:

> I put the image of the PENCIL near a fence . . . the one down the street, you know. But what happened was that the image fused with that of the fence and I walked right on past without noticing it. The same thing happened with the word EGG. I had put it up against a white wall and it blended in with the background. How could I possibly spot a white egg up against a white wall? [Luria, 1968, p. 36]

S. could also solve certain problems very well if the solution required visualization. For example, consider the following account, from the interviews with S., of one of his problem-solving triumphs.

> You remember the mathematical joke: There were two books on a shelf, each 400 pages long. A bookworm gnawed through from the first page of the first volume to the last page of the second. How many pages did he gnaw through? You would no doubt say 800—400 pages of the first volume and 400

of the second. But I see the answer right off! He only gnaws through the two bindings. What I see is this: the two books are standing on the shelf, the first on the left, the second on the right of it. The worm begins at the first page and keeps going to the right. But all he finds there is the binding of the first volume and that of the second. So, you see, he hasn't gnawed through anything except the two bindings. . . . [Record of May, 1934]

However, one need not envy S. his powerful memory and his brilliant images—for he had shortcomings stemming from the same source. S. suffered from definite abnormalities of thought. For example, he was asked to interpret a simple sentence, "The work got under way normally." As Luria comments, "Could there be anything complicated about such a sentence? We would have thought S. could have no trouble with it, but he found it very difficult to grasp." The nature of his difficulties is seen in another record:

> I read that 'THE WORK GOT UNDER WAY NORMALLY.' As for WORK, I see that work is going on . . . there's a factory . . . But there's that word NORMALLY. What I see is a big, ruddy-cheeked woman, a NORMAL woman. . . . Then the expression GET UNDER WAY. Who? What is all this? You have industry . . . that is, a factory, and this normal woman—but how does all this fit together? How much I have to get rid of just to get the simple idea of the thing [Luria, 1968, p. 128].

As Luria says, "Each word he read produced images that distracted him and blocked the meaning of a sentence. When it came to texts that contained descriptions of complex relationships, formulations of rules, or explanations of causal connections, S. fared even worse" (p. 129).

MEMORIZATION

At this point, it is possible to understand the significance of memorizing. It is a process by which meaningless and disorganized information can be stored for later retrieval. In order to memorize a list, the subject's best method is to develop images for each item, and then relate these images either by using a well-learned scheme (like the street used by Luria's S.) or by finding some special set of connections between elements (like the *fish* sitting at a *table*).

If a person has a rapid flow of images or associations, he may become able to remember almost anything. However, the memory used for memorizing is quite different from the more abstract or scientific sort of memory. When abstract memory is involved, a person studies material to find its own significance and then fits this new information to a specific understanding of the situation. The nature of the information determines how it is to be understood and where in memory it is to be placed. In memorizing, on the contrary, one is not concerned with the nature of the information memorized (which is often nonsensical) but instead forms an image based on some sort of superficial property and then fits the image, not into a general understanding, but into an arbitrary system or structure having nothing to do with the meaning of what is learned.

To memorize information a person often must find some artificial way of recalling it upon an arbitrary demand. This is typical of school performance, in which the teacher may demand all sorts of information, in no particular order and not as part of any meaningful ongoing process. The student facing such demands is well advised to acquire mnemonic systems of various sorts. A mnemonic system is extraneous—it is a system that can be used to learn all sorts of things, and the system itself remains the same no matter what is being learned. For that reason, it is inflexible and insensitive to the inner characteristics of the information to be remembered. When a person does not understand what he is to remember, he must still have some system. If the inner pattern of the material to be remembered will not emerge as a structure, then the learner is likely to impose some other, extraneous system upon it. If he has no such system, he simply does not learn, or soon forgets. If he has such a system, then he can remember the material.

Of course, memorizing something has little to do with understanding it. In fact, since memorized material is already fitted into an extraneous system, it may be almost impossible to study it to extract the appropriate underlying pattern of meaning.

If the student fully understands the limitations of memorizing, he may still feel that there are times when he must memorize masses of meaningless material and should learn ways of doing so. Examples of meaningless material include telephone numbers, names of people, and so forth.

Effective memorizing systems seem to have a few general characteristics in common. First, they tend to use imagery: one is advised to generate and connect images. Second, they frequently use a memorized structure on which to hang new information. An alphabetical list such as "arrow," "bird," "cat," "dog," . . . integrated into a story can provide an arbitrary serial listing to which other things can be attached. An acquaintance of the author's, majoring in history, carefully memorized the English kings from about 1000 A.D. onward and then tied every other event in European history, as he read it, to the English king reigning at that time. This enabled him to remember dates with great precision and to organize a large mass of information. Luria's subject S. placed his images along an imaginary walk and used that geographical structure to recall.

Third, associations are often bizarre, nonsensical, or humorous, and thereby can avoid confusion with other material memorized at another time. In every case, memorizing is an active process, closely related to imagination.

FORGETTING

Everyone has the experience of forgetting what was learned—college students perhaps more than most people. A failure to remember is to some extent a reflection on how well the material was learned in the first place; when we test for memory, we test the joint accomplishments of learning and retention. If we understand the process of forgetting, we can modify or improve learning so as to avoid forgetting.

Interference and Decay

A computer memory can lose information in two ways: because the stored information is destroyed by some electronic accident or because some new information has been written over what was to be remembered. The same possibilities exist for the human memory: they are called "decay," meaning spontaneous loss of information over time, and "interference," which is the forgetting of one thing because the person is trying to learn or remember another.

Everyone has had the experience of forgetting, all too often; but how are we to know whether forgetting depended on decay of the trace or interference? The answer is, through an experiment. The design of such experiments is one of the finer accomplishments of experimental psychology.

Working on a friend's political campaign, I attended a committee meeting and learned the names of the people there. Then the next night I attended a meeting of the local chapter of the Audubon Society and learned the names of the people there. A week later the political committee met again, and to my horror I discovered that I could remember only half the names. Was this because a week had elapsed or because of the Audubon Society meeting? This particular situation cannot be unraveled; but it is possible to get valid experimental information about the general question and then use it to decide whether decay or interference was the likely factor in my case.

Divide twenty college students into two groups—at random, which will make the groups of approximately equal ability in learning and remembering. Then devise some suitable memory task for both; perhaps have them try to memorize a list of twenty-five common adjectives. All the subjects are treated the same and learn exactly the same list to the same criterion of learning on the first day. On the second day, half the subjects (the experimental group) will be given an interfering task; the other half (the control group) will spend their time at some innocuous task like naming the colors of pieces of construction paper or reading jokes in old *New Yorker* magazines. The interfering task given to the experimental group will be something quite like the original task—for example, learning another list of twenty different adjectives. On the third day, all the subjects are called back to the laboratory and tested, the question being how well they have remembered the original twenty-five common adjectives. All the subjects will be tested on exactly the same task and in exactly the same way.

The result might come out in either of two ways. Suppose that the two subgroups perform about equally well. This means that the interfering task—learning the second list of adjectives—did not affect memory more than the unrelated activity, and this in turn would mean that forgetting may be akin to mere decay—the 48 hours between learning and test were enough to produce the forgetting. At least we could say that a serious effort to demonstrate interference had failed.

The other possibility is that the experimental group would have more trouble remembering the first list than the control group. This result, if large enough to signify a general trend, would indicate that learning the second list of adjectives produced interference and the forgetting was probably caused by such interference. In fact, in almost every possible experiment run carefully enough and with enough subjects, it is found that interference does occur—that learning the second list does interfere with remembering the first list.

Wait a minute, you may say; does this experiment really prove that forgetting occurs through interference? To answer this question, we start by considering two alternatives. First, does this experiment disprove a simple decay theory? Second, is there some other interpretation that might affect the results, like the intelligence or talent of the subjects, tiredness, interest in the material, etc.?

Table 13.1 shows a diagram of the experiment that can help us discuss the possible interpretations. Task A is the original list of adjectives. Task B is a similar task that will be used as a possible source of interference with A. Task X may be no task at all or some totally irrelevant activity like naming colors or reading cartoons. We shall soon see how the experiment uses task X.

Now consider the effects of simple decay. The time between the first task and the test is the same in both groups, and on the average we may expect both groups of subjects to spend about the same amount of time asleep and awake, eating, reading, listening to lectures, etc. Therefore, as

Table 13.1   Experimental design for retroactive interference

	First task	Interpolated task	Test
Experimental group	A	B	A
Control group	A	(X)	A

regards whatever the factors affect decay, the experimental and control groups are equal.[2] The two groups, then, must be equal at the time they are tested on task A. But the actual result is that the experimental group, which has been subject to interference, will not remember as much as the control group. This difference cannot be explained by decay.

What about other factors; such as the intelligence or talent of the subjects? It must be remembered that the subjects were divided *randomly* into two groups. These two subgroups can be somewhat different in average ability, but it is very unlikely that a random division of the subjects would result in subgroups that are consistently very different in ability. In fact, this question is handled by ordinary statistics, for the theory of statistical tests tells just how likely it is that we will get a given difference between two groups based solely on chance. Since the subjects were divided randomly, any difference in their ability or talent occurs solely by chance.

What about fatigue or interest in the material? This seems to be a possible factor, for the control group has only had to learn one list of adjectives, whereas the experimental group has had more work to do, having learned two lists. The effort expended by the two groups was nearly equated by introducing the "dummy" task X, a task that did not interfere with memory but that occupied as much time and effort as the interfering task B. Also, the final test was given 24 hours after the interpolated task, B or X, and therefore all the subjects had ample time to rest and recover from the small amount of work done the day before. Now, common sense indicates that if 1/2 hour of memorizing, 24 hours earlier, has a sizeable effect on ability to remember, this is probably not mere fatigue or boredom but must be a more specific effect on memory. Perhaps it is not possible to completely eliminate the "boredom" hypothesis; but the experimenter designs his experiment so that the experimental and control groups must be very close as regards level of

---

[2]Strictly speaking, the groups are not equal. Since the subjects were assigned at random, the two groups differ; but the difference is a random variable. This produces variance within each group and also will produce a difference in performance between the two groups. The standard methods of statistical analysis enable us to determine whether an observed difference in performance between groups can reasonably be attributed to this kind of random variability or must be considered definite evidence that the experimental conditions (in our case, interference versus control) have an effect.

boredom and then concludes that a large difference between the groups must be caused by interference specific to the memory task, not to some condition as general as boredom.

This discussion illuminates the importance of the experimental design: it shows why the two groups of subjects are chosen randomly from a population, why the two groups learn exactly the same task A, are tested on it in exactly the same way and after exactly the same retention interval, and why the control group is given the dummy task X that takes as long as the interfering task B. All these fine points of experimental control are meant to eliminate possible alternative interpretations of the result and force everyone to agree that forgetting is caused by interference.

The experiment shown in Table 13.1 was a test of what is called "retroactive interference." This is an old term for interference that acts backwards in time. What this means is that the interfering task, B, acts on something that was learned earlier than itself; therefore, its direction of action is backwards in time. It is not the only form of interference possible; there is also "proactive interference." The experimental design for proactive interference is shown in Table 13.2. Everything in Table 13.2 is the same as in Table 13.1 except that the interfering task B is now given before task A is learned rather than after. The experimental subject first learns the interfering task B, then the next day learns A, and then a day later tries to remember A. The control group spends the first day on the dummy task X, the second day learning A, and the third day being tested for memory of A.

Proactive interference does occur experimentally, but it is weaker than an equal amount of retroactive interference. Common sense would suggest that retroactive interference would be greater than proactive interference, mainly because in the retroactive paradigm task B is in the place where it can do the most harm—right between learning and testing A. In the proactive paradigm, the interfering task occurs a day before the main part of the experiment and is not in a position to cause as much trouble. On the other hand, most retroactive interference consists of one or a few tasks between learning and remembering, whereas a person can pile up vast amounts of proactive interference over his whole lifetime from birth to learning a given task.

Table 13.2 Experimental design for proactive interference

	Interference	Learning	Memory test
Experimental group	B	A	A
Control group	(X)	A	A

There is still one loose end to tie up. In both these experiments the experimental group forgets more rapidly than the control group, and this shows the effects of interference. However, in most of these experiments, the control group also forgets, somewhere between 25 and 75 percent of the material in 24 hours. Does this not prove that some of the forgetting is the result of decay?

Various experimenters have tried to prove that all forgetting in these experiments can be attributed to some sort of interference. To do so, they must find some source of interference for the control group. One source, particularly relevant when the subjects are college students, is retroactive interference from the ordinary activities of the day. The college student may memorize and rehearse words during his ordinary working day, and these tasks are close enough to the usual laboratory task to result in some interference. A second source is proactive interference. A historical study of years of research by B. J. Underwood (1957) showed that control subjects forgot much more in early research around 1910 or 1920, than they did in more recent research—say, in 1950 or 1960. Underwood was reluctant to conclude that the human memory was evolving so rapidly that people in 1920 would forget 75 percent of a list in 24 hours but that their children in 1950 forget only 25 percent.

What Underwood found was that in most early experiments, the laboratory only had a few people available—the professor, perhaps one assistant, and a laboratory class of ten or so students. For this reason, all subjects would be tested day after day, perhaps for months, learning lists and being tested with and without interfering material. After a couple of weeks of this regimen, a subject would have memorized many lists of adjectives, nonsense syllables, or whatever the experimenter was using, and would have built up massive proactive interference. By 1950, psychology classes were large, and each subject in an experiment would be tested only for one session. These subjects had far less proactive interference, and remembered about 75 percent of a standard list. From this and a few experiments using massive proactive interference, Underwood concluded that this sort of interference can build up for a long time. It is interesting to note that a subject who has learned many such lists can learn a new list faster and faster but will also forget such lists faster and faster.

All this early research leads to the conclusion that ordinary forgetting does not result from simple decay over time but rather almost entirely from interference—from learning other material of the same kind. In detail, this sort of interference is different from interference in the computer. For one thing, in a computer the only possible kind of interference is retroactive; that is, some later information B is written over the original information A. In a computer this interference occurs when tasks A and B have the same addresses in memory, whereas in the human interference occurs when A and B have similar information content. In the human, proactive interference can be demonstrated; but it is impossible in the computer.

Several theories have been put forward to explain how interference results in forgetting. The simplest idea is that interference amounts to putting new information into old addresses and thereby writing over the old information, which is therefore forgotten. But this is surely wrong, for several reasons. First, the interfering material does not have to have exactly the same address (stimulus terms, in paired-associates learning) as the original material. There is considerable interference when the interfering task is merely similar to the original learning. Second, when an exact "writing-over" experiment is run (Barnes and Underwood, 1959), it is found that subjects frequently know and can recall both the response originally learned and the new interfering response, when shown a stimulus. This proves that attaching a new response to a stimulus does not necessarily "write over" the original response.

Another form of interference theory suggests that when a new response to a stimulus is learned, the old response tends to be "unlearned" or "extinguished." However, Postman (1961) has shown in many studies that the amount of interference depends not only on individual items common to the two lists but also on the general similarity of "context"—whether the lists are learned in the same general way, in the same room, etc.

Forgetting is studied with material that is barely or incompletely learned, and usually with disorganized lists of words or syllables. Such material is pronounceable, and the subject has plenty of time to process each item up to the point of pronouncing and (if it is a word) recognizing it and knowing its meaning. However, the construction of the lists is such that it is not easy to integrate beyond this item-by-item level.

In the usual memory experiment, the subject is trained only until he can remember about half the items or (at a maximum) until he has once got through the list without error. Detailed studies show that subjects cannot usually repeat the whole list again—many of the items were just barely held in memory, not highly organized. If the subject is given a few more trials, he begins to develop more specific and higher-level codings and ties the material into higher-level organizational possibilities. The process is slow and painful, because the materials are nonsensical in any ordinary or literal sense and the subject must invent some meaning. Given a little time, though, many college students can invent a fairly well unified meaning.

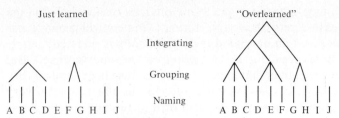

Figure 13.4 Organization of a list of words when barely learned and when "overlearned."

Figure 13.4 is a schematic picture of a list of words and the organization structure developed by a subject when trying to learn it. Notice that after the list, or major parts of it, is "overlearned," items are tied to high-level structures.

Now consider what happens in a retroactive-interference experiment. A second list, somewhat like the first, is given after the first. If the first list is integrated only to a low level, then most of its organizational ties are actually terminated when the interfering list is learned. This means that the first list is no longer in an active state in any way and cannot be reconstructed after interference. On the other hand, suppose that the first list is quite well integrated, as through overlearning. Then when the interfering list is learned, it can be integrated into much the same higher-order structure used for the first list. These higher-order integrations of the first list therefore survive during learning of the interfering list, and the first list is not lost.

The survival of a well learned list is shown in Figure 13.5, which shows the original list being well integrated into a tree, then the second list being fitted into the same tree, and then how the first list can be retrieved.

Why must the interfering list be similar to the original list if it is to

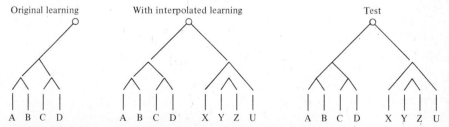

Figure 13.5 When the original list (ABCD) is well learned, a higher-order structure has emerged. When an interpolated or interfering list is added, it is fitted into a compatible organization. When the original list is tested, memory is excellent because the original structure is still active.

produce large amounts of interference? One obvious reason is that in the experiment to measure retroactive interference, the control group learns the original list, is given an unrelated task, and finally is retested; and its performance is the experimenter's *definition* of "no interference." But there is more to the fact than that logical point, because in general all very dissimilar interpolated lists have a small interfering effect, and all very similar interpolated lists cause a great deal of interference.

Here we must realize that the subject is doing many things in his life, and they are compartmentalized. He eats, but the act of eating is not integrated with taking a shower, or studying for an examination, or laundering clothes. Two behavior systems that are connected to very different high-level motivational systems would almost never interact in any way. If two systems are both disorganized but are so similar that they cannot be placed in separate categories, then they will interfere. Otherwise, they can be related together as alternative behavior systems and can both remain available.

Chapter 14

Serial Patterning

A person who speaks English words but places his words in nongrammatical order is not intelligible. A musician who disorders the notes of a song, a protocol officer who introduces people in the wrong order, a child who makes the motions of walking but without coordinating them into the correct order, and a spider who tries to connect the cross-lines of its web before securing the main radial framework—all will be completely ineffective. Many activities of animals and men require that partial acts be arranged in a certain serial order.

CHAINS OF RESPONSES

How can serial behavior be integrated? Let us first consider this question from the point of view of a simple stimulus-response theory. A single response unit, reflex, or habit is the response to a stimulus. Once the sequence S-R has occurred, the system merely waits for a new stimulus S. This approach permits a detailed analysis of a single response but does not itself provide any basis for a coordinated sequence of responses.

Theory of Chains of Responses

To handle strings of responses, S-R theorists have said that a response usually produces a stimulus. Either the muscular movement itself, or the changed position of the body, or some change in the environment may be perceived. Thus, one can say that a response R produces a characteristic stimulus S. This leads to a theory of response chaining, as follows: Let us signify the connection between a stimulus and a response, the reflex or habit, by a dash (—), and the connection between a response and its stimulus aftereffects by a dot, (.). Then, a chain of responses would arise from the schematic formula

$$S—R.S—R.S—R.S$$

and so forth. If the organism learned to make a given specific response R_1, this would put him in a feedback loop, as follows:

$$S—R_1.S_1—R_1.S_1—R_1 \text{ etc.}$$

In other words, the response R_1 would be repeated over and over again, indefinitely, or until the response was either fatigued or—through failure to produce a favorable result—became extinguished.

If two responses each become conditioned to the stimulus produced by the other, then simple alternation should result:

$$S—R_1.S_1—R_2.S_2—R_1.S_1—R_2.$$

and so forth. Finally, a chain can be made up of all different responses hooked to one another:

$$S—R_1.S_1—R_2.S_2—R_3.S_3—R_4$$

and so forth.

When a musician plays a melody on the violin, is this the form of control the brain exercises? Would it be fair to say that one note follows another?

One difficulty with such a theory is that a person may be able to "think" a melody without actually playing it and then enter into actual performance in the middle. In such a case it appears that the necessary stimulus somewhere along in the sequence, like S_4, occurs without the response R_4 that would have produced it. If this is possible, it follows that the structure is not necessarily a chain of stimuli and responses but might be a chain of "images" of tones.

According to the theory of simple behavior flows, as developed in

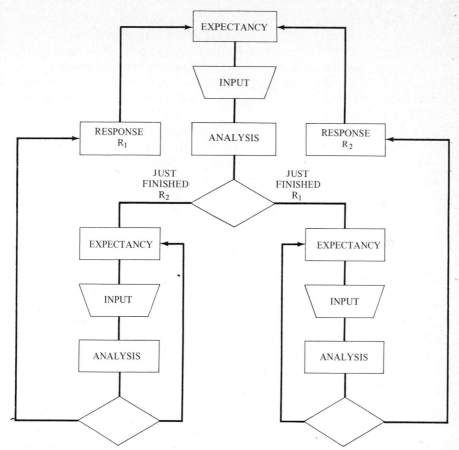

Figure 14.1 Flowchart of the behavior flow producing simple alternation between R_1 and R_2.

this book, repetition of a response would arise from a simple behavior flow in which the aftereffect of the response returns the flow to its beginning and the stimulus input consists of the results of the response. This would be similar to the simple S-R reflex theory, except for the complication of expectancies and analysis. These complications, however, do not change the overall structure of serial organization.

Alternation, however, would be explained another way by a behavior-flow theory. The two responses being alternated would have separate behavior flows, and there would be a higher-order behavior flow to decide which to use. The aftereffect of one response would be the cue, at the higher level, to call in the other behavior flow. The general structure is shown in Figure 14.1.

The difference between Figure 14.1 and the simple S-R chain lies in the use of a higher-level behavior flow that serves to decide which response to make next. This reveals that at the higher level, the analysis the subject must make is based on which response he has just completed. This requires that the subject have some memory of what response he has *just* completed. (It would not be enough to remember that the response has been made at some time in the past—the discrimination must be of the immediately past event.)

A completely heterogeneous chain of responses, R_1—R_2—R_3—R_4—R_5—, and so forth, is a natural extension of the simple response-chaining theory. However, notice that in the behavior-flow theory this could lead to a rather complicated structure of behavior flows; in fact, it is not at all obvious how to construct such a system. Therefore, if animals and men can readily organize chains of different responses into complex behavior structures, this would support the S-R reflex theory and produce real embarrassment for the cognitive, behavior-flow theory.

On first glance, it appears that S-R theory is, then, surely correct. A skilled musician can play or sing any of a tremendous variety of different notes. A mature speaker can say any of a huge—perhaps infinite—variety of possible English sentences. It seems that any response can be attached to any other. However, when we think of it, there do seem to be preferences, so that some behaviors "naturally" follow others, making easy sequences, whereas others do not fit together and would lead to awkwardness. A skilled musician can play a melody more smoothly than a jumble of unrelated notes, and one can recite a sentence more easily than a string of unrelated words. Does this present any difficulty for the idea of an S-R chain?

At first, no. Clearly, it is possible for some responses to be attached, selectively, to others. One reason would be that when R_2 follows R_1, the result is successful or reinforcing, and therefore a strong association is formed. Another possibility is that the stimulus resulting from R_1, which we would call S_1, is a natural stimulus for response R_2. There could be an innate, unlearned reflex connection, or the form of S_1 might so resemble the form of R_2 that one naturally arouses the other.

The Serial-Position Curve

A basic experimental technique is rote serial learning. The subject is shown a sequence of nonsense syllables or unrelated words, and as he sees one he is to anticipate the next. The same list is repeated over and over until the subject has mastered it. In this experiment, the most obvious and invariable finding is called the "serial-position curve," a plot of the difficulty (for example, the number of failures made by the average subject) of the various items in a serial list. If the items are all of the same type and equally easy to learn, and if there is no systematic order within

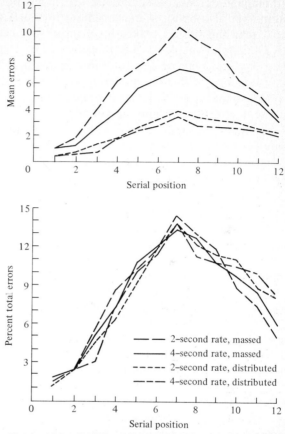

Figure 14.2 Serial-position curves in verbal learning. (*McCrary & Hunter, 1953.*)

the list of items, then the middle items in the list are much more difficult than those at the beginning and end. A typical serial-position curve is shown in Figure 14.2.

The interesting fact which emerges from such experiments (McCrary & Hunter, 1953) is that the shape of the serial-position curve is always the same for any simple list of appropriate length. If the materials are easy to learn, then there will be few errors, but they will be distributed proportionally just as in Figure 14.2. Fast and slow learners, trained at high or low rates, learning difficult nonsense syllables or easy family names, will learn at very different rates but produce the same serial-position effect.

This suggests that there may be a profound reason for the shape of the curve. The simple S-R chain hypothesis seems, at first, to offer no explanation. However, as has been known since the early work of

Ebbinghaus (1886), associations are made not only between adjacent items but also between more remote items. If the items are R_1, R_2, R_3, etc., then the subject makes his primary associations between R_6 and R_7 (for example) but also makes associations between R_6 and R_8, between R_6 and R_9, etc. One reason for this (Atkinson, 1957) is that the stimulus consequence of R_6 does not disappear immediately but may remain for a while, so that when R_9 occurs, some of the trace of the stimulus S_6 is still present, and the two may be connected.

One might suppose that the first item of the list would have the most interfering remote associations, the second would have fewer, etc. In a ten-item list, R_1 has remote associations with the eight items R_2 to R_{10}, whereas R_8 has only one remote association (with R_{10}), and R_9 has no remote associations. The serial-position curve, however, shows that the first item is very easy to learn; it is the items just past the middle that are most difficult.

Another consideration is this: if the stimuli from old items remain to become associated with remote responses, then traces of old items are present when the subject tries to respond later: when he has just made response R_5 and has produced trace S_5, which is mainly associated with R_6, he also has traces S_4, S_3, and so forth, which have not yet cleared out of his mind. These stimulus traces also will produce wrong responses, and the old stimulus traces accumulate more at the end of the list than at the beginning. This produces a possible prediction that it should be the last items in the list that would be most difficult.

It is possible to construct an explanation for the serial-position effect by taking the two factors together—that early items are relatively safe from stimulus traces, and that items late in the list are relatively safe from remote associations. The theory is quite complicated but can explain the shape of the data curves, at least to a close approximation (Atkinson, 1957).

When experimenters look closely at the performance of subjects learning serial lists, however, they see a different pattern. Feigenbaum and Simon (1962) have put forward the following idea. A subject can hold only about six items in short-term storage; in the case of nonsense syllables with unconnected letters, this amounts to two syllables. The subject first puts the first two items of the list into short-term memory and (probably) learns them. These items, along with the pause between lists, constitute "anchors," and the subject systematically focuses his attention on items adjacent to anchors. Thus, either he may learn item R_3, which is next to the R_1, R_2 block he has already learned, or he may learn the last item (say, R_{10}). Having learned R_{10}, he will then work back to R_9. In this way, step by step, the subject will work from anchors toward the middle

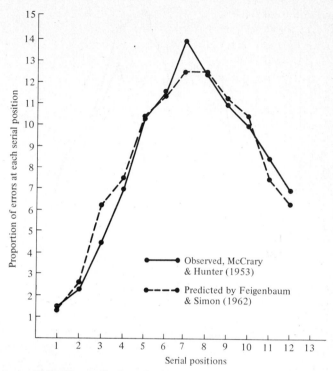

Figure 14.3 Theoretical and observed serial position curves, showing close fit of the Feigenbaum-Simon model.

of the list. His slow performance on items near the middle of the list is explained by the fact that he does not really try to learn them until the items nearer the ends of the list have already been learned. This model closely predicts the typical form of serial-position curves, as is shown in Figure 14.3.

If Feigenbaum and Simon's approach to the serial-position curve is correct, at least in its main outlines, it helps explain why a person usually has more difficulty with the middle of a long serial task than with the beginning or end: he works on the ends first, they being anchors, and only after he has learned an initial or terminal segment can he extend his knowledge in toward the middle. If an anchor is placed somewhere in the middle, learning is faster and can also begin near the anchor. In an experimental test, just such a dip has been found, as is shown in Figure 14.4. This might explain why a person learning a long musical piece—for example, a sonata—may find that he has relatively great difficulty learning the middle of each movement; the division into movements provides several anchors, and learning proceeds outward from each such anchor.

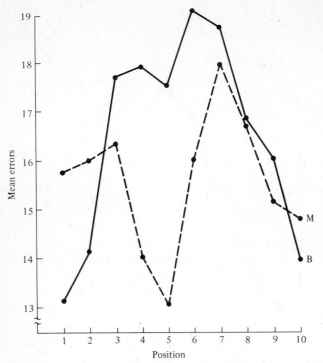

Figure 14.4 Curve B is a normal serial position curve. Curve M is produced by subjects told that the first syllable they saw was the middle of the list. Note that the easy items are those the subject *thinks* are the end ones. (*Glanzer and Dolinsky, 1965.*)

THE ORGANIZED SEQUENCE

When a college student tries to learn a serial list of twelve nonsense syllables, he must go through the list five or six times, spending at least 1/2 hour altogether. Furthermore, serial rote learning is a difficult and painful experience. Does this mean that serial organization of behavior is always difficult to learn?

Examples of Organized Sequences

The college student can read ten or fifteen pages an hour, even of fairly difficult material, and this will result in several thousand words per hour. It is true that he cannot give a perfect verbatim account of what he has read; yet he seems to be establishing some sort of serial organization. Even more impressive is the rate of speech: something like four words per second in rapid speech, normally consisting of ten phonemes (distinct speech sounds) per second. In speech, sounds must be arranged according to strict sequential orders; the sound "eachp" will not substitute successfully for "peach." Reading new material, and speaking spontaneously, are not very difficult or painful tasks for most college students; and certainly they handle much more than twelve syllables in 1/2 hour—in fact, they speak at nearly a thousand times the rate of learning nonsense syllables.

This huge discrepancy might be explained by two peculiarities of rote serial learning: first, such learning is verbatim word by word, not merely a matter of getting the gist of the information; second, a serial list, as used in laboratories, is senseless and contains no information in it—it lacks a "pattern."

The discussion of memorizing in Chapter 13 emphasized "finding a pattern." Is it possible that people perform easily and efficiently when the serial organization of the task involves a pattern? This seems possible; speech is governed by a complex set of rules, its syntax (grammar), and this set of rules determines which words can follow others, what groupings are acceptable, etc. For example, one can say "The cows are on the porch" but not "The are cows porch on the." In fact, there are relatively few possible grammatical arrangements of any set of words, and the arrangements are controlled by highly systematic rules of grammar.

Similarly, playing a musical instrument involves the rapid execution of a sequence of complicated movements, in precisely the correct order and timing, and with the proper force or form. How is this possible? One thing that comes at once to a musician, or to anyone learning music, is that some passages are relatively easy (such passages appear in "first books"); others are difficult (such passages might appear in J. S. Bach); and certain passages, not being "understood," are essentially impossible (as, perhaps, in unfamiliar experimental modern music).

Most of the behavior flows we have described in this book have the property of analyzing a specific stimulus input and selecting a response accordingly. The theory has emphasized that the person searches for information rather than merely accepting what comes to him, and analyzes the information rather than merely taking it at face value. But the behaviors we have worked with so far have all been directed, at every stage, by external stimuli. When a person speaks, or uses a typewriter, or runs down a football field, he is still affected by external stimuli; but it also appears that his responses are themselves coordinated. Behavior is controlled by plans, and is not merely reactive to external stimuli—or at least, so it seems.

The first issue is whether organized sequential behavior is always directed by external stimuli or can be controlled by some sort of inner pattern. The method used to answer this question is to take an example of serial behavior and attempt to determine what external stimuli might control it. We first try to eliminate the obvious possibilities of external control; if this is successful, then it is reasonably probable that some sort of internal, pattern control may exist. Then we try to determine the nature of this patterning. If the nature of the internal pattern is clearly revealed and all obvious candidates for external stimulus control have been eliminated, then everything will point to a form of serial patterning or coordination in such behavior. The concept of a behavior flow will then have to be changed to give a clear account of such forms of behavior that are not under the direction of external stimuli.

Lashley (1951), who first clearly formulated the theory of serial patterning, gives some examples of a research method from his own experience:

> For some time I have kept records of errors in typing. A frequent error is the misplacing or the doubling of a letter. *These* is typed t-h-s-e-s, *look* as l-o-k-k, *ill* as i-i-l. Sometimes the set to repeat may be displaced by several words. The order is dissociated from the idea. Earlier, in preparing this paper, I wrote the phrase "maintain central activities." I typed *min,* omitting the *a,* cancelled this out and started again; *ama.* The impulse to insert the *a* now dominated the order. I struck out the *a* and completed the phrase, only to find that I had now also dropped the *a* from *activities.* This example suggests something of the complexity of the forces which are at play in the determination of serial order and the way in which conflicting impulses may distort the order, although the primary determining tendency, the idea, remains the same [Lashley, 1951; in Slamencka, 1967, p. 67].

Notice that in this passage, Lashley is performing a familiar task with a limited number of responses (the typewriter keys) that must be combined in the correct order. He centers his attention on *errors* in typing: what kinds of errors are made, and how frequently. In particular, he is interested in those errors that may show what process is going on in the behavior system. His general idea is that the errors arise from applying a general rule in the wrong place or at the wrong time. Lashley does not merely cancel out the first "a" in "ama"; he applies a more general operation of canceling an initial "a," and this general tendency erroneously and accidentally obliterates the first "a" in "activities."

Data like these are not completely convincing, because they are collected unsystematically, and the particular error an individual may make could have a multitude of explanations. Could Lashley merely have moved or tipped his hand so as to make it temporarily less likely that he would type "a," which is at the extreme left of the keyboard? Is it true that in his mind words do not so often begin with "a"? Does he perhaps have some associations, habits, or other tendencies that could produce this combination of errors? Or are they perhaps simply random occurrences that he has happened to select out to fit his hypothesis? A more systematic experimental method is needed to eliminate these alternative interpretations and convince us of the exact nature of these serial control mechanisms.

Serial-Pattern Learning: Hierarchical Rules

In a series of experiments carried out in the author's laboratory (Restle & Brown, 1970) college students had to anticipate which of six lights, numbered 1 to 6, in a panel in front of them would come on next. There was a pushbutton under each light; the subject was to push a button under the light he thought would come on next. In fact, the lights came on in a sequence that repeated over and over; for example, 6 5 4 2 3 4 4 5 4 3. Subjects had about 2 seconds to anticipate each light, and after a few times through the pattern they would be able to anticipate most, if not all, of the lights.

What might direct the responses? An S-R theory would say that when the first light (6) comes on, it is the stimulus to the next response, which is to press button 5. When light 5 comes on, it is the stimulus to push button 4. In a simple behavior flow, much the same concept can be applied: the stimulus input is a light coming on; this is analyzed by the subject, and the location of the light is picked out as the key property. The subject will have established an expectancy, for example, that light 5 will follow light 6, having seen such a succession before and singled out this "pattern." When light 6 comes on, it is identified, and this leads to the expectancy that light 5 will come on next. The subject, having such an expectancy, makes the response of pushing the button under light 5.

However, the sequence 6 5 4 2 3 4 4 5 4 3 (Figure 14.5) cannot be learned by such a simple S-R association or behavior flow. Consider the

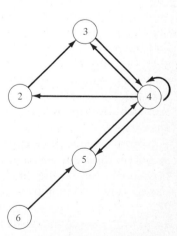

Figure 14.5 Associations in the sequence 6 5 4 2 3 4 4 5 4 3.

Table 14.1

Stimulus (position)	Response
S_{P1}	R_1
S_{P2}	R_2
S_{P3}	R_3

third light, which is light 4—what response will become associated with this stimulus? At various points in the sequence, light 4 is followed by lights 2, 3, 4, and 5. An S-R theory must say that all these responses are learned. Thus when the subject comes to light 4 in the sequence, he has four different things to do next, and there is no way for him to select the correct one consistently. A simple behavior flow also finds that the subject, through past experience, has identified the successions 4-2, 4-4, 4-5, and 4-3, which give him four behavior flows leading to four responses. Again, there is no way to select the correct response. In the experiment, of course, the subjects *are* able to select the correct response at each location.

This observation shows that subjects do not make their predictions on the basis of only the previous light.

Another possibility is what may be called the "serial-position" hypothesis. According to this, the subject does not attach his response to the previous event in the series but instead he "knows where he is in the sequence" and learns the response to his position in the list. He would then know the last part of the sequence 6 5 4 2 3 4 4 5 4 3 by means of associations like "at position 6, make response 4; at position 7 make response 4; at position 8 make response 5"; etc. The stimulus terms are positions. The whole list of stimulus-response associations would start off as in Table 14.1. This structure can be learned; since every serial position is a separate stimulus, you can attach any response you like to each.

This serial-position hypothesis has been used as an explanation for the shape of the serial-position curve in serial rote learning. The idea is that the positions at the beginning and end of the sequence are discriminable; the subject easily knows which is first and which is last. The middle positions, on the other hand, are much more difficult to discriminate, perhaps because the ends of the sequence are anchors and therefore are well discriminated but the middle of the list is without nearby anchors.

Is this an adequate explanation for serial-pattern learning of lights? If so, then different sequences of lights should produce similar "serial-position curves," the first and last events being easiest, etc. In one experiment we compared two sequences:

6 5 4 2 3 4 4 5 4 3
6 5 4 3 5 4 5 2 3 4

These are fairly similar sequences, but they produced quite different serial-position curves, as shown in Figure 14.6. It appears that the difficulty of learning a particular light depends not merely on where it appears in the sequence but also on the whole pattern of lights.

A third hypothesis is the "compound-stimulus" theory: the response is associated not just with a single stimulus but with a whole sequence of two or more previous events. If you play the piano, you might agree that you do not seek one key on the basis merely of the previous key struck but might base your next response on a sequence of previous notes, perhaps two or three notes back.

It is almost impossible to disprove this hypothesis, at least unless it states exactly what past events are used by the subject. However, in our experiment we were able to calculate how many past stimuli a subject would have to remember to be able to choose a correct response. This differs considerably from one point to another in the sequences; for example, in 6 5 4 2 3 4 4 5 4 3, the fifth event (the 3 right after 2) can be learned merely by associating with light 2, since light 2 comes on only once in the sequence. On the other hand, to predict the last event, 3, one must remember the whole past subsequence 4 5 4, because earlier in the sequence the correct response after 6 5 4 is a 2. It would not be enough to remember the single past event 4, or the double past event 5 4; one must remember three events. We found, upon analyzing the data, that our subjects did not systematically need more trials to learn items requiring a long memory. The evidence is not decisive and does not disprove this hypothesis about compound stimuli; but we certainly did not find data that strongly support the hypothesis.

Another idea about problems of this type is that the subjects find some things hard and others easy because they do not really learn a new sequence but merely find some other sequence, already in their memories, that they can use. This would be something like memorizing. For example, if your home telephone number was 234-4543, you could learn the above sequence merely by saying to yourself, "6-5-4—and then my phone number." This is an example of mastering the sequence by transfer of learning from some previously learned sequence.

To test the transfer hypothesis, we varied these sequences by moving them one light to the left; varying the sequence given above in this way yields:

5 4 3 1 2 3 3 4 3 2

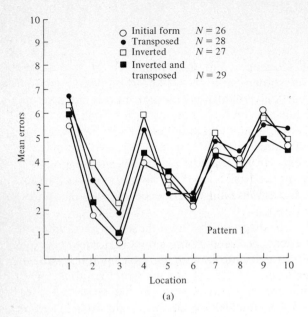

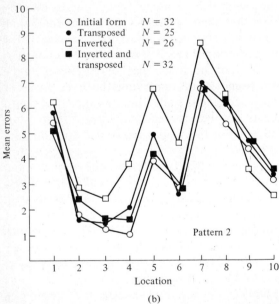

Figure 14.6   (a) Serial position profiles of a sequence and different variations of it. (b) Profile of a different sequence and its variations. Shape of the profile depends on the structure of the sequence. (*Restle and Brown, 1970.*)

Then we also inverted the responses in the six-button box left-for-right, producing

    2 3 4 6 5 4 4 3 4 5

and

    1 2 3 5 4 3 3 2 3 4

If one of these was your telephone number, house number, social security number, etc., then none of the others would be. On the other hand, many of the internal relationships between the lights were kept, and in fact the four "patterns" were almost identical. Various subjects learned each of the varieties of this sequence, and they all produced almost exactly the same data; this showed that it was the internal pattern or structure, not any accidental correspondence between the sequence and the outside world, which affected learning.

It has slowly emerged, in the last few years, that a person does not learn a sequence at all; he learns a system of rules by which he can generate the sequence.

A rule is a way of going from one event to another; but a rule, unlike a mere association, applies to many particular transitions. In music, an *association* would be between C natural and E flat. A *rule* including that association might be, "Ascend by a minor third," the same rule that would also go from E flat to G flat, thence to A natural, and so forth.

Let us consider what simple rules might exist for notes in music. First, one can repeat the same note, going from A to A. Any note can be repeated, as can any chord or, in fact, any other musical entity. Second, one can transpose upward or downward. If the transpositions are related by a simple scale, then repeated transposition of a note produces a "run," or scale: A, B, C, D, etc. This is a very simple element of a melody. Finally, one can alternate between two notes, by making a transposition and then the inverse back to the original note: C, D, C, D, C, . . . a "trill."

These three musical entities, the repeated note, the run, and the trill, are almost unique in that they can be generated by the repeated application of a simple rule, although the trill, which requires the subject to alternate between two opposite transpositions, is somewhat more complicated than the repetition or the run. Sequences containing repetitions, runs, and trills should, then, be fairly easy to learn; and generally speaking, that is what has been found in experiments. The experimental results are more detailed, however. First, subjects make very few errors near the end of a run but make many errors just after a run. In the sequence A B C F . . . very few errors would be made on B and C, but subjects would make many errors at F. This suggests that they are learning the run. Moreover, one particular error, making the response "D" at the fourth position instead of "F," will occur excessively often. In other words, subjects will tend to overextend the run. This can be interpreted to mean that they apply the rule of transposing even when it no longer applies. Similar results are found when a note is repeated (C C C), except that subjects have a considerable tendency to anticipate the end of the repetitions and make errors late in the block. There is a weak though noticeable tendency for subjects to pick up "trills" like C D C D . . . , but it is not as strong as the tendency to pick up runs or repetitions.

A natural way to handle a sequence is to break it up into parts. Bower and Winzenz (1969) have shown that a given sequence of digits is different if it is grouped differently: that is, if you memorize 23-5469-31, you may not recognize 235-46-931 as the same sequence. When learning a sequence it is helpful to group it in some rhythmic way, so that you will always group it the same way both in studying it and in being tested. If you try to rehearse a string of random digits in a monotone, they may group themselves perceptually in different ways on different trials, and the result will be a great waste of time.

Our research on rules has shown that there is sometimes a "natural" phrasing or grouping of such digits (Restle, 1972). In a sequence like 1 2 2 3 1 2 2 3 the experimenter might put the main pause between the two halves, making the easy pattern 1223 1223; or he might put pauses elsewhere—for example, 122 31223, which is relatively difficult. It is also possible to put longer pauses between major divisions and smaller pauses between minor divisions, and this is even more effective: for example, 12 23 12 23. This may be contrasted with the following phrasing, which is harmful: 122 3 1 223. Simply letting a subject *see* a sequence phrased wrongly will make it more difficult for him to learn it later. Good phrasing was found to be helpful, though in the experiments it was but little better than even spacing of lights in time. This may have happened because the sequences are so simply organized that the subjects could grasp them without the aid of phrasing (Restle, 1972).

This research, taken all together, shows that long serial tasks are handled by being broken up into parts, and that the most natural "parts" are those that can be generated by simple rules. Breaking a sequence into wrong parts may be worse than leaving it alone, provided that it is otherwise well organized. One function of the system of response-generating rules, then, is to divide a task into subtasks, each of which is controlled by a relatively simple system of rules.

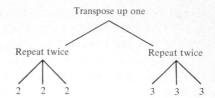

Figure 14.7 Structure of the sequence 2 2 2 3 3 3.

This statement naturally leads to the question of how the subject is going to string the subsequences together. A natural approach might be through *associations,* but this will lead to a mixed theory; since associations alone cannot give a reasonable account of lower-level learning of individual items, how could the association theory be sufficient for tying together larger subunits? What other possibility is there? As we have seen, single events may be grouped together because they can be generated by a single rule. The "hierarchical" theory of serial-pattern learning states that there are higher-order rules which may generate the subsequences themselves.

To illustrate this, consider the little sequence 2 2 2 3 3 3. It consists of two subsequences, 2 2 2 and 3 3 3, each of which is generated by the rule "Repeat twice." Let us call these two subsequences A and A', since they are closely related. What rule will generate the whole sequence? It might be the following: Transpose up one on the subunits; and the subunits are generated by repeating twice.

This structure can be described as in Figure 14.7. For the subject to use such a structure to generate his sequence, he would start at the top of the tree and first take the left branch. This would take him down to "Repeat twice," and again he would take the left branch. This leads to the event "2," his first response. Then he would go up to the next level and apply the rule, which would lead to a repetition and another response "2." Again he would go up one level and then generate his third "2." At this point, when he returns to the second level he finds that rules at this level have been used up. Therefore, he must go to the higher level, which says, "Transpose up one." He therefore prepares to generate the same structure, but now transposed, and makes response "3," which he then repeats twice as before, going to the lower-level branch. When that is finished, the subject has nowhere to go. (In the actual experiments, he would go back to the beginning, because he could know that the sequences repeat over and over. That is, the subject would actually be using a tree with a still higher level that says, "Repeat over and over.")

This theory can explain many interesting errors that subjects make. It was mentioned earlier that many subjects overextend a run. Many other, more complicated errors, are made; and sometimes the cause of the error

is quite far removed from the response itself. An example is the sequence
1 2 2 3 6 6 6 6 2 3 3 X . . . in which many subjects will make the response
"4" at the place marked X. They seem to carry over the pattern 1 2 2 3
from the beginning of the sequence; and that itself is the transposition of 1
(1 2), itself transposed (2 3). When they see 2 3 after the block of 6s, their
tendency is to transpose that subsequence, because that falls into a
regular tree in which the subsequence 1 2 2 3 is later transposed to 2 3 3 4.

In these sequences, subjects seem to generate errors as follows:
They absorb part of the sequence and find a rule that would generate that
part. If their rule system leads to errors, they look at the errors and try to
change the rule system, often by complicating it, so as to handle the
exceptions. In this way they gradually develop a rule system that is more
and more complicated, seeking higher-order rules governing when other
rules will apply.

These "rules" are the college student's form of behavior flow in these
experiments. Each rule requires that the subject determine his situation
within the sequence, analyze it to see if he is where he thinks he should
be, and then respond accordingly. Furthermore, the idea of having rules
that determine when other rule systems apply is the same thing as having
a behavior flow which controls other behavior flows. The college student
trying to anticipate a series of lights may build structures with rules
controlling rules, up to a tree with five levels. Since this is accomplished in
a few minutes while learning a trivial task in a laboratory, a five-level
hierarchical tree must not be anywhere near the limits of the human mind.

Serial Patterning of Complex Behavior

What other examples of serial organization of behavior can we study?
One example, surely, is the simple motor skill: for example, an animal
walking or running. Biological studies of walking and swimming in
animals, particularly in fish and insects, show that the individual limb can
make periodic responses even when its nerve supply from the rest of the
body is removed. In lower animals, the lowest levels of motor program-
ming appear to reside in the limb itself, or at least to be separate from the
main body. These systems receive some "feedback" information from
motions of the limb and from resistance to movement and respond
accordingly. However, isolated limbs cannot walk normally, because they
do not have either the vigor or the coordination required in walking. In an
insect, opposite pairs of legs affect one another and maintain coordination, and then a more central system determines which pair of legs will
operate next. As each of the individual limb actions is carried out,
feedback returns to the higher systems, which then send out further
information. Coordination requires several levels of organization, with

simpler behavior flows being controlled, in their application, by higher ones. It may be inappropriate to use words like "expectancy" with respect to the left middle leg of a beetle; but the point to be made is that hierarchical organization of behavior systems exists even at relatively low levels.

How large are the functioning systems in acts like walking, sitting down, and so on? Many of us have been victims of the childish trick of pulling a chair out from under a person who is about to sit down. Even though the person sees or hears the chair being moved at a time when his balance is upright, and even though he has the ability to move a leg backwards to catch himself, he will often sit heavily on the floor. The total act of sitting, which involves the coordination of several movements and postural adjustments, evidently begins with what one might call an "intention" to sit down, which initiates the operation of a large system of smaller adjustments. The whole act of sitting down is based upon the presence of the chair, since one always checks that a chair is there when he starts to sit down. However, once the process is begun, and the hips are thrown backwards, the legs are bent, the body leans forward, and the knees are flexed, the coordination of the act of sitting no longer depends upon the chair—in effect, the lower behavior flows are not checking for the position of the chair, nor is the system so constructed that it returns to the "top level" during the act. The result is that the person feels himself helplessly sitting down on nothing. But very few children are tricked very often in this way; apparently, then, it is not very difficult to reorganize the sitting process to include repeated checks on the presence of the chair.

Athletes and people who must respond quickly in their work often notice that they cannot respond quickly to a really unexpected stimulus. This is a great problem in driving an automobile, especially on super highways where cars may travel at 65 or 70 miles per hour. If another vehicle is stopped unexpectedly on the highway ahead of a driver, he may drive right into it; this is in fact a fairly common source of serious accidents. Why? The actions of driving are integrated into a smooth and elaborate behavior-flow system with certain expectancies: (1) that the road, nearby buildings, etc., will all remain fixed with respect to one another; and (2) that all cars, trucks, and other vehicles on the road will also move pretty much together. This system enables the driver to control his speed with respect to traffic, slipping smoothly by other cars and not being distracted by highway signs. All unmoving things are used as parts of a general frame of reference for finding the road; and all vehicles are part of a second, dynamic environment within which the driver seeks a safe place. When a vehicle stops on the highway, it may still be interpreted by the driver as part of his second stimulus system, in which case the fact that he is driving toward it at 70 miles per hour is totally unexpected. His behavior flow loops a few times, trying to figure out the relative speed of the truck, and before he can realize that he must reclassify it as unmoving, he may have driven right into it.

This leads us to the realization that skills and quick responses are parts of a large system, usually organized hierarchically. A person can respond with great skill and speed if the successive responses are all planned and are all run off by a single behavior-flow system. In baseball, everyone has seen a good outfielder "start with the crack of the bat" and run swiftly and unerringly to the point the ball will reach; in football, a runner in the broken field will make each "move" so that he escapes the immediate tackler and also finds an opening downfield. A tennis player may develop a combination of shots, placing a drive and at once moving to the net to make a volley he knows should be possible, considering the position he has forced his opponent into. In boxing, combination punches are the mark of skill, and the best boxers integrate defensive parrying with counterpunching into a single smooth act.

In all these examples, the individual motions are not separate or controlled by "reflexes" but are parts of a much more complex behavior-flow system. The ability to integrate and coordinate very complicated responses is one of the signs of the good athlete. In many sports, particularly competitive ones, the complex system of behavior flows is controlled by external stimuli provided by the opponent, and the game may evolve into an interactive behavior system in which the players become coordinated together. This is done consciously within teams in such sports as basketball, soccer, and football; but coordination of the behavior of two opponents, as in boxing or tennis, may also be observed, and a fine competitive game may often develop into a dance—to the great pleasure of both players.

A closely related and even more complex form of serial behavior is music in its various forms: dance, song, and instrumental music. A pianist's fingers move with incredible speed and sureness, meanwhile controlling the most delicate shades of timing and force so as to phrase the music properly. How can such a behavioral stream be controlled? In music theory one is taught that a piece may be divided into movements, the movements into parts, the parts into themes, and even the themes into phrases and motives. These segments function in the pianist's control of his playing. Some pianists, who are thought of as scholarly, may be able to define the parts of a piece systematically and describe its structure according to a general theory; they may also know the composer's organizational methods, the ideas current at the time the music was composed, and the way the organization of the music relates to other compositions. Other pianists, who are considered more "intuitive," may be unable to mark the score in a coherent way and may know relatively little of the theory or history of the music; but they show in their playing that they "understand" and can express the organization of the music.

One simple experiment that convinces most musicians of this is to require them to begin playing a composition in the middle. If the starting point is at the division between major parts, this is not a difficult task; but if the starting point is at a subsidiary phrase, the task may be very difficult. If the subject is asked to start halfway through a phrase or motive, he can accomplish the task only by active imagination: he must go back to a major division, imagine the music up to the place where he must start, and then actually begin playing at that point.

The research described above on serial-pattern learning would lead us to expect precisely this. According to the experiments, the learner extracts a pattern from the sequence, finds rules that will generate that pattern, and then performs the sequence by applying his rule system. The lowest-level rules are controlled by higher-level rules, and so forth, so that the system as a whole is a highly organized "tree" structure. If the musician tries to start in the middle of such a structure, he does not have available the conditions to begin the correct set of rules, indicating which parts of the piece have already been played, which are to come, and "where he is" in the structure.

GRAMMAR

Speech is the most remarkable of human traits. All human societies have and use language, and all languages are of great grammatical complexity. The human ability to speak and, even more remarkable, to hear and understand speech is the single best example of serial patterning. This ability is so universal, and so permeates human life, that we often neglect it.

Linguists divide speech into "phonemes"—significant speech sounds. An example is /b/, the first sound and last sound of "bulb." Physically, those two sounds are quite different, but in our language they have the same "meaning" and we ordinarily hear them as alike. A phoneme is a class of sounds classified by the language as linguistically the same. In ordinary speech, a person produces approximately ten phonemes per second, shading each sound appropriately into the next. This is no circus act but a normal activity, though the reader is encouraged to listen to an excited teen-ager and try to appreciate the incredible speed and flexibility of the human lips, teeth, tongue, palate, larynx, lungs, and diaphragm, and to remember that these organs are manipulating a vibrating column of air.

Not only are the sounds produced quickly; they are also selected strictly so as to constitute words and phrases. Most possible series of phonemes are meaningless, but the speaker selects unerringly among the correct ones.

Furthermore, the words are arranged into sentences, in grammatical order. Although the concept of grammatical order is a matter of theoretical linguistics, not psychology, the psychology of speech must come to grips with grammar, since people speak and understand language within a grammatical framework.

A grammar, according to Chomsky (1964), is a set of rules which if applied in all combinations would generate all possible grammatical sentences and no ungrammatical ones. A grammar of English would be enormously complex and rich and could never be fully investigated, but much of linguistic theory deals with various problems in that undertaking.

Several grammars can be constructed that build upon the order of words or the dependence of one word on the context of past words. Such "grammars" parallel the various simple association theories refuted earlier in this chapter and need not occupy further attention here.

Phrase-Structure Grammars

A reasonably useful grammar is what is called a "phrase-structure" (or constituent-structure) grammar.

Let us first see how it deals with a simple sentence like "The wind almost capsized the sailboat." The phrase-structure grammar tries to develop the grammatical structure. The sentence consists of two main constituents, a subject ("the wind") and a verb phrase ("almost capsized the sailboat"). The verb phrase consists of a verb phrase and an object. A tree structure is now constructed, starting with the whole sentence S and dividing it into noun phrase (NP), verb phrase (VP), articles or determinants (D), nouns (N), verbs (V), adverbs (Adv), and other structural elements. The tree structure for this sentence is shown in Figure 14.8.

The rules embodied in Figure 14.8 are "rewrite rules". In such a rule,

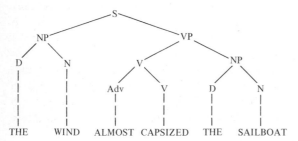

Figure 14.8 Phrase structure of a simple sentence.

one can replace any symbol (shown on the left) by something else (shown on the right). The symbol "+" merely means that one symbol is to follow the other. Thus:

$$S \rightarrow N + VP$$

$$NP \rightarrow D + N$$

$$VP \rightarrow V + NP$$

$$VP \rightarrow (Adv) + VT$$

The parentheses around "Adv" mean that the insertion is optional. There are also various rules for coming to actual words, "lexical insertion rules." Examples are:

$$D \rightarrow the$$

$$Adv \rightarrow almost$$

$$VT \rightarrow capsize$$

$$N \rightarrow wind$$

$$N \rightarrow sailboat$$

There is a simple relationship between rewrite rules and phrase markers (structural trees like the one shown in Figure 14.8). The phrase marker is built from the top, starting with S and putting down branches to NP and VP. The rewrite rule says "S→NP + VP," which is equivalent to saying that from S in the tree we can put down two branches labeled "NP" and "VP."

The phrase structure of a sentence has definite psychological reality. For example, notice in Figure 14.8 that the sentence goes from "the" to "wind" at a low level of the tree; but to go from "wind" to "almost" it must go to the very top. When subjects in an experiment try to recall a sentence verbatim, they fail at major divisions of the tree more often than at lower levels of the tree (Johnson, 1965). An actual sentence from Johnson's experiment, with phrase structure and probabilities of errors, is shown in Figure 14.9. This sentence uses an additional rule, an optional insertion of adjectives:

$$N \rightarrow (Adj) + N$$

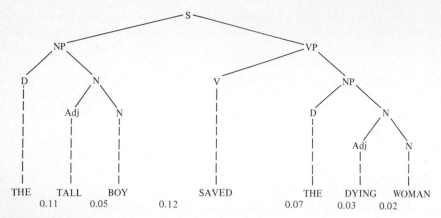

Figure 14.9 Phrase structure of a sentence along with error probabilities from test of recall of the sentence. Higher error frequencies occur at major boundaries of the structure.

The proportions below the sentence are what Johnson calls "transitional error probabilities"; they represent the probability that the subject will fail to produce the next word, given that he has produced the whole sentence correctly up to that point. They are an index of the overall difficulty of the location; but since the subject may hear the sentence several times before he is "tested" on the later words (since it takes that long before he gets to them), one must expect transition-error probabilities to be relatively high early in the sentence and relatively low toward its end.

Obviously, there are a great many particular sentences that have exactly the tree structure ("phrase marker") as the one shown in Figure 14.9. A few examples are:

The new saw felled the pine tree.
An angry man chased the fleeing thief.
A clear voice shouted a ringing slogan.
The small box held a mildewed book.

Given a particular phrase marker, there are a great many possible "lexical substitutions" if one uses an unabridged dictionary with 200,000 words and makes all grammatical substitutions without worrying about the semantic meaningfulness. However large this collection of substitutions might be, however, at least it is finite. The phrase marker, then, is presumably finite; even if all 200,000 words could be substituted for each of the n words of a sentence, this would produce $200{,}000^n$ possible actual sentences—and if n is, say, 20, this is a truly enormous but nonetheless finite number.

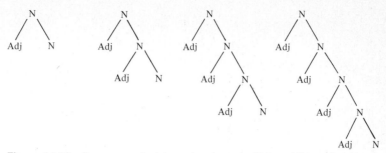

Figure 14.10 Sequence of phrase structures built by adding adjectives.

However, when we start to enumerate the possible phrase markers, the situation is more complex. Consider, for example, the use of the optional rule

N→(Adj) + N

which is called a "recursive" rule because it takes in a noun *(N)* and puts out an expression that contains a noun. Figure 14.10 shows a sequence of phrase markers that can be produced by applying the optional rule once, twice, three times, etc. The following sentences might result:

The tall boy saved the dying woman.
The tall boy saved the dying old woman.
The tall boy saved the dying old black woman.
The tall boy saved the dying old black Baptist woman.

Each of these has its own, different phrase marker. Now, how many such phrase markers are there? If you told me there were 100, I would say, "Well, if you can string that many adjectives before a noun, you surely can put in one more; therefore, there are not 100 but at least 101." This form of argument can be used to hold that there can be no finite number of phrase markers, because the application of optional rules (for one thing) permits extension of any given phrase marker into another.

Another way to build large phrase markers is with recursive sentences. Consider the sentence "I saw John call Bill." Its phrase structure is as shown in Figure 14.11. Notice the circled sentence marker; what "I saw" is represented by a sentence—as indeed it should be, since it is a complete action. However, this means that one of the rules of rewriting should be

VP → V + S

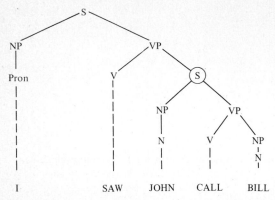

Figure 14.11 Phrase structure of a self-embedded sentence.

and this in turn means that after we have developed a sentence down to the verb phrase VP, we can then insert a sentence and start the derivation all over again. When we come to the VP of that embedded sentence, it is possible to insert another sentence. This produces, not a grammatical monstrosity, but only a quite normal and sensible sentence: "Horace saw the man that (shod the horse that (shied at the dog that (chased the cat that (caught the mouse that (ate the cheese that (came from the milk that (the old goat gave)))))))." This sentence comes from a tree eight sentences deep but is clearly grammatical and fairly intelligible. It is correct, I think, to argue that if the above sentence is possible, then it could be expanded by one more level—for example, it could begin with "I know a fellow named Horace who . . ." If so, then the number of possible phrase structures is unbounded, and a theory must be propounded to tell us where they all come from.

Transformational Grammars

Chomsky's basic position is that phrase structures are made from one another by transformation rules. For example, from the sentence "Tom pushed the Mikado," one can obtain the passive form "The Mikado was pushed by Tom." The new passive phrase marker is obtained from the old by a general rule to the effect that

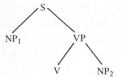

can be transformed into

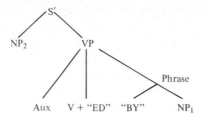

In the example, NP is "Tom," NP$_2$ is "the Mikado," and V is "pushed." The auxiliary verb is "to be," taking the original tense of V in the first sentence. This transformational rule seems fairly complicated, but it can be stated so as to handle quite complicated sentences, e.g., "The mouse that . . . was caught by the cat that . . . . This suggests the system by which a complex self embedded sentence will be modified by a passive transformation centering on "The cat that caught the mouse that. . . . There are several transformations: negation, question ("Did Horace see the man . . .?"), and conjunction (forming "Tom and Bill went home" from "Tom went home and Bill went home"). Self-embedding of sentences is also the product of a transformation. The English language has a number of transformations but apparently only a fairly small, finite set. By applying various combinations of such transformations, a speaker can generate a very large number of phrase structures. In fact, the transformations permit a speaker to generate new variations of any phrase structure he may have, and therefore there is no limit to the number of possible phrase structures. Thus the concept of transformations provides a relatively simple basis, in a system of transformation rules, on which the infinite language capacities of the human being can be erected.

Some of the earliest studies of modern psycholinguistics were concerned with showing the effects of these transformations on the behavior of laboratory subjects. In one interpretation of Chomsky's transformational grammar, there is one class of "kernel" sentences that are simplest—these are the sentences using the minimum allowable transformational rules to develop the phrase structure. Such kernel sentences have the superficial form of positive declarative sentences ("John flew the jet airplane"). Such a sentence can be made passive ("The jet airplane was flown by John"), negative ("John did not fly the jet airplane"), or interrogative ("Did John fly the jet airplane?"). It is possible, then, to construct sentences that use two such transformations: for example, negative passive ("The jet airplane was not flown by John") and even negative passive interrogative ("Wasn't the jet airplane flown by

John?"). If subjects were required to remember such sentences briefly, they found that the difficulty of reproducing the sentence depended on how many transformations had been used in producing its phrase structure, and their errors usually consisted of giving a sentence with fewer transformations than they had heard. This led George Miller (1962) to the hypothesis that the sentence was held in memory as a kernel sentence, and then a set of transformations were appended as "tags."

Although these efforts to study transformations are recent they came before laboratory studies of phrase structures had progressed very far. One difficulty with the laboratory studies of transformation is that linguistic details of a sentence are soon shed by the memory, and only the semantic information meaning is kept. Possibly, to study the effects of transformations on memory is to ask the wrong question. It would be more appropriate to see what transformations a person uses in fluent speech, and how the transformations required to generate the phrase structure of a sentence affect how easy it is to understand the sentence. Unfortunately, such experimental methods must be invented and refined for the specific purpose of studying psycholinguistics. It is reasonable to hope that psycholinguistics will continue its present rapid development, at least for the next five or ten years.

SUMMARY

Behavior often shows serial patterns, and important examples include simple motor coordinations, athletics, music, and language. Serial patterns are coordinated by dividing a sequence into parts and relating the parts to one another. A sequence is easy to learn to the extent that it can be generated by coherent systems of rules. Such rules may generally be "rewrite rules" that result in a hierarchical tree, like the phrase markers of grammar.

Such rule systems give some concept of what is meant by an organized sequence yet do not restrict a person or animal to rigidly prescribed responses. Rule systems do restrict the set of patterns that may be performed, but their main impact is "generative." That is, they provide a systematic way of laying out a whole range of possibilities and combinations, without at the same time saying which specific combination will occur. Such "theories" are not like the theories of physics: in physics a theory is intended to say exactly what will happen under specified conditions; but generative theory merely indicates possibilities without singling one out as a prediction or even listing all possibilities (which may be infinitely numerous).

The idea of a generative theory is appealing as an approach to the general theory of cognitive structures. On the other hand, theories of how a given structure gives rise to behavior are more like conventional physical theories in that they make specific predictions. It is too early to know whether cognitive theories should be strictly generative, strictly predictive, or a combination of both.

Chapter 15

Choice and Decision

One of the things that add spice to psychology is the fact that we cannot really predict what people will do—at least, not when they are being interesting. This has to be true, when you think about it, because we are not interested in habitual behavior, repeated over and over in the same circumstances. We may be interested in the fact that people are creatures of habit, but when they manifest this tendency we turn away. Some responses are much more significant and tell us something about the person: these are the results of decisions or choices.

Why is a decision more interesting than a habitual response? One reason is that the outcome is less predictable, and therefore we are interested to know what it will actually be. *Information*, in both a technical and a literary sense, is to be obtained from a choice. It is the uncertainty itself that makes a choice interesting; the study of choice becomes, then, to a degree, a study of uncertain behavior.

Within the general theory of behavior flows, particularly as presented in Chapters 13 and 14, it is difficult to see how behavior can really be uncertain. There are cognitive organizations to control behavior, and higher-order structures to control lower-order ones; everything seems nicely organized. Where will the uncertainty come in?

Uncertainty and choice arise whenever two or more different behavior flows, both of which can operate in the same situation, are not coordinated. This leaves the subject with two different responses, either (but not both) of which can occur, and no higher-order structure to decide which will be used. The subject cannot be expected to do exactly the same thing every time but instead will vacillate and vary from one occasion to another, at least until a higher-order control emerges.

TYPES OF DECISION SITUATIONS

There are three basic forms of "conflict" that require decision: the "approach-approach" conflict, between two attractive alternatives; the "avoidance-avoidance" conflict, between two repulsive alternatives; and the "approach-avoidance" conflict, arising when the same object or situation is both attractive and repulsive. The distinction between these three types of situations was made by the Gestalt theorist Kurt Lewin (1931) and has been developed theoretically and experimentally by Neal Miller (1944, 1959).

Lewin thought of the person as being in a field acted upon by forces: a conflict would arise if the person were acted upon by opposite forces that would impel him to opposite or incompatible actions. Lewin also held that as one came closer to a positive goal, its attractiveness would increase; and as one approached a negative goal, its repulsiveness would increase.

Approach-Approach Conflict

In an approach-approach conflict, two forces tend to pull the person toward two different activities, both attractive. As the person comes nearer one goal than the other, the closer goal becomes more attractive and the farther goal becomes less attractive, so that he is pulled still closer to the former. Even if the forces are exactly balanced at the start, the situation is like a pencil balanced on its point—the slightest imbalance tips the system over, and the person should go toward one goal or the other without delay or vacillation. (See Figure 15.1.)

Miller refines this theory somewhat by defining a "gradient" of attraction, higher near the goal and lower farther away. The net force toward a goal (or the net strength of the response of going toward that goal) is represented by the height of the gradient. The approach-approach conflict is represented in Figure 15.2.

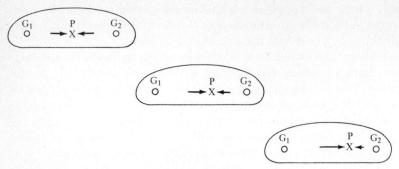

Figure 15.1 Approach-approach conflict with unstable equilibrium, leading to rapid resolution.

These theories indicate a smooth consistency of behavior that is not usually found. A third way of talking about conflict uses probability theory (Bower, 1959). A probability theory usually distinguishes only a few of the positions the organism can take in the situation. For example, in the approach-approach conflict, the person can be neutral, can be in the process of approaching either goal A or goal B, or can actually have arrived at either goal. These states are shown in Figure 15.3. The probabilities of transition between the various positions can be guessed in advance or determined by observation.

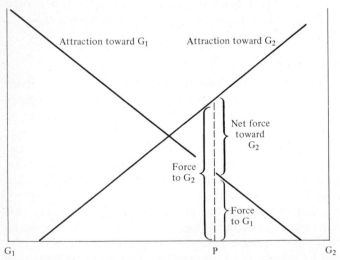

Figure 15.2 Dual approach gradients. Since P is nearer G_2 there is a net force to approach G_2 rather than G_1.

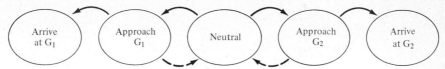

Figure 15.3 Probability model of approach-approach conflict.

In the usual experimental situation, the probabilities of transition from "approach" to "arrive" are quite high; there is, then, only a low probability of vacillation—switching back and forth. Once the organism approaches a goal, he rarely turns back. Once the organism arrives at a goal, the trial is terminated and there is no turning back.

Hovland and Sears (1938) trained college students to move a pencil either to the left or to the right across a piece of waxed paper toward a light. They then ran one "conflict" trial for each subject. The approach-approach conflict simply consisted of turning both of two lights on. Over half the subjects (57.5 percent) simply moved toward one of the lights; 21.3 percent made a double response, moving to one light and then quickly to the other; 12.5 percent made a compromise response between the two lights; and only 8.7 percent failed to respond. Compared with other conflicts, this was a very large percentage of responses to one light, as would be expected by the unstable equilibrium.

One conclusion from both theory and experiment is that in an approach-approach conflict most people and animals should take one choice or the other with little delay or difficulty—and if the situation permits them to take both choices, they may. This is not a situation in which the person is "locked in" between two alternatives, unable to decide.

Avoidance-Avoidance Conflict

A person might have to decide between studying and doing the dishes, between cowardice and death on the battlefield, between Scylla and Charybdis: in Lewin's formulation, the person is then in a field between two sources of repulsion. If he moves nearer one, it becomes more repulsive than the other; as a result, he is pushed back into the middle. However, if the person moves out of line between the two repulsive positions, he will be forced out of the field. The only thing that would keep a person between two such repulsive situations is a psychological barrier that prevents escape. See Figure 15.4.

Neal Miller (1944) points out that one way to establish a negative situation is to put a rat in a runway and then shock it at some point in the runway. If a rat has a history of having been shocked at a certain place in

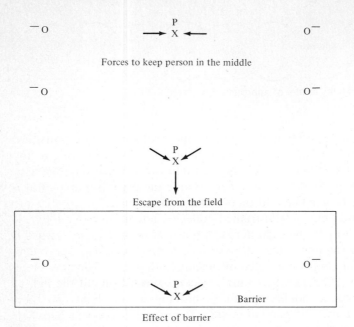

Figure **15.4** Avoidance-avoidance or double-negative conflict, showing that P will leave the field unless a barrier prevents him.

the runway and is then put down nearby, it will move away. The strength of the response can be measured by putting a little harness on the rat and measuring the strength with which it pulls away. Miller found that the closer the animal was to the place where it had been shocked the harder it pulled; it pulled especially hard if it was put down on the shock grid. The gradient, though high, was also steep: that is, once the rat had got a short distance from the danger spot, it stopped pulling. The gradients for an avoidance-avoidance conflict are shown in Figure 15.5. From this one would predict that an animal might safely wander around over a considerable area between the two danger spots in an apparatus where shock was administered at two places. The probability theory, in this case, would hold that when the animal approaches one of the danger spots, he has very low probability of going to it but otherwise is not much affected. The result is free "random" movement in the middle area and some approaches to the two danger spots, but a very low probability of going into a danger spot. See Figure 15.6.

Hovland and Sears (1938) set up this kind of conflict in their motor-performance task (see page 289) by first instructing subjects to move not toward a light on a board but toward the corner of the board that

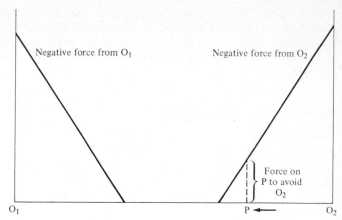

Figure 15.5 Gradients of avoidance-avoidance conflict: P will stay in middle region.

did not have a light. Therefore, the subject was to make a specific response to a light, but the response was to avoid it. On the test trial, the experimenters turned both of two lights on. Only 17.5 percent of the subjects made a single response to one light; only 17.5 percent made a double response; and only 5.0 percent compromised—the remaining 72.5 percent failed to go to either corner.

Neal Miller describes the behavior of rats that had been trained to escape an electric shock by running away from whichever end of the alley was distinguished by a light and buzzer, and were then placed in an avoidance-avoidance conflict by having lights and buzzers turned on at both ends of the runway:

> When released a considerable distance away from the center, all of the animals started by avoiding the nearest light. After running in one direction these animals stopped and turned back, remaining in conflict between the

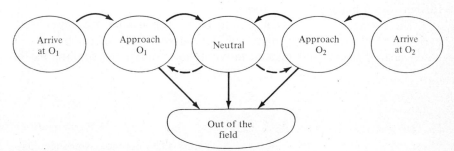

Figure 15.6 Probability model of avoidance-avoidance conflict.

two lights. When released at the center, they started more slowly than the approach-approach animals, vacillated much more, and remained nearer the starting point. In the avoidance-avoidance conflicts, the animals showed a definite tendency to try to escape to the side and up out of the alley [1944, p. 445].

Approach-Avoidance Conflict

In approach-approach situations, there is no real conflict. In avoidance-avoidance situations, conflict arises only if the subject is hemmed in. But when a situation is both attractive and dangerous, the subject can be locked into a long-term conflict. The general form of the conflict, in Lewin's terms, is shown in Figure 15.7. This diagram does not tell us what will happen to the subject. If he moves closer to the place G, the force of both the attraction and the repulsion will increase. Does this mean that he will simply approach slowly, that he will slowly drift away, or that he will come part of the way and then get stuck?

This is the main problem Miller worked on. Working with Brown (1940) on rats in harnesses, he found that approach tendencies seemed to produce a relatively flat gradient; the rat pulled when it was far from the food. Avoidance gradients, obtained by shocking the rat, were steep; the rat pulled only when very near the shock grid but if the shock was intense would pull very hard. A typical approach-avoidance situation is shown in Figure 15.8: the rat is fed in one place, then shocked at the same place, and then put down by the experimenter somewhere in the alley. According to Figure 15.8, the rat will approach the food until it gets quite close, because the approach gradient is flat. When the rat reaches point E, the equilibrium point, the avoidance and approach tendencies are equal. If the rat gets closer to the goal than point E, the avoidance gradient is higher than the approach gradient, and the animal should retreat. According to this theory, then, the rat will ordinarily stick at a position just "out of danger," unwilling either to go closer, for fear of the shock, or to go farther away, because of the food.

The probability approach should be useful in analyzing approach-avoidance behavior, since many subjects in such an experiment do not stand near the goal, but instead move about, sometimes running as far

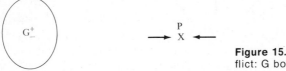

Figure 15.7 Approach-avoidance conflict: G both attracts and repels P.

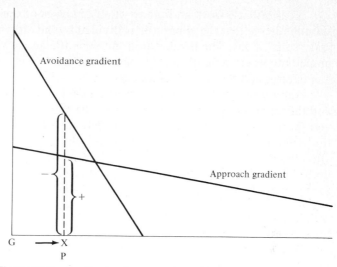

Figure 15.8 Gradients of approach-avoidance conflict. Notice that avoidance gradient is steeper. P will stop at point where gradients cross.

away as possible and other times coming right up to eat the food. The *average* position of a rat in the runway can be predicted by gradients, although rats are actually found all along the length of the runway. However, the simple probability approach given above says very little about approach-avoidance conflict—except, perhaps, that the subject will tend to approach but not to arrive at the goal.

In approach-avoidance conflict, the subject has two behavior flows that lead to opposing behavior. For rats in a runway, one behavior flow is simple food getting, and the animal expects to find food in the goal box. The second behavior flow is avoidance of shock, for the animal also expects a painful shock. These two expectancies conflict and, we assume, are not integrated into a single structure. If this is true, then the animal will sometimes have an expectancy of food, and sometimes have an expectancy of shock, but it will not characteristically expect both at the same time. The situation will match either expectancy quite well, since both food and shock have been received in the runway.

The theoretical question about approach-avoidance conflict is, therefore, which expectancy will be aroused at what time? When the expectancy of food is aroused, the situation will be analyzed appropriately, the input will match the expectancy, and the animal will approach food. When the expectancy of electric shock is aroused, the animal will again analyze the situation appropriately, find a match, and retreat.

Neal Miller's work and many other analyses of the rat's response to shock indicate that the apparatus is divided by the rat into "danger" areas and "safe" areas. The danger area includes the actual shock grid and its immediate environment; the safe area includes areas in which the animal has determined that no shock occurs.

Apparently, in the danger area the expectancy of shock takes over, and the animal retreats. In the safe area, the animal does not expect shock and therefore is controlled by the expectancy of food. This should place the animal right outside the edge of the danger area. If there is some stimulus marking the edge of the danger area—as, for example, a change in the color of the walls of the runway—this will be used by animals. If the expectancy of food is strong because the animal is very hungry, then the animal may enter the danger area but continue the expectancy of food. In this case the animal may resolve the conflict by eating, overcoming its fear.

ON MAKING PRUDENT DECISIONS

The theory that there are three types of decisions is based on the assumption that the decision maker has only two or three expectancies. Human beings, faced with the difficult major decisions of life, may have a great many conflicting expectancies and may have to deal with both a tangle of motivations and a morass of possible consequences of each alternative. Imagine a head of state deciding whether to declare war: although it might be true to say that he is in an "approach-avoidance conflict," that description is too oversimplified to be of much interest.

In economics, psychology, political science, and management science there has arisen a theory of how decisions *ought* to be made. Such a theory is not a psychological theory of how decisions actually *are* made; but it tells us what possible methods a person might use and gives us a basis for evaluating how well decisions are made, apart from the question of how well a decision happens to work out in practice.

A *rational* decision maker acts in such a way as to get the most of whatever he most values. If he does not get what he wants, or if he produces harmful aftereffects, then he is irrational or imprudent. "Irrationality" implies that a person has correctly predicted the consequences of his acts, but that the consequences were not what he wanted. "Imprudence" usually implies that he was trying to satisfy his own wants but erred, probably by having formed mistaken expectations of consequences. Irrationality, then is a failure in evaluating desires, and imprudence is a failure in estimating probable consequences.

If the process of decision making is idealized, it may be divided into three stages: analysis of the situation, evaluation of the possible consequences, and deciding.

Analysis of the Situation

The first step in making a prudent decision is to identify the possible alternatives. In many cases, the decision-making process does not begin unless the alternatives have already been developed by some other person or agency. Often, in a bureaucracy, a higher-level official makes decisions regarding proposals that come from lower levels or from the outside world. A motorcycling association may petition the headquarters of a national forest to lay out trails through the forest for motorcycling. The head forester considers the petition but then is faced by opposition from conservation groups. The two sides define the decision problem, and the forester is thereby given his set of alternatives. Similarly, the jury in a court of law is asked to decide for the plaintiff or the defendant, and its set of possible alternatives is decided by the attorneys for the two parties and by the judge. It is quite possible, in such cases, that the best alternative is never presented and does not enter into the decision process.

Sometimes the decision process is simplified by convention or fiat. For example, a complex business decision may be simplified so that it becomes a question of what price will be asked for a basic product; negotiations between labor and management may come down to a decision about wage rates; a writer may decide simply how many hours a day he will work on his book. These simplifications make it quite easy to scan the possible alternatives and thus give the decider confidence that there is a single decision, perhaps in the middle of his subjective range. Of course, however, there may be another possible decision entirely apart from the dimension chosen.

Surprisingly, the theory of choice and decision making has very little to say about systematic methods of deciding what the alternatives may be. One general idea is to have interested or naïve people "brainstorm" and see what alternatives they may devise. In brainstorming, a group of people work together in a very informal atmosphere, sometimes using alcohol or other relaxing drugs, and trying to think up the most unusual, outlandish, or bizarre ideas possible. This process is disciplined to the extent that no criticism is admitted, new ideas are accepted whether or not they are good, and any tendency for systematic development of one line of thought is discouraged. In this way, the widest possible range of ideas is developed for later consideration.

It would also seem that a complete set of relevant alternatives could be developed by systematic application of rules. This might consist of a mnemonic system for retrieving possibilities that may have been tried in the past, or a way of working out all alternatives. If the decision to be made is similar to decisions in the past, then one way to get a set of alternatives is by a historical search. This requires some mnemonic system, either natural or artificial, that permits the decider to generate a complete set of historical instances. The search of documents can be particularly helpful for this purpose. The method to be used would consist of a conventional "search of the literature," using general sources, reference methods of libraries, and references from one publication to others as a method of finding, in a fairly systematical way, a complete body of historical precedents. Lawyers, as well as historical and literary scholars, have many techniques for developing such sets of possibilities.

Such methods are not discussed in the theory of decision making, because much of modern decision theory arises from game theory. There are many aspects to game theory; one is that it thinks of decisions in real life as comparable to the strategies of players in games, particularly in competitive gambling games of strategy, like poker. An older form of game theory, which has had a profound effect, is the theory of chess. Although chess is apparently an infinitely complex game, in which the human capacity for foresight is completely employed, the particular alternatives open to a player at any one moment can quickly be enumerated. He need only look at each of his pieces (never more than sixteen) and see what moves are possible for each piece. In a typical position, there may often be only fifty or fewer moves possible within the rules of the game. In a game of poker, the player is free to make any bet, but otherwise most of his decisions are one-dimensional. In a card game like bridge, the player at a given moment can make one of a small set of possible bids or play exactly one of the cards in his hand. In all games, there exists at every move a set of possible alternatives, well defined and delimited, within which the player may operate. The rules of the game *give* the player his set of possible alternatives and outlaw such otherwise reasonable choices as sweeping the pieces to the floor, cursing the opponent, offering bribes, etc. If decision theory is thought of as an extension of the theory of games, then it is natural to begin the discussion of a decision with a given set of alternatives. In the real world, however, the set of alternatives is not given, and the wise decider is often characterized by the ability to invent a new alternative.

The following problem illustrates an example of the problems inherent in systematic ways of making decisions. One is given a three-by-three matrix of dots, as in Figure 15.9; the problem is to draw four straight lines connected (without lifting one's pencil from the paper) that will pass through all nine dots. The reader who does not already know this problem may find it difficult. There is a natural tendency to try to devise various

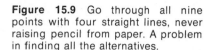

Figure 15.9 Go through all nine points with four straight lines, never raising pencil from paper. A problem in finding all the alternatives.

four-line pathways satisfying the rules of the problem, testing each to see if it goes through all the points. We may think of this as a very simple decision problem, in which many alternatives exist that are clearly unsatisfactory, and (perhaps) one alternative exists that is satisfactory. The reason this problem may be difficult is that many people generate their alternatives using an unnecessary rule that seems, somehow, to apply—namely, that the lines all remain within the square outlined by the dots. The solution to the problem requires only that the person let his pencil move outside that region a little bit. But a semisystematic method of generating alternatives can easily be mistaken and may fail to generate the correct solution.

Tracing Consequences

When the alternatives have been worked out, the person is not yet ready to decide, because he must consider the consequences of his various actions. If he does not foresee such consequences and evaluate their significance correctly, he may obtain a "short-run advantage" that is disastrous in the longer run. This is the opposite of prudence.

Psychologically, we are here considering a complex system of expectancies. In a chess game, I may notice that a certain move of my queen would capture a bishop. I do not take the move at once, however; I must at least look ahead and see if my opponent could then take my queen. That more remote consequence would outweigh the benefits of winning a mere bishop.

Similarly, a retail store owner might want to raise prices to increase his income. However, he might foresee that his competitors would take away his customers, leaving him with only a fraction of his earlier profit.

The Decision Tree   Game theory, as derived from both chess and poker, is particularly helpful in telling us how to foresee these more complicated possible consequences of our actions. A systematic method of working out such consequences is to develop a "tree," as follows.

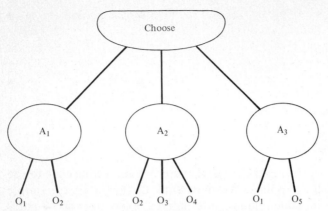

Figure 15.10 Simple tree of choice alternatives and possible outcomes.

Begin with your own possible alternatives, say, A_1, A_2, and A_3. If you choose A_1, then there are several possible outcomes. Lay these out under A_1. Similarly, lay out the possible outcomes under alternatives A_2 and A_3. This produces the tree shown in Figure 15.10.

Further analysis of the situation may reveal that you can plan responses to each of the above branches, and that each of your responses, in the context of the earlier response and the earlier outcome, itself has predictable outcomes. Going ahead two levels produces the tree in Figure 15.11. Even though Figure 15.11 represents a situation much simpler than even an easy chess position as analyzed by a child, notice that the branches of the tree have become prolix. One must realize that a wise decider can foresee the consequences of an act far into the future: it is not enough to see ahead one or two "moves." A government that sees economic prosperity for the next five years, but does not see exhaustion of natural resources and accumulation of pollution, may be elected but is not wise. Still, in many cases long-term consequences are very remote, and their full exploration would require developing trees with thousands of branches—perhaps millions or more. Even if there are only two alternatives available at each stage, and only two possible outcomes, at every level of the tree each branch proliferates into four twigs. In that case, if one looks ahead n stages, one must build a tree with 4^n branches; to foresee even five moves ahead, for example, requires a tree with $4^5 = 4 \times 4 \times 4 \times 4 \times 4 = 1,024$ branches.

Nevertheless, such trees and their branches often must be studied if one is to arrive at prudent decisions. Complexity is inconvenient, but there is no way to simplify many decisions without courting disaster.

Psychologically, a complicated tree of this sort might exist in long-term memory, but it would be most difficult to search and consider. If a person is actually to trace all consequences, he usually must write down the possibilities or (better yet) program them into a computer. In a chess game, the player does not write down the possibilities; indeed, chess players clearly do not even consider all possibilities. Instead, they usually work from "positions," relatively complex patterns of interaction and possibility, in a highly organized but mysterious way.

A tree might consist of a network of expectancies: for example, "If A_1 is chosen and O_2 results, then the choice of A_2 will result in outcome O_3," and so forth. These expectancies could have the form of simple associations, as between alternative A_2 and outcome O_3. If so, the tree would exist as a great tangle of such associations, all quivering in the mind and extremely difficult to invoke when needed. Another possibility is that each branch of the tree would consist of a kind of serial structure, as discussed in Chapter 14. However, most of these sequences may have no particular pattern, and it would be very difficult to find the pattern in all branches of the tree at once.

In summary, the logic of decision making insists that all branches of this tree of consequences should be traced out, but we have no psycho-

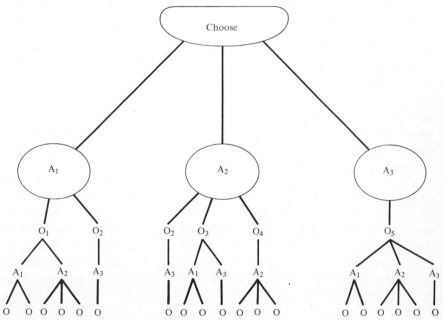

Figure 15.11 Tree showing further ramifications of choice, here involving two-stage strategies.

logical theory of how this can be done. The situation is unsatisfactory, but its resolution awaits further research.

Evaluation of the Tree   Some of the consequences are almost sure to follow, and some are very unlikely. In a chess game I may have available a move to which my opponent could make a very foolish response, giving me the game. However, if my opponent is skillful, that branch of the tree is very unlikely and hardly requires consideration. If I am a dairyman thinking of cutting the price of milk, I may believe it is very likely that my competitors would retaliate, because the same thing happened across town three months earlier and all dairies responded within a day.

The value of any branch of a tree depends in part on the *subjective* probability of each of the branches. The reference here is to the decision maker's estimate of the probabilities, not to the correct or objective probabilities. In most actual decisions, the various considerations are so complex and so nearly unique that true probabilities are very difficult to determine; still, the decider must somehow evaluate the probability of every branch of the tree.

In a very simple experiment, it appears that the person may estimate these probabilities by searching his long-term memory for some expectancy. For example, he thinks of choosing alternative A_1 and then wonders about the probability of O_1 versus O_2. He may search long-term memory for a past experience in which an alternative like A_1 was chosen (either by himself or by someone else). The memory need not conform perfectly to the present situation; it need only match with respect to the dimensions of the situation that the person analyzes, and this depends upon the behavior flow in operation at the time. If the person first finds a memory in which O_1 occurred, then he at that moment expects O_1. In many experiments, it seems that the subject bases his choice upon the outcome expected (Estes, 1962).

In a very important decision the person may take more time and attempt to obtain a more precise estimate of the subjective probabilities of O_1 and O_2. To do this he might continue his search of long-term memory, dredging up a number of memories of situations with a response like A_1, and accumulating several expectancies of memories of both O_1 and O_2. He may eliminate some because he thinks that the past situation was too unlike the present one, and in other ways he may process these accumulated memories and arrive at some estimate of subjective probability.

If this is the process of estimating a subjective probability, it appears that a person will not ordinarily make accurate estimates of the subjective probabilities of all possible branches of the decision tree. To simplify the calculation, a person could expunge sections of the tree, thinking of them as too unlikely to require further analysis; or he might assign some arbitrary probability based on a general rule rather than on the use of memories. A gambler might disregard the consequences of losing a large bet on the basis that "Luck never forsakes me when I most need her," even though this generalization might not agree with the actual contents of long-term memory if it were searched.

The next step in evaluating the tree, after the subjective probabilities are assigned, is to determine the utilities or values to be assigned to each branch. A person cannot choose wisely unless he knows what he wants, and a "rational" choice is one that has the best chance of satisfying the wishes of the chooser.

Utility theory—the theory of how a decision is made, or should be made, so as to maximize the utilities of the chooser—does not come from psychology. It seems to be traceable more directly to certain theories in economics, particularly to what used to be called "liberal" and now could better be called "free-enterprise" economics. According to this theory, the purpose of any economic control system is to get producers to produce enough of the right things to meet society's needs. The direction of what is produced is controlled by the market—people presumably will pay more for what they want more. Since higher prices constitute higher rewards, that market encourages a producer to make goods that are wanted, and thereby shapes production to fit needs. Since the market does not pay for what is not delivered, everyone is motivated to produce. Furthermore, no external controls need be placed on the system— everyone merely acts to satisfy his own wants and thereby keeps the system humming smoothly along.

For the system to work optimally, it is important that people be willing to pay for what they really want. This raises the question of what people really want. In effect, utility theory says that a numerical utility can be assigned to every outcome, indicating the degree to which the person wants it. Of two alternatives, he will choose the one with the higher utility. The best measure of the real wants of a person is his actual choices rather than his verbal expressions, since the latter may be intended more for social effect—to enhance his status or obtain a competitive advantage—than as true self-analyses. Such a theory appears to be circular: the utilities are derived from choices and then serve as a major basis for predicting choices. However, it is possible to measure utilities in certain simple experimental situations and from those measurements to predict choices in more complex situations. Furthermore, if a person's choices can be reconciled with the idea that he has underlying utilities, then certain regularities will be observed that are useful in making direct predictions. For example, if you choose a beagle over a cat as a pet, and a cat over a white rat, then the three utilities must be ordered with the beagle highest and the rat lowest. If so, utility theory can predict that you would choose a beagle over a rat. Such predictions, it must be admitted, might be made without the apparatus of a highly complicated mathematical theory, but it is generally held that an obvious prediction is better than no prediction at all.

To arrive at a very good prediction, it is not enough to have utilities for all outcomes. It is possible that you would prefer to receive a dinner followed by a dessert rather than a dessert followed by a dinner, or a full life before a sudden death rather than a sudden death before a full life. As the person considers each path through the tree of possibilities, he must not merely add the utilities of the outcomes; instead, he must estimate the utility of the entire path, considering the alternatives chosen, the outcomes obtained, and the order in which these events occur.

Decision

Each path through the tree now has a subjective probability and a utility. How does this help a person make his first immediate choice? The overall value of an alternative can be thought of as the expected utility of the whole subtree descended from that alternative. Each path that starts with A_1 is a possible future history of the person, and he has estimated its probability and evaluated its utility. He adds all the paths from A_1 together, the utility of each path being weighted by its subjective probability. For example, if a student decides to major in geology, he might discover a gold mine. The utility of this outcome is high, but its subjective probability may be very low. The tendency to major in geology, then, is equal to the high utility multiplied by the low subjective probability—a moderate result.

In the idealized world of utility theory, this calculation—multiplying the probability of each path in the tree by its utility and then adding these values for all paths descended from an alternative—yields a numerical value called the "subjectively expected utility" (SEU) for that alternative. Having an SEU for each alternative, a person is advised to choose the alternative with the highest SEU. In this way, it is said, he makes a prudent and rational choice, thinking of the consequences of each alternative and then distributing his resources so as to obtain the best possible expected return. Even though one cannot know for sure what the future will bring, this theory leads one to make reasonable choices, going with the probabilities rather than against them.

DYNAMICS OF DECIDING

The theory of prudent decisions is somewhat philosophical and tells how decisions should be made. The psychological study of decisions has suggested a different viewpoint and calls the SEU theory into question as a satisfactory normative theory, that is, a satisfactory theory of how decisions should be made.

One fact about psychological data, in situations of choice as in other situations, is that choices are only probable, not certain. SEU theory can handle this fact only by saying that somehow the subjective probabilities or the utilities vary from time to time.

In an experiment, since judgments tend to vary from trial to trial, the data consist of the probability that alternative A_1, A_2, etc., will be chosen. It has been very natural to think that if A_1 is almost always chosen over A_2, it must be much better; and that if A_1 is chosen over A_2 only, say, 55 percent of the time, then A_1 is only slightly better than A_2 in terms of its SEU.

There is another factor involved, however, which has been described theoretically (Restle, 1961) and shown in some experiments (Coombs, 1958; Restle & Greeno, 1970; Tversky, 1972). If two alternatives and their consequences are qualitatively similar, and one is better than the other, the better one will have some advantage and the worse one will quite possibly have no advantage at all. For example, you might be offered either A_1, a basket of fruit, or A_2, a basket of fruit plus a candy bar. The probability of choosing A_2 is almost certain, for there is no reason to choose A_1 (assuming only that you have some desire for the candy bar). A small difference in SEU leads to very consistent responding.

In contrast, consider a choice between A_1, a basket of fruit, and A_3, a good leather wallet of approximately the same price as the basket of fruit. In this choice, the alternatives are qualitatively different and have quite different consequences. The fruit is immediately pleasant, is healthful, and can be shared with friends; the wallet has none of these characteristics. On the other hand, the fruit will be eaten or spoiled within a few days, whereas the wallet will remain useful for a year or two. Such a choice is relatively uncertain, even if the wallet has a substantially greater SEU than the fruit, and the probability of choice will be near 0.50.

Why is a subject inconsistent when deciding between qualitatively different alternatives like a wallet and fruit? He has good reasons for preferring the wallet, because it has at least one valued attribute (a long period of usefulness) not shared by the fruit. To the degree that the person's analysis yields such an attribute, he will choose the wallet. The

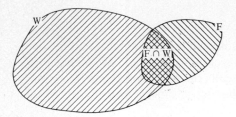

Figure 15.12   Choice between two relatively dissimilar alternatives, pictured as sets of valued aspects.

fruit also has valued attributes (healthfulness and sociability) not shared by the wallet. The situation may be pictured as in Figure 15.12. This is a Venn diagram of three sets of valued attributes; those favoring the wallet (W-F), those favoring the fruit (F-W), and the overlap (F ∩ W).

In Figure 15.12 the total set F is larger than the set W, but W-F is still substantial. The overlap, F ∩ W, is relatively small. Contrast this with Figure 15.13, in which the sets W and F remain the same size but F ∩ W is greatly increased.

In each case, the probability of choosing W is the number of valued attributes in W-F relative to F-W. If the number of elements in the set W-F is written N(W-F), then

$$\text{Probability of choosing } \mathbf{W} = \frac{N(\mathbf{W-F})}{N(\mathbf{W-F}) + N(\mathbf{F-W})}$$

Notice that the elements in F ∩ W do not count. Being attributes of both alternatives, they can have no influence on a choice between them.

There are two ways in which this probability of choice might come about. A person might discard *attributes* one at a time at random until all those left pointed unambiguously to one alternative or the other (Restle, 1961). If the person ends up with an attribute common to both alternatives, he would have to start over. Or the person might pick an attribute and eliminate all *alternatives* that do not have it (Tversky, 1972). If the attribute chosen is in W-F, like permanence, the person discards the fruit, which does not have that attribute, and chooses the wallet. If he first tries

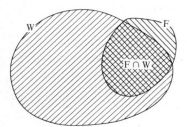

Figure 15.13   Choice between two relatively similar alternatives.

an attribute in F-W, like healthfulness, he discards the wallet and chooses the fruit. If he chooses an attribute shared by both (e.g., being a token of affection), then he cannot discard either alternative and must consider another attribute. This produces exactly the same probabilities as the first situation.

Tversky's theory permits systematic predictions of complex choices, and also is psychologically more realistic than SEU theory. However, as Tversky points out, a subject who follows his method of choosing, with a random selection of aspects, may make some very unfortunate choices. The best choice may not be best in all ways and might easily be eliminated in the process of choosing because it lacks a relatively trivial attribute. Tversky rightly considers this a flaw in his formulation. A truly wise person would not throw away a diamond merely because he happened to hit upon size as a valued aspect and a diamond is small. But how would he avoid such a blunder? He would have to know that quality of gems is a property that overrides mere size. This does not mean that he disregards size: a two-carat diamond is to be chosen over a one-carat diamond of similar quality.

What a wise decision maker must do is to arrange his values appropriately, so that he does not delete a good choice on the basis of a trivial consideration. If the various aspects can be clearly ranked so that the most important is put first, then it is possible to arrive at reasonable decisions by Tversky's method. The most important aspect would be tested first, and all choices that can be eliminated on that basis would be deleted. If more than one choice remains, the decider shifts to the second most important aspect.

This method of going from more to less important aspects will work only if the aspects are very strongly ordered, so that the first is more important than all the others combined, the next is more important than all below it, and in general each aspect is more important than the sum total of all aspects ranked below it. This is certainly an exceptional situation, and a decision-maker cannot expect the world to conform to so convenient a configuration.

Generally, there will be some sort of value conflict that should, ideally, be resolved. Some higher-order behavior flow must be called upon to generate expectancies in an appropriate order. A person with strong political values might evaluate choices on the basis of loyalty or power considerations; a religious person might seek to carry out the will of God; an altruist might evaluate his choices by how they benefit others; an "economic man" might seek profits. Such *value systems* may be thought of as very high-order behavior flows that serve to generate lower-order values, which in turn are used to narrow down the range of choices.

References

Adams, J. A., & Montague, W. E. Retroactive inhibition and natural language mediation. *Journal of Verbal Learning and Verbal Behavior,* 1967, **6,** 528–535.

Allison, J. Response deprivation and "reinforcement." Lecture at Indiana State University, October 26, 1972.

Allison, J., & Timberlake, W. Instrumental and contingent saccharin licking in rats: Response deprivation and reinforcement. (Submitted to *Learning and Motivation,* 1973.)

Anderson, J. R., & Bower, G. H. *Human Associative Memory,* Washington, D.C.: Winston, 1973.

Anderson, R. C. Encoding processes in the storage and retrieval of sentences. *Journal of Experimental Psychology.* 1971, **91,** 338–340.

Atkinson, R. C. A stochastic model for rote serial learning. *Psychometrika,* 1957, **22,** 87–96.

Atkinson, R. C., & Estes, W. K. Stimulus sampling theory. In R. D. Luce, R. R. Bush, & E. Galanter (Eds.), *Handbook of mathematical psychology.* Vol. 2. New York: Wiley, 1963.

Atkinson, R. C., & Shiffrin, R. M. Human memory: A proposed system and its control processes. In K. W. Spence & J. T. Spence (Eds.), *The psychology of learning and motivation: Advances in research and theory.* Vol. II. New York: Academic Press, 1968.

Barnes, J. B., & Underwood, B. J. "Fate" of first-list associations in transfer theory. *Journal of Experimental psychology,* 1959, **58,** 97–105.

Bartlett, F. C. *Remembering.* Cambridge, England: Cambridge University Press, 1932.

Bobrow, S. A., & Bower, G. H. Comprehension and recall of sentences. *Journal of Experimental Psychology,* 1969, **80,** 445–461.

Bolles, R. C. Species-specific defense reactions and avoidance learning. *Psychological Review,* 1970, **77,** 32–48.

Bourne, L. E. *Human conceptual behavior.* Boston: Allyn and Bacon, 1965.

Bourne, L. E., Jr., & Restle, F. Mathematical theory of concept identification. *Psychological Review,* 1959, **66,** 278–296.

Bower, G. H. Choice-point behavior. In R. R. Bush and W. K. Estes (Eds.), *Studies in mathematical learning theory.* Stanford, Calif.: Stanford University Press, 1959.

Bower, G. H. A multi-component theory of the memory trace. In K. W. Spence & J. T. Spence (Eds.), *The Psychology of Learning and Motivation.* Vol. 1. New York: Academic Press, 1967.

Bower, G. H. Mental imagery and associative learning. In Lee Gregg (Ed.), *Cognition in learning and memory.* New York: Wiley, 1970. (a)

Bower, G. H. Organizational factors in memory. *Cognitive Psychology,* 1970, **1,** 18–46. (b)

Bower, G. H., Clark, M. C., Lesgold, A. M., & Winzenz, D. Hierarchical retrieval schemes in recall of categorized word lists. *Journal of Verbal Learning and Verbal Behavior,* 1969, **8,** 323–343.

Bower, G. H., & Holyoak, K. Encoding and recognition memory for naturalistic sounds. *Journal of Experimental Psychology,* 1973, **101,** 360–366.

Bower, G. H., & Springston, F. Pauses as recoding points in letter series. *Journal of Experimental Psychology,* 1970, **83,** 421–430.

Bower, G. H., & Winzenz, D. J. Group structure, coding, and memory for digit series. *Journal of Experimental Psychology,* 1969, **80,** (No. 2, Part 2).

Bransford, J. D., Barclay, J. R., & Franks, J. J. Sentence memory: A constructive versus interpretive approach. *Cognitive Psychology,* 1972, **3,** 193–209.

Bransford, J. D., & Franks, J. J. The abstraction of linguistic ideas. *Cognitive Psychology,* 1971, **2,** 331–350.

Breland, K., & Breland, M. A field of applied animal psychology. *American Psychologist,* 1951, **6,** 202–204.

Breland, K., & Breland, M. The misbehavior of organisms. *American Psychologist,* 1961, **16,** 681–684.

Breland, K., & Breland, M. *Animal behavior.* New York: Macmillan, 1966.

Brown, J. S. Generalized approach and avoidance responses in relation to conflict behavior. Unpublished doctoral dissertation, Yale University, 1940.

Brown, R., & McNeill, D. The "tip of the tongue" phenomenon. *Journal of Verbal Learning and Verbal Behavior,* 1966, **5,** 325–337.

Bruner, J. S. The course of cognitive growth. *American Psychologist,* 1964, **19,** 1–15.

Bush, R. R., & Mosteller, F. *Stochastic models for learning.* New York: Wiley, 1955.

Butler, R. A. Discrimination learning by rhesus monkeys to visual-exploration motivation. *Journal of Comparative and Physiological Psychology,* 1953, **46,** 95–98.

Butler, R. A. Curiosity in monkeys. *Scientific American,* 1954, **190,** 70–75.

Chomsky, N. *Syntactic structures.* The Hague: Mouton, 1957.

Chomsky, N. *Aspects of the theory of syntax.* Cambridge, Mass.: M. I. T. Press, 1965.

Chumbley, J. I. Hypothesis memory in concept learning. *Journal of Mathematical Psychology,* 1969, **6,** 528–540.

Collins, A. M., & Quillian, M. R. Retrieval time from semantic memory. *Journal of Verbal Learning and Verbal Behavior,* 1969, **8,** 240–247.

Collins, A. M., & Quillian, M. R. How to make a language user. In E. Tulving & W. Donaldson (Eds.), *Organization of Memory.* New York: Academic Press, 1972.

Conrad, E. Acoustical confusion in immediate memory. *British Journal of Psychology,* 1964, **55,** 75–84.

Conrad, R. Acoustic confusions in immediate memory. *British Journal of Psychology,* 1964, **55,** 75–83.

Conrad, R. Interference or decay over short retention intervals? *Journal of Verbal Learning and Verbal Behavior,* 1967, **6,** 49–54.

Coombs, C. H. On the use of inconsistency of preferences in psychological measurement. *Journal of Experimental Psychology,* 1958, **55,** 1–7.

Craik, F. I. M., & Lockhart, R. S. Levels of processing: A framework for memory research. *Journal of Verbal Learning and Verbal Behavior,* 1972, **11,** 671–684.

Dawes, R. M. Cognitive distortion. *Psychological Reports,* 1964, **14,** 443–459.

Denny, M. R. Relaxation theory and experiments. In F. R. Brush, *Aversive conditioning and learning.* New York: Academic Press, 1971.

DeRosa, D. V., & Morin, R. E. Recognition reaction time for digits in consecutive and nonconsecutive memorized sets. *Journal of Experimental Psychology,* 1970, **83,** 472–479.

DeSoto, C. B., & Kuethe, J. Subjective probabilities of interpersonal relationships. *Journal of Abnormal and Social Psychology,* 1959, **59,** 290–294.

DeValois, R. L., Morgan, H. C., Polson, M. C., Mead, W. R., & Hull, E. M. Psychophysical studies of monkey vision. I. Macaque luminosity and color vision tests. *Vision Research,* 1974, **14,** 53–67.

Dufort, R. H., Guttman, N., & Kimble, G. A. One-trial discrimination reversal in the white rat. *Journal of Comparative and Physiological Psychology,* 1954, **47,** 248–249.

Ebbinghaus, H. *Memory: a contribution to experimental psychology.* H. A. Reiger & C. E. Bussenius (Trans.), 1913. New York: Teachers College, Columbia University, 1885.

Estes, W. K. Statistical theory of spontaneous recovery and regression. *Psychological Review,* 1955, **62,** 145–154.

Estes, W. K. Theoretical treatments of differential reward in multiple-choice learning and two-person interactions. In J. H. Criswell, H. Solomon, & P. Suppes (Eds.), *Mathematical models in small group processes.* Stanford, Calif.: Stanford University Press, 1962.

Estes, W. K. Probability learning. In A. W. Melton (Ed.), *Categories of human learning.* New York: Academic Press, 1964.

Estes, W. K., & Skinner, B. F. Some quantitative properties of anxiety. *Journal of Experimental Psychology,* 1941, **29,** 390–400.

Feigenbaum, E. A., & Simon, H. A. A theory of the serial position effect. *British Journal of Psychology,* 1962, **53,** 307–320.

Feigenbaum, E. A., & Simon, H. A. Brief notes on the EPAM theory of verbal learning. In C. N. Cofer and B. S. Musgrave (Eds.), *Verbal behavior and learning: Problems and Processes.* New York: McGraw-Hill, 1963.

Ferster, C. B., & Skinner, B. F. *Schedules of reinforcement.* New York: Appleton Century Crofts, 1957.

Fillmore, C. J. The case for case. In E. Bach & R. T. Harmes (Eds.), *Universals in linguistic theory.* New York: Holt, Rinehart and Winston, 1968.

Franklin, B. *The autobiography of Benjamin Franklin.* Boston: Houghton Mifflin, 1923. First English edition, 1793.

Freedman, Jonathan L., & Loftus, Elizabeth F. Retrieval of words from long-term memory. *Journal of Verbal Learning and Verbal Behavior,* 1971, **10,** 107–115.

Frisch, K. von. *The dancing bees.* London: Methuen, 1954.

Garcia, J., & Koelling, R. A. Relation of cue to consequence in avoidance learning. *Psychonomic Science,* 1966, **4,** 123–124.

Gelman, R. Conservation acquisition: A problem of learning to attend to relevant dimensions. *Journal of Experimental Child Psychology,* 1969, **7,** 167–187.

Geyer, L. H., & DeWald, C. G. Feature lists and confusion matrices. *Perception and Psychophysics,* **14,** 471–482.

Gibson, E. J. Principles of perceptual learning and development. New York: Appleton Century Crofts, 1969.

Gibson, E. J., Gibson, J. J., Pick, A. D., & Osser, H. A developmental study of the discrimination of letter-like forms. *Journal of Comparative and Physiological Psychology,* 1962, **55,** 897–906.

Glanzer, M., & Clark, W. H. The verbal loop hypothesis: Binary numbers. *Journal of Verbal Learning and Verbal Behavior,* 1963, **2,** 301–309.

Glanzer, M., & Dolinsky, R. The anchor for the serial position effect. *Journal of Verbal Learning and Verbal Behavior,* 1965, **4,** 267–273.

Greeno, J. C. How associations are memorized. In D. A. Norman (Ed.), *Models of human memory.* New York: Academic Press, 1970.

Gregg, L. (Ed.) *Cognition in learning and memory.* New York: Wiley, 1970.

Grice, G. R., & Hunter, J. J. Stimulus intensity effects depend upon the type of experimental design. *Psychological Review,* 1964, **71,** 247–256.

Grings, W. W. Verbal-perceptual factors in the conditioning of autonomic responses. In W. F. Prokasy (Ed.), *Classical conditioning: A symposium.* New York: Appleton Century Crofts, 1965.

Guthrie, E. R. *The psychology of learning.* New York: Harper and Row, 1935.

Guttman, N. Operant conditioning, extinction, and periodic reinforcement in relation to concentration of sucrose used as a reinforcing agent. *Journal of Experimental Psychology,* 1953, **46,** 213–224.

Harlow, H. F. Responses by rhesus monkeys to stimuli having multiple sign values. In Q. McNemar & M. A. Merril (Eds.), *Studies in personality.* New York: McGraw-Hill, 1942.

Harlow, H. F. The formation of learning sets. *Psychological Review,* 1949, **56,** 51–65.

Harlow, H. F. The nature of love. *American Psychologist,* 1958, **13,** 673–685.

Harlow, H. F., McGaugh, J. L., & Thompson, R. F. *Psychology.* San Francisco: Albion, 1971.

Harlow, H. F., & Zimmerman, R. R. Affectional responses in the infant monkeys. *Science,* 1959, **130,** 421–432.

Hearst, E. Some persistent problems in the analysis of conditioned inhibition. In R. A. Boakes and M. S. Halliday (Eds.), *Inhibition and learning.* New York: Academic Press, 1972.

Hearst, E., & Jenkins, H. M. *Sign-tracking: The stimulus-reinforcer relation and directed action.* Austin, Texas: The Psychonomic Society, 1974.

Hediger, H. *The psychology and behaviour of animals in zoos and circuses.* New York: Dover, 1968.

Heider, F. Attitudes and cognitive organization. *Journal of Psychology,* 1946, **21,** 107–112.

Heider, F. *The psychology of interpersonal relations.* New York: Wiley, 1958.

Hilgard, E. R., & Bower, G. H. *Theories of learning.* New York: Appleton Century Crofts, 1966.

Hillman, B., Hunter, W. W., & Kimble, G. A. The effect of drive level on the maze performance of the white rat. *Journal of Comparative and Physiological Psychology,* 1953, **46,** 87–89.

Honzik, C. H. Delayed reaction in rats. *University of California Publications in Psychology,* 1931, **4,** 307–318.

House, B. J., & Zeamon, D. Position discrimination and reversals in low-grade retardates. *Journal of Comparative and Physiological Psychology,* 1959, **52,** 564–565.

Hovland, C. I., & Sears, R. R. Experiments on motor conflict. I. Types of conflict and their modes of resolution. *Journal of Experimental Psychology.* 1938, **23,** 477–493.

Hunt, H. F., & Brady, J. V. Some effect of punishment and intercurrant "anxiety" on a simple operant. *Journal of Comparative and Physiological Psychology,* 1955, **48,** 305–310.

Hunter, W. S. The delayed reaction in animals and children. *Behavior Monographs,* 1912, **2,** 1–85.

Johnson, N. F. The psychological reality of phrase structure rules. *Journal of Verbal Learning and Verbal Behavior,* 1965, **4,** 469–475.

Kintsch, W. *Learning, Memory, and conceptual processes.* New York: Wiley, 1970.

Krechevsky, I. (Now David Krech.) "Hypotheses" in rats. *Psychological Review,* 1932, **39,** 516–532.

Krechevsky, I. The docile nature of "hypotheses." *Journal of Comparative Psychology,* 1933, **15,** 429–443.

Krueger, W. C. F. The effect of overlearning on retention. *Journal of Experimental Psychology,* 1929, **12,** 71–78.

Lashley, K. S. *Brain mechanisms and intelligence.* Chicago: Chicago University Press, 1929.

Lashley, K. S. The mechanism of vision. XV. Preliminary studies of the rat's capacity for detail vision. *Journal of General Psychology,* 1938, **18,** 123–193.

Lashley, K. S. The problem of serial order in behavior. In L. A. Jeffress (Ed.), *Cerebral Mechanisms in Behavior.* New York: Wiley, 1951.

Laughery, K. R. Computer simulation of short-term memory: A component decay model. In G. H. Bower and J. T. Spence (Eds.), *The Psychology of learning and motivation.* Vol. 6. New York: Academic Press, 1971.

Lawrence, D. H. The applicability of generalization gradients to the transfer of a discrimination. *Journal of General Psychology,* 1955, **52,** 37–48.

Leary, R. W. Analysis of serial discrimination learning by monkeys. *Journal of Comparative and Physiological Psychology,* 1958, **51,** 82–86.

Levin, H., & Turner, E. A. Sentence structure and eye-voice span. *Project Literacy Reports,* September, 1966, No. 7, 79–87.

Levine, M. Hypothesis theory and non-learning despite ideal S-R reinforcement contingencies. *Psychological Review,* 1971, **78,** 130–140.

Levine, M., & Harlow, H. F. Learning sets with one- and twelve-trial oddity problems. *American Journal of Psychology,* 1959, **72,** 253–257.

Levinson, B. Oddity learning set and its relation to discrimination learning set. Doctoral dissertation, University of Wisconsin, 1958.

Levison, M. J., & Restle, F. Effects of blank-trial probes on concept-identification problems with redundant relevant cue solutions. *Journal of Experimental Psychology,* 1973, **98,** 368–374.

Lewin, K. Environmental forces in child behavior and development. In C. Murchison, *A handbook of child psychology.* Worcester, Mass.: Clark University Press, 1931.

Locke, J. C., & Locke, V. L. Deaf children's phonetic, visual, and dactylic coding in a grapheme recall task. *Journal of Experimental Psychology,* 1971, **89,** 142–146.

Lorenz, K., and Leyhausen, P. *Motivation of human and animal behavior.* New York: Van Nostrand, 1973.

Loucks, R. B. Efficiency of the rat's motor cortex in delayed alternation. *Journal of Comparative Neurology,* 1931, **53,** 511–567.

Luria, A. R. *The mind of a mnemonist.* New York: Basic Books, 1968.

Mandler, G. Organization and memory. In K. W. Spence & J. T. Spence (Eds.), *The Psychology of Learning & Motivation.* Vol. 1. New York: Academic Press, 1977.

Martin, E. Stimulus meaningfulness and paired-association transfer: The encoding variability hypothesis. *Psychological Review,* 1968, **75,** 421–441.

Massaro, D. W. Preperceptual auditory images. *Journal of Experimental Psychology,* 1970, **85,** 411–417.

Massaro, D. W. Effect of masking tone duration of preperceptual auditory images. *Journal of Experimental Psychology,* 1971, **87,** 146–148.

Masserman, J. H. *Behavior and neurosis.* Chicago: University of Chicago Press, 1943.

McCrary, J. W., & Hunter, W. S. Serial position curves in verbal learning. *Science,* 1953, **117,** 131–134.

McGaugh, J. L. Time-dependent processes in memory storage. *Science,* 1966, **153,** 1351–1358.

Meyer, D. E. On the representation and retrieval of stored semantic information. *Cognitive Psychology,* 1970, **1,** 242–300.

Meyer, D. R. Intraproblem-interproblem relationships in learning by monkeys. *Journal of Comparative and Physiological Psychology,* 1951, **44,** 162–167.

Miller, G. A. The magical number seven, plus or minus two: Some limits on our capacity for processing information. *Psychological Review,* 1956, **63,** 81–97.

Miller, G. A. Some psychological studies of grammar. *American Psychologist,* 1962, **17,** 748–762.

Miller, G. A. A psychological method to investigate verbal concepts. *Journal of Mathematical Psychology,* 1969, **6,** 169–191.

Miller, G. A., Galanter, E., & Pribam, K. H. *Plans and the structure of behavior.* New York: Holt, Rinehart and Winston, 1960.

Miller, N. E. Experimental studies of conflict. In J. M. V. Hunt (Ed.), *Personality and the behavior disorders.* New York: Ronald Press, 1944.

Miller, N. E. Liberalization of basic S-R concepts: Extensions to conflict behavior, motivation, and social learning. In S. Koch (Ed.), *Psychology: A study of a science.* New York: McGraw-Hill, 1959.

Mishkin, M., Prokop, E. S., & Rosvold, H. E. One-trial object-discrimination learning in monkeys with frontal lesions. *Journal of Comparative and Physiological Psychology,* 1962, **55,** 178–181.

Moon, L. E., & Harlow, H. F. Analysis of oddity learning by rhesus monkeys. *Journal of Comparative and Physiological Psychology,* 1955, **48,** 188–194.

Moore, J. W., & Gormezano, I. Effects of omitted versus delayed UCS on classical conditioning under partial reinforcement. *Journal of Experimental Psychology,* 1963, **65,** 248–257.

Morton, J. Interaction of information in word recognition. *Psychological Review,* 1969, **76,** 165–178.

Munn, N. L. *Handbook of psychological research on the rat.* Boston: Houghton Mifflin, 1950.

Neisser, U. *Cognitive Psychology.* New York: Appleton Century Crofts, 1967.

Norman, D. A. *Models of human memory.* New York: Academic Press, 1970.

Olds, J. Physiological mechanisms of reward. In M. R. Jones (Ed.), *Nebraska Symposium on motivation.* Vol. 3. Lincoln: University of Nebraska Press.

Paivio, A. Mental imagery in associative learning and memory. *Psychological Review,* 1969, **76,** 241–263.

Paivio, A. *Imagery and verbal processes.* New York: Holt, Rinehart and Winston, 1971.

Paivio, A., & Csapo, K. Concrete image and verbal memory codes. *Journal of Experimental Psychology,* 1969, **80,** 279–285.

Paivio, A., Smyth, P. C., & Yuille, J. C. Imagery versus meaningfulness in paired-associate learning. *Canadian Journal of Psychology,* 1968, **22,** 427–441.

Palermo, D. S. Imagery in children's learning: Discussion. In H. W. Reese (Chm.), Imagery in children's learning: A symposium. *Psychological Bulletin,* 1970, **73,** 383–421.

Paris, S. G. Propositional logical thinking and comprehension of language connectives: A developmental analysis. Unpublished doctoral dissertation, Indiana University, 1972.

Pavlov, I. P. *Conditioned reflexes.* G. V. Anrep (Trans.) London: Oxford University Press, 1927.

Payne, B. The relationship between a measure of organization for visual patterns and their judged complexity. *Journal of Verbal Learning and Verbal Behavior.* 1966, **5,** 338–343.

Penfield, W. Memory mechanisms. *Transactions of the American Neurological Association,* 1951, **76,** 15–31.

Peterson, L. R., & Peterson, M. J. Short-term retention of individual verbal items. *Journal of Experimental Psychology,* 1959, **58,** 193–198.

Philipchalk, R. P., & Rowe, E. J. Sequential and nonsequential memory for verbal and nonverbal auditory stimuli. *Journal of Experimental Psychology,* 1971, **91,** 341–343.

Picek, J. S., Sherman, S. J., & Shiffrin, R. M. Cognitive organization and coding of social structures. *Journal of Personality and Social Psychology,* 1974, in press.

Polson, M., Restle, F., & Polson, P. G. Association and discrimination in paired-associates learning. *Journal of Experimental Psychology,* 1965, **69,** 47–55.

Polson, P. G. A quantitative study of the concept identification and paired associates learning in the Hull paradigm. Unpublished doctoral dissertation, Indiana University, 1967.

Posner, M. I., Boies, S. J., Eichelman, W. H., & Taylor, R. L. Retention of visual and name codes of single letters. *Journal of Experimental Psychology,* 1969, **79,** No. 1, Part 2.

Posner, M. I., & Mitchell, R. F. Chronometric analysis of classification. *Psychological Review,* 1967, **74,** 392–409.

Postman, L. The present status of interference theory. In C. N. Cofer (Ed.), *Verbal Learning and Verbal Behavior,* New York: McGraw-Hill, 1961.

Postman, L. Short-term memory and incidental learning. In A. W. Melton (Ed.), *Categories of human learning.* New York: Academic Press, 1964.

Potts, G. R. A cognitive approach to the encoding of meaningful verbal material. Unpublished doctoral dissertation, Indiana University, 1971.

Potts, G. R. Information processing strategies used in the encoding of linear orderings. *Journal of Verbal Learning and Verbal Behavior,* 1972, **11**, 727–740.

Premack, D. Reinforcement theory. In D. Levine (Ed.), *Nebraska symposium on motivation.* Vol. 13. Lincoln: University of Nebraska Press, 1965.

Prytulak, L. S. Natural language mediation. *Cognitive Psychology,* 1971, **2**, 1–56.

Raser, G. A. False recognition as a function of encoding dimension and lag. *Journal of Experimental Psychology,* 1972, **93**, 333–337.

Reitman, J. S. Mechanisms of forgetting in short-term memory. *Cognitive Psychology,* 1971, **2**, 185–195.

Rescorla, R. A. Pavlovian conditioning and its proper control procedures. *Psychological Review,* 1967, **74**, 71–80.

Restle, F. Discrimination of cues in mazes: A resolution of the "Place-versus-response" question. *Psychological Review,* 1957, **64**, 217–228.

Restle, F. A survey and classification of learning models. In R. R. Bush & W. K. Estes (Eds.), *Studies in mathematical learning theory.* Stanford, California, Stanford University Press, 1959.

Restle, F. *Psychology of judgment and choice: A theoretical essay.* New York: Wiley, 1961.

Restle, F. The selection of strategies in cue learning. *Psychological Review,* 1962, **69**, 329–343.

Restle, F. The relevance of mathematical models for education. In E. R. Hilgard (Ed.), *Theories of learning and instruction.* Chicago: University of Chicago Press, 1964. (a)

Restle, F. Sources of difficulty in learning paired associates. In R. C. Atkinson (Ed.), *Studies in mathematical psychology.* Stanford, California: Stanford University Press, 1964. (b)

Restle, F. Significance of all-or-none learning. *Psychological Bulletin,* 1965, **64**, 313–325.

Restle, F. Theory of serial pattern learning: structural trees. *Psychological Review,* 1970, **77**, 481–495.

Restle, F. Serial patterns: The role of phrasing. *Journal of Experimental Psychology,* 1972, **92**, 385–390.

Restle, F. Critique of pure memory. In R. Solso (Ed.), *Theory in Cognitive Psychology: The Loyola Symposium.* Potomac, Maryland: Lawrence Erbaum, 1974.

Restle, F., Andrews, M., & Rokeach, M. Differences between open- and closed-minded subjects on learning-set and oddity problems. *Journal of Abnormal and Social Psychology,* 1964, **68**, 648–654.

Restle, F., & Brown, E. Organization of serial pattern learning. In Bower, G. H. *Psychology of learning and motivation.* Vol. 4. New York: Academic Press, 1970.

Restle, F., & Emmerich, D. Memory in concept attainment: Effect of giving several problems concurrently. *Journal of Experimental Psychology,* 1966, **71**, 764–799.

Restle, F., & Greeno, J. G. *Introduction to mathematical psychology.* Reading, Mass.: Addison-Wesley, 1970.

Revusky, S., & Garcia, J. Learned associations over long delays. In G. H. Bower (Ed.), *The Psychology of learning and motivation.* Vol. 4. New York: Academic Press, 1970.

Richter, C. P. Experimentally produced behavior reactions to food poisoning in wild and domesticated rats. *Annals of the New York Academy of Science,* 1953, **56**, 225–239.

Riopelle, A. J., & Churukian, G. A. The effect of varying the intertrial interval in discrimination learning by normal and brain-operated monkeys. *Journal of Comparative and Physiological Psychology,* 1958, **51**, 119–125.

Riopelle, A. J., Francisco, E. W., & Ades, H. W. Differential first-trial procedures and discrimination learning performance. *Journal of Comparative and Physiological Psychology,* 1954, **47**, 293–295.

Rock, I., & Heimer, W. Further evidence of one-trial associative learning. *American Journal of Psychology,* 1959, **72**, 1–16.

Rokeach, M. *The open and closed mind.* New York: Basic Books, 1960.

Rosenberg, S., & Jarvella, R. J. Semantic integration and sentence perception. *Journal of Verbal Learning and Verbal Behavior,* 1970, **9**, 548–553.

Rosenblatt, F. The perceptron: A probabilistic model for information storage and organization in the brain. *Psychological Review,* 1958, **65**, 386–408.

Rozin, P., & Kalat, J. W. Specific hungers and poison avoidance as adaptive specializations of learning. *Psychological Review,* 1971, **78**, 459–486.

Santa, John L., & Rauken, H. B. Effects of verbal coding on recognition memory. *Journal of Experimental Psychology,* 1972, **93**, 268–278.

Sasson, R. Y. Interfering images at sentence retrieval. *Journal of Experimental Psychology,* 1971, **89**, 56–62.

Schoeffer, M. S. Probability of response to compounds of discriminated stimuli. *Journal of Experimental Psychology,* 1954, **48**, 323–329.

Schrier, A. M., Harlow, H. F., & Stolnitz, F. (Eds.) *Behavior of nonhuman primates.* New York: Academic Press, 1965.

Schusterman, R. J. Transfer effects of successive discrimination-reversal training in chimpanzees. *Science,* 1962, **137**, 422–423.

Selfridge, O. G., & Neisser, U. Pattern recognition by machine. *Scientific American,* Aug. 1960, **203**, 60–68.

Sheffield, F. D., Wulff, J. J., & Backer, R. Reward value of copulation without sex drive reduction. *Journal of Comparative and Physiological Psychology,* 1951, **44**, 3–8.

Shepard, R. N. The analysis of proximities: Multidimensional scaling with an unknown distance function. *Psychometrika,* 1962, **27**, I: 125–140, II: 219–246.

Shiffrin, R. M. Memory search. In D. A. Norman (Ed.), *Models of Human Memory.* New York: Academic Press, 1970.

Shiffrin, R. M. Information persistence in short-term memory. *Journal of Experimental Psychology,* 1973, **100**, 39–49. (a)

Shiffrin, R. M. Short-term store: Organized active memory. Paper presented at Midwestern Psychological Meetings, Chicago, Ill., 1973. (b)

Shiffrin, R. M., & Schneider, W. An expectancy model for memory search. Paper read at Midwestern Psychological Association, Chicago, Ill.,

1973. Indiana Math Psych Program Report 72-9, Submitted to *Memory and Cognition.*

Skinner, B. F. *The behavior of organisms.* New York: Appleton Century Crofts, 1938.

Skinner, B. F. *Walden Two.* New York: Macmillan, 1948.

Skinner, B. F. *Beyond freedom and dignity.* New York: Knopf, 1971.

Slamencka, N. J. *Human learning and memory: Selected readings.* New York: Oxford University Press, 1967.

Solomon, R. L., Kamin, L. J., & Wynne, L. C. Traumatic avoidance learning: The outcomes of several extinction procedures with dogs. *Journal of Abnormal and Social Psychology,* 1953, **48,** 291–302.

Solomon, R. L., & Wynne, L. C. Traumatic avoidance learning: The principles of anxiety conservation and partial irreversibility. *Psychological Review,* 1954, **61,** 353–385.

Sperling, G. The information available in brief visual presentation. *Psychological Monographs,* 1960, **74**(Whole No. 498).

Sternberg, S. High-speed scanning in human memory. *Science,* 1966, **153,** 652–654.

Sternberg, S. Two operations in character-recognition: Some evidence from reaction-time measurements. *Perception and Psychophysics,* 1967, **2,** 45–53.

Sternberg, S. Memory-scanning: Mental processes revealed by reaction-time experiments. In J. S. Antrobus (Ed.), *Cognition and affect.* Boston: Little Brown, 1970.

Stevens, K. N., & Halle, M. Remarks on analysis by synthesis and distinctive features. In W. Wathen-Dunn (Ed.), *Models for the perception of speech and form.* Cambridge, Mass.: M. I. T. Press, 1967.

Strong, P. N., Jr. Memory for object discriminations in the rhesus monkey. *Journal of Comparative and Psychological Psychology,* 1959, **52,** 333–335.

Suci, G. The validity of pause as an index of units in language. *Journal of Verbal Learning and Verbal Behavior,* 1967, **6,** 26–32.

Theios, J. Reaction time measurements in the study of memory processes: Theory and data. In G. H. Bower (Ed.), *The Psychology of Learning and Motivation.* Vol. VII. New York: Academic Press, 1973.

Timberlake, W., & Allison, J. Response deprivation: An empirical approach to instrumental performance. *Psychological Review,* 1974, **81,** 146–164.

Tinbergen, N. *The study of instinct.* Oxford: Clarendon Press, 1951.

Tinklepaugh, O. L. An experimental study of representative factors in monkeys. *Journal of Comparative Psychology,* 1928, **8,** 197–236.

Tolman, E. C. *Purposive behavior in animals and men.* New York: Appleton Century Crofts, 1932.

Tolman, E. C., & Honzik, C. H. "Insight" in rats. *University of California Publications in Psychology,* 1930, **4,** 215–232.

Townsend, J. T. Theoretical analysis of an alphabetic confusion matrix. *Perception and Psychophysics,* 1971, **9,** 40–50. (a)

Townsend, J. T. Alphabetic confusion: A test of models for individuals. *Perception and Psychophysics,* 1971, **9,** 449–454. (b)

Trabasso, T. R. Stimulus emphasis and all-or-none learning in concept identification. *Journal of Experimental Psychology,* 1963, **65,** 398–406.

Trabasso, T. R., & Bower, G. H. *Attention in learning.* New York: Wiley, 1968.

Trapold, M. A., & Spence, K. W. Performance changes in eyelid conditioning as related to motivational and reinforcing properties of the UCS. *Journal of Experimental Psychology,* 1960, **59**, 209–213.

Tulving, E. Subjective organization in recall of "unrelated" words. *Psychological Review,* 1962, **69**, 344–354.

Tulving, E. Episodic and semantic memory. In E. Tulving & D. Donaldson (Eds.), *Organization of memory.* New York: Academic Press, 1972.

Tulving, E., & Donaldson, W. (Ed.) *Organization of Memory.* New York: Academic Press, 1972.

Tulving, E., & Thompson, D. M. Encoding specificity and retrieval processes in episodic memory. *Psychological Review,* 1973, **80**, 352–374.

Turvey, M. T. On peripheral and central processes in vision: Inferences from an information-processing analysis of masking with patterned stimuli. *Psychological Review,* 1973, **80**, 1–52.

Tversky, A. Elimination by aspects: A theory of choice. *Psychological Review,* 1972, **79**, 281–299.

Uhr, L. Pattern recognition. In L. Uhr (Ed.), *Pattern recognition.* New York: Wiley, 1966.

Underwood, B. J. Interference and forgetting. *Psychological Review,* 1957, **64**, 49–60.

Underwood, B. J. Attributes of memory. *Psychological Review,* 1969, **76**, 559–573.

Underwood, B. J., & Postman, L. Extraexperimental sources of interference in forgetting. *Psychological Review,* 1960, **67**, 73–95.

Vitz, P. C., & Todd, T. C. A coded element model of the perceptual processing of sequential stimuli. *Psychological Review,* 1969, **76**, 433–449.

Weber, R. J., & Castelman, J. The time it takes to imagine. *Perception and Psychophysics,* 1970, **8**, 165–168.

Weinstein, B. The evolution of intelligent behavior in rhesus monkeys. *Genetic Psychology Monographs,* 1945, 31.

Wickelgren, W. Rehearsal grouping and hierarchical organization of serial position cues in short-term memory. *Quarterly Journal of Experimental Psychology,* 1967, **19**, 97–102.

Wickens, D. D. Encoding categories of words: An empirical approach to meaning. *Psychological Review,* 1970, **77**, 1–15.

Winzenz, D., & Bower, G. Subject imposed coding and memory for digit series. *Journal of Experimental Psychology,* 1970, **83**, 52–56.

Wollen, K. A., & Lowry, D. H. Effects of imagery on paired-associate learning. *Journal of Verbal Learning and Verbal Behavior,* 1971, **10**, 276–284.

Woodworth, R. S. *Experimental psychology.* New York: Holt, 1938.

Young, M. N., & Gibson, W. B. *How to develop an exceptional memory.* Philadelphia: Chilton, 1962.

Yngve, V. H. A model and a hypothesis for language structure. *Proceedings of the American Philosophical Society,* 1960, **104**, 444–466.

Zeaman, D. Response latency as a function of the amount of reinforcement. *Journal of Experimental Psychology,* 1949, **39**, 466–483.

Index

Index